HOW TO LOVE YOUR *Life*

Hey Troy,
Great to meet you!
I hope you truly
love your life & see
good days!
[illegible signature]

Hey Troy,

Great to meet you!

I hope you family

love your life to see

good days!

Dave [illegible]

Endorsements

Heather Sanford has written a book that is a wake-up call on how to really enjoy your life, what is real and what is not. She shows you how to reach your dream in life; it is before you, it is your choice and it is possible. Only someone who has experienced and obtained her dream to love her life can share such insight with you. Learn how to love *your* life!

- Armond Morales
Four time Grammy winner with The Imperials,
seventeen Dove Awards, Gospel Music Hall of Fame

Heather Sanford beautifully navigates you through your own journey to loving your life in this practical and inspiring book. *How to Love Your Life* ignites an eternal perspective of your God-given purpose and offers empowering action steps to embracing the life God has planned for you. The scriptural truths and spiritual wisdom that Heather shares within this book are life-changing. Every person who desires to live an exciting and abundant life must read this motivational book!

- Judy Jacobs
Internationally known psalmist,
author, mentor and pastor

Thank you, my friend, for putting into words so many things that I have long sensed with my heart! In drawing from your lifetime of personal experiences and observations, you have beautifully distilled in this masterful volume what I believe is the longing of our Father's heart for each of His children. This labor of love is a gift to the body of Christ, and is certain to change the lives of all those who open themselves to the eternal truths revealed in these pages. How gracefully you have dressed the wick and lit the path for how to love *my* life; I know I will not be the same for having allowed your heart to touch mine through the pages of this book.

- Cindy Duvall
Shekinah Glory Ministries International

Heather Sanford has written a fantastic book on how to love your life. I have found in my years of travels that most people simply go through life without living their life. In Heather's book she teaches that we can actually live in the moment every day and gives us the steps to do so. This book will not only leave you feeling better, but living better.

- Tim Storey
Author of Comeback & Beyond

There seems to be a never-ending barrage of advertisements aimed at encouraging us to have more, be more, do more, entitled to more, all leading us down the path of dissatisfaction with our life's journey. Heather Sanford beautifully and practically presents us with biblical truth to counter the deception of unrealistic expectations, in "How to Love Your Life". This is not another "how to" book based on someone's opinion, but rather on the Truth of God's Word. We are all on this "journey" of life and I believe the road map provided within the pages of this book will help any reader to not only learn to love life, but also have joy in the journey.

- Anne Marie Ezzo
Speaker and co-author of Growing Kids God's Way
and other parenting curricula

An awesome book of inspiration and instruction for your walk with God; a must read that you will not be able to put down.

- Steve Brock
Pastor, revivalist and international Gospel recording artist

HOW TO LOVE YOUR *Life*

Heather Sanford

WestBow Press books may be ordered through booksellers or by contacting:

WestBow Press
A Division of Thomas Nelson
1663 Liberty Drive
Bloomington, IN 47403
www.westbowpress.com
1-(866) 928-1240

ISBN: 978-1-4497-2404-7 (sc)
ISBN: 978-1-4497-2397-2 (hc)
ISBN: 978-1-4497-2396-5 (e)

Library of Congress Control Number: 2011913769

Printed in the United States of America

WestBow Press rev. date: 8/9/2011

Dedicated To:

My loving Lord and Savior Jesus Christ.

Lord, it is my honor to dedicate to You
the first fruits of all my labor.

Generation after generation stands in awe of Your work;
each one tells stories of your mighty acts.
Psalm 145:4

The Message Translation

Table of Contents

Foreword

In over thirty years of ministry life I have had the opportunity to read many good books that can help people succeed at their desired dreams. The subjects may vary, but the principle of information gathering is the same. If you want to grow, develop, succeed, and last, you must learn, learn, learn. All talented, brilliant, successful people will affirm this great truth. As I see it, success, satisfaction, and significance in life is directly related to your willingness to learn, acquire information, and discipline yourself to apply good living practices.

This brings me to the foreword for my dear friend, Heather Sanford, and her fabulous new book, *How to Love Your Life.* If there was ever a person who is qualified to write on such a vital, sensitive, and special subject as family and marriage, it is Heather Sanford. Heather has lived and experienced all the joys and challenges of marriage, child rearing, physical attacks on her health, church-building in several nations, and ministry to countless hurting and needy people. She has counseled some of the wealthiest people in society and some of the poorest. In both worlds, Heather's zeal for solutions has never waned. Heather and Kevin, her husband of many years, have transferred a great wealth of information from their own vast reservoir of experience and godly wisdom to many others.

When I was first learning to golf, a friend of mine said, "Do not try to hit the ball so far. Just learn to hit it straight!" After a short time of immense frustration with my game, I talked to an instructor about how to hit a golf ball straight forward. Then, I bought golf swing videos and began to seriously learn from others what I needed to know. The best way for me to learn was to read, listen to the advice of others, and then practice over and over. This principle is so important, because in Heather's book, *How to Love Your Life,* you will learn how to straighten out a life that may need help to succeed. Heather's knowledge and inspiring instruction will surely help you "straighten out your swing" to become a powerful, self-motivated wife or husband that can be fully prepared for whatever life's experiences bring to you. You will learn how to be prepared in advance when the "ifs and whens" of life try to destroy your joy.

There are occasionally things that you will experience in life that you have no time to train and prepare for. Heather's book, *How to Love Your Life,* will help you be mature, strong, and well equipped to overcome the most difficult of family and marital challenges. This valuable preparation will cause you to build a life of confidence, positive faith, and inspiration for all those who come in contact with you.

I have learned that my successes in life have come because of the time I have spent in preparation, acquiring knowledge, and then being a doer of those things. Heather's book is a world of information and inspiration that will help you be prepared, informed, and ready to succeed. Your family can excel and surpass all your dreams and goals if you will put into practice the powerful, easy to grasp principles in this wonderful book.

I encourage you to read this "game changing" book and become a doer of the things Heather recommends to you. You will be so inspired to win at life.

In Christ,

Walter Hallam, M. Div
Senior Pastor
Abundant Life Christian Center, La Marque, Texas

Acknowledgments

I want to give special thanks to my husband Kevin Sanford. His input and additions into the book were invaluable! This book would not be the same without you. Thank you, honey, for all your patience and also for taking up the slack with the kids while I spent late hours finishing this up. I love you so very much and truly appreciate you!

I also want to thank my four adorable children for their love, prayers and, yes, patience during this project. Thank you so much for letting mommy work so many extra hours. Thank you to Hannah and Abbey for helping with the younger two and for having such great attitudes. Thank you to Matthew for being such a good sport through it all. And thank you to my precious, little two-year old, "Lilly Beth" for all those late night hugs and kisses that really kept me going. The four of you are the best kids anyone could have ever been blessed with.

Very special thanks to Christen Hubbard. Her insight, design, and help with the book are appreciated beyond words. I am honored to have someone as gifted as she to help with the book. Christen, I love you dearly and appreciate you so much. This book would never have been finished without you. You are very special to me. You will be greatly missed. You have left an indelible imprint on all our lives.

Special thanks to Yasmin Reid. Her enthusiasm about the book was encouraging and contagious and opened the door for the book to be published. Yasmin, thank you so much for all your love, support, and diligence. I love you dearly.

Special thanks to Kathie Kennemer. Without your support, this book would have never been a reality. Kathy, what a gift from God you have been to me. Thank you for believing in me.

Special thanks to Sarah Katherine Harless for coming in at the last minute, typing in all of the final edits and the many, many final changes. Thank you for being so joyful through the process of finishing the book and journal and helping with our children's camp at the same time. You have been a tremendous addition to our staff! Thank you.

Special thanks to Lynia O'Brien for taking on the extra office work, while I was working on the book. You carried the extra load with such grace and helped us keep moving forward in everything we did. I love you dearly and so appreciate your heart of service.

Special thanks to Anne Campion for your typing during our "all-nighters." You typed tirelessly and with great heart. Anne, your love and dedication is inspirational. You are a gem God has blessed us with. We love you.

Special thanks to the women of Abundant Life Church, Galway Ireland, for being such a joy to teach "How to Love Your Life" to. Your hunger for the Word always draws the best out of me. I love you and am so glad you are in our lives.

Thank you to Kelly Dunn for photography, Natalie Renfro for make-up, and Wendy Marthers for hair. Thank you for making me look good and having fun at it!

Lastly, but importantly, I want to give a heartfelt thank you to Rodney, Betsy, Joel, Brian, Jason and the whole Westbow/Thomas Nelson team.

I've been impressed and tremendously blessed by your professionalism and joy, and I have loved every minute of working with you all. I would recommend you to all! Thank you so much for making my first book such a great experience!

Letter to the Reader

"For he that will love life, and see good days,
let him refrain his tongue from evil, and
his lips that they speak no guile:
Let him eschew evil, and do good; let him seek peace, and ensue it."
1 Peter 3:10–11 (KJV)

My Dear Reader,

How would you like to love your life and see good days? I know I do! The God of the universe that created *all* certainly created happiness, and it is not illusive. If He created happiness, then it is to Him we must go to find it in this war-torn world. God is good and will withhold no good thing from us (Psalm 84:11). So how do we learn to receive the good from the hand of a loving God? It just may be easier than you think. In order to put certain principles in action, you may have to let go of your standard modus operandi and old ways of thinking. If all your old ways were working, you would likely not have picked up this book.

Let me reassure you that this book was not written by someone who has a perfect life or enjoys perfect circumstances. This book was born from the heart of adversity. In the midst of challenges, hardships, and disappointments, I began to discover that there is a way to love your life that is indescribable.

I was already a Christian for years and a pastor's wife, and yet on many days joy was lacking. I felt such pressure and responsibility. I loved my family and my church and worked hard to make everyone else love their lives. But if I was 100 percent honest, many days I didn't love mine. I knew that that was not God's highest, so I didn't give up until I learned how to love my life. Do I love it perfectly every day? No, but when I start slipping back into the old me, I once again pick up the principles in this book and everything changes!

Therefore, please allow me to give you some friendly, "straight-shooting" Bible-based information with some revolutionary thoughts that can challenge the way you look at life. The chapters of this book are honest, direct, and filled with more and more stories with every page. I believe with all my heart that you will love this book.

Enjoy! My gift to you is for you to learn *How to Love Your Life*!

Heather Sanford

P.S. My dear reader, though this book is written from a Christian perspective, if you are not a Christian, do not let that put you off. Please keep reading, for you will discover many life-changing truths that I believe you will miss if you put this book down. So if a few things do not at first make sense to you, they will as you read on.

"For he that will love life, and see good days,
let him refrain his tongue from evil,
and his lips that they speak no guile:
Let him eschew evil, and do good;
let him seek peace, and ensue it."

1 Peter 3:10–11 (KJV)

Chapter One

The Enemy: Dissatisfaction

Now the serpent was more crafty than
any beast of the field which the
Lord God had made. And he said …
Genesis 3:1a

"To love life and see good days" is the heart's desire of all regardless of race, creed, religion, and education level. From the rainforest to the university, from those living on the streets to those possessing the highest offices in the lands there is a yearning from deep within the human heart to love life. Something within our hearts cries out, "This life was meant to be good! I was meant to be happy!" And so you were. So why can loving one's life seem so elusive at times? What caused peace, tranquility, ease, enjoying each other and enjoying life to turn into stress, confusion, anger, wars, etc.?

Before I begin, let me set the foundation upon which this book was predicated: God is good! He is for you, and He is not against you. He loves you and is not angry at you. He desires that you love your life and see good days even more than you desire these things. Now with that thought in mind, let's go back to the beginning:

God's original plan was never for mankind to know pain and heartache.

How do I know this? Because God created mankind in a perfect environment. If He had intended us to originally learn through pain and disappointment, God would have put us in a world much like we live in today. According to the Genesis account, however, that is not how it all began.

"Then the LORD God formed man of dust from the ground, and breathed into his nostrils the breath of life; and man became a living being" (Gen. 2:7). Then Scripture tells us that God placed man in a garden He had created for him. In this garden were beautiful trees with beautiful fruit for him to eat. "The LORD God commanded the man, saying, 'From any tree of the garden you may eat freely; but from the tree of the knowledge of good and evil you shall not eat, for in the day that you eat from it you will surely die'" (Gen. 2:16–17).

Woman is then wonderfully created and life is as it should be for the new couple, Adam and Eve. They are the perfect couple living a perfect life in the perfection of Eden. Then … the serpent entered. We all know the rest of the story about how he cunningly and audaciously convinced Eve that God was holding out on her, not giving her the very best life had to offer. He convinced her to be dissatisfied with the amazing life she had, and so Eve ate from the Tree of Knowledge of Good and Evil. She and Adam lost everything, and the saddest part was that they in fact already possessed the knowledge of good, but had been spared from being tainted by the knowledge of evil. Evil always brings death, and God had wanted to protect mankind from this fate.

You may ask, then why did God put that tree there at all? Well, without choices, people never mature. God, contrary to some people's common belief, is not a control freak. If He had not provided an opportunity of choice, then we would have been no better than a mere robot, and God created children, not robots.

What was the result of Adam and Eve's disobedience? First, fear. They were even afraid of God, and then fear in general entered (Gen. 3:10). Second, blame entered (Gen. 3:12–13), and we have been blaming everybody else but ourselves ever since. Third, spiritual death and subsequent darkness arrived, which we will talk about later.

Please notice what tool the Enemy chose when he wanted to dislodge Adam and Eve from their perfect life—dissatisfaction. Again, let's remember that the garden was a perfect environment. They had everything they needed there to be happy, blessed, and successful. Out of every weapon at the Devil's disposal, he chose this powerful driver from his arsenal because it is, as he is, a subtle and effective thief. He began to "talk" to them about the one and only thing they didn't have in order to take their eyes off of everything else that they did have. (Sound familiar? How many of us have fallen for that trick?) Once a hunger for the forbidden was stirred in their souls, the Devil led them along with this carrot like a sheep to the slaughter, right out of the wonderful life that had been prepared for them.

Truth:

Dissatisfaction may seem harmless, or even appropriate, but it is the number-one killer of successful, godly lives.

You hear about it all the time; someone has it all: a beautiful family, a good job, a nice house, and then dissatisfaction takes hold and they have an affair. They lose everything—their family, their house and sometimes even their job, and for what? A lie? Dissatisfaction? The fantasy never plays out the way they expect it to. Like Pinocchio, the reality of their decisions is often a harsh and shocking wake-up call, but unlike Pinocchio, we are not always offered a second chance.

Dissatisfaction (which can also be referred to as fantasy) can and will displace us from a wonderful life if we let it. When we desire a life that was not designed for us, we will stray from the life that was. God has created every soul for a purpose and already has an intended direction for each life. This great calling is your God-given dream. This differs greatly from a fantasy. A fantasy is a lie, a distraction. In fact, *Merriam-Webster's Dictionary* defines a fantasy as "…the power or process of creating especially unrealistic or improbable mental images in response to psychological need <an object of fantasy>; also: a mental image or a series of mental images (as a daydream) so created."[1]

Fantasy (dissatisfaction) causes us to detour from the life that God intends for us. Fantasy is by its very definition in direct contradiction to Truth. Even if what you want is essentially good or noble, if it is not your "calling," your destiny, it is a fantasy. God has a dream for you, and Heaven's true blessing will only be found on the road He has called you to travel.

So how do we discover the difference between our own fantasies and the path God has prepared for us? How do we move past dissatisfaction toward loving our lives today? Let's journey together through this step-by-step process of loving the life you've been given and discovering the life that is available to you. That starts where you are right now.

Truth:

No one can live your life as well as you can! No one can be you as well as you!

God knew exactly what He was doing when He made you. Here is the truth from God's Word: "Shall the potter be considered as equal with the clay? … Or what is formed say to him who formed it, 'He has no understanding?'" (Isa. 29:16b).

You may not realize it, but when you say, "God, why couldn't I have been that other person over there?" you're insulting God. You are saying, "God, you do not know what You created." You're saying, "You made a mistake when You made me." The truth is that no one can live your life as well as you can, and no one can be you as well as you. This is true even if you find it hard to believe. The trick then lies in learning to love being you!

I have never had my china bowl, sitting on the table, look up and say, "Well I am fat! You made a mistake, Wedgewood! Why did you make me?" I've never had any of my china call up the Wedgewood Company to complain. I've never had my Tupperware complain about storing my leftovers. They are simply doing what they were designed to do. And what a blessing it is.

We do not see anything in creation complaining—the lions do not complain, and even the rats do not complain. No one complains but us. Mankind is often caught complaining over and over and over, "God, you made a mistake." To complain is to claim equality with the Creator, but we are not equal with God. To begin to love your life you have to begin to trust that you were not a mistake, that you were wonderfully made.

> "For You formed my inward parts; You wove me in my mother's womb. I will give thanks to You, for I am fearfully and wonderfully made; Wonderful are Your works, And my soul knows it very well. My frame was not hidden from You, When I was made in secret, And skilfully wrought in the depths of the earth; Your eyes have seen my unformed substance; And in Your book were all written the days that were ordained for me, When as yet there was not one of them. How precious also are Your thoughts to me, O God! How vast is the sum of them! If I should count them, they would outnumber the sand. When I awake, I am still with You" (Psalms 139:13–18).

The next time you are tempted to complain, instead say, "No! God did not make a mistake with me or my life. I am fearfully and wonderfully made."

Now with all that in mind, take a deep breath! Okay, are you ready for this next question?

If your life *never* changed, could you be happy?

Now that question alarms most people, so if that's you, you're normal. Do not panic; this is not a book about how to "survive" a miserable life and be happy in the midst of it. This book is about learning to love the life you were given and realize the only person you can change is you. This book is about how to be a successful *you.*

Truth:

You can still have dreams for tomorrow, but you do not have to wait for tomorrow to be happy and fulfilled.

So often when we set our hearts on certain things happening we are not truly happy until they come to fruition, and we miss out on today! We spend our lives waiting for each new change, living our lives with the ever-evasive fantasy of the future instead of living our lives for today and what God has for us today.

There is so much incredible potential in each day. Though goals, direction, hopes, and dreams are important, we cannot be so focused on them that we miss today. In this uptight world of trying to keep up with the Joneses or the pressing desire to put "life" on hold for a dream that has now become a fantasy, we can miss the laughs, the joys, and the small things that make life worth living, the blessing that each day holds.

Truth:

The more perfect life has to be for you to find happiness, the more happiness will elude you.

However, when the things that we have withheld our true happiness for do finally happen, they are almost never like we expected, and deep in our hearts we can be disappointed. That's true for everyone at some point or another. This is especially true, however, when a person imagines an event down to the very conversations that will be spoken and the positive reactions people will have. These people will always be disappointed. Life is not that predictable. The happy people are those that didn't have an unrealistic image in their mind of the event before they went into it. They had a good but a realistic idea of what their experience could be. Stress, anxiety, and disappointment come when your identity is wrapped up in the execution of the event and not in the people included in the event.

Truth:

Fantasy sets up false expectations and ruins moments that should be happy.

So stop it. Do not fantasize. Have a plan. Work for the plan, and then enjoy the moment.

Let's look at some real life examples where people can get caught up in the fantasy, the "perfect," and miss the present moment. Keep in mind, the dreams you have had the longest have the greatest potential to become a fantasy; be it a spouse, children, promotion, etc.

- **The "Perfect" Wedding**
  The first fantasy we will touch on is your wedding day. Single ladies, this one is especially for you. (Single men, I will get to you.) Sometimes weddings do not turn out *exactly* the way they are pictured by the bride. So what happens? Many brides are dissatisfied. Every bride thinks her wedding day should be about her, and in theory it should be, but many brides experience setbacks on the big day, such as parents and in-laws fighting at the wedding, unhappy guests, dissatisfaction with the hotel service, or rainy weather that makes her hair flop. Many things *can* go "wrong," *but* you should realize that all of these things do not have to be "perfect" for you to be happy on your wedding day. Be careful not to miss the whole reason you're getting married, and that is to enter into a covenant with a life-long partner. It is not really about the dress. It's not! It is not really about the cake. So what if it turned out ugly? That can certainly happen, but it is

not really important. If everything has to be "perfect," then your day has a greater chance of being ruined. It is great to have a spirit of excellence, but you cannot be so caught up in the details that your world is destroyed and your whole wedding day is stolen from you, if it does not turn out a certain way. Single ladies, you need to decide that on your wedding day you are going to laugh in the face of mishaps. Whatever they might be, remember that they are not what's important. If you do all the prep ahead of time to make the day great, then all that's left is to put it in the hands of God and enjoy it! Have fun on your special day!

- **The "Perfect" Marriage**

  There is no such thing as a perfect marriage. There are good marriages, even great marriages, but there are no perfect marriages. They are all "working marriages". Any marriage is a lot of work. So what happens? People get married, and because married life is not as perfect as they had imagined, they are disappointed! I hate to tell the single people this, but guys have an ideal image of marriage as well as girls—and the two worlds do not match. He's dreaming of breakfast in bed, she's dreaming of breakfast in bed, and they both go hungry! No one's getting anyone's slippers, and suddenly we've got a problem here. That's called marriage. Every couple has to figure out how to make it work for them. People think, "Gosh, this is not perfect. It must be wrong!" This thought process can start a terrible and destructive chain of events. Do you see how you can begin to make mistakes because of this imagined perfection? There is, however, nothing in life as fulfilling as marriage so long as the fantasy is dealt with properly.

- **The "Perfect" Family**

  Single men, this one is for you. Many single men have a fantasy of what being the "head of the house" looks like. Many men think their decisions will never be questioned and that their needs and desires will be at the top of everyone's list. Some dreamy young men have even gone so far as to think having essentially "sired" children means a house full of servants who will bring the "king of the castle" breakfast in bed. Then marriage happens and the reality check comes in. You may get breakfast in bed on Father's Day and/or your birthday, but usually the king is busy fighting for, financing, or guarding his kingdom. So much for resting!

- **The "Perfect" Baby/Child**
  People think they are going to have the "perfect" baby. They say things like:
  - "My baby is going to be wonderful!"
  - "My baby will never cry all night."
  - "My baby is never going to throw a fit like that."
  - "My child is going to be the next president."
  - "My child is going to take on the family business."
  - "My child is going to live next door."

  The truth is that your child is going to be who they were born to be by the grace of God. And perfect children do not exist. My husband once commented to my mother that someone's child was such a "good baby." She responded, "All babies are good. Some are just easier than others." I've found this to be true. So enjoy your child for who he or she is and be careful not to compare them to someone else's child or even to your own preconceived destinations for them.

- **The "Perfect" Parent**
  People also dream (and this is one of my favorites) about being the "perfect" parent. They look at their sweet little baby and say, "I do not understand all these other parents. I would never lose my temper with this precious one." Then before they know it, their halo falls off; they raise their voice to their child, and they

begin to feel disappointed and think, "God does not love me because I was not the perfect parent."

No one is a perfect mother or father. No one has lived free from losing his or her cool and responding without grace at some point or another. I remember one particular day in 1999 when Samuel, a little boy from Nicaragua whom we fostered for five years, was seven. He barely spoke English at the time, and our eldest daughter, Hannah, was only two and I was very pregnant with our second child, Abigail. There was not anything the children did right that day. They broke everything, they spilled everything; it was a horrible day. My husband Kevin (a pastor) had been at the church office all day, and when he drove up from work I was sitting on the front porch. He asked, "Where are the children?" and I said, "They are inside somewhere. I was about to lose it, so I thought the best thing I could do was sit and wait for you. They are all yours." And I left. I took a walk. I came back about an hour later after Kevin had put them to bed and said, "Okay, how is everything? I am good now." I think I scared Kevin a little bit, but I was too pregnant; I couldn't go there. I felt like I was more harm to them than anything in the kitchen! So understand that perfect parenting is out. We can learn to be a *good* parent, and we should! We need to "study to show ourselves approved"[2], but perfect parenting does not exist. (Fantastic parenting material, and my personal favorite, can be found in the "Baby Wise" series. It goes all the way to "Teen Wise." Please see "List of Recommended Resources" at the back of this book.)

- **The "Perfect" Anniversary**

  This one is hilarious, because people can get ideas in their minds about everything being perfect to the point that they just cannot enjoy anything. I know from experience. On our first anniversary, we traveled to the States for a preaching engagement in Missouri.

I was seven months pregnant at the time with our first baby. Kevin and I were in the process of moving from Managua, Nicaragua, where we had been pastoring, to Galway, Ireland to pioneer another church. We stopped in the States on the way. I do not know what I had imagined for our first anniversary, but certainly preaching was not at the top of my list. I gave all my preconceived ideas to the Lord and we ended up having a lovely couple of days.

The following year, Pastor Hallam, our pastor from Houston, came to Ireland to preach at our church. It just so happened to fall on our second anniversary! This happened every year after for the first five or six years of our marriage, and amazingly, each year it was purely co-incidental. You know what I learned? I learned the day didn't matter as long as the anniversary was celebrated. And now, we have taught our children that same lesson. Sweet little Abigail has never celebrated her birthday on the actual day since we began Christian Camp of the Arts (our church's annual community-based summer camp). Because of the community calendar, CCA always falls on her birthday, but she is genuinely happy about it. She gets a party a month ahead or a week later *and* celebrated at camp. She has discovered that the actual party is usually bigger and more fun if it is not on her birthday when things are hectic with the camp. Our youngest, Elisabeth, had her first birthday party in September, once all our friends were finally back from their vacations, but she was born in August! We've learned to be flexible, especially in the ministry! If you can learn to be flexible instead of rigid, you can learn to enjoy the grace that God has for you. We have a sign in our office for our staff that says, "Blessed are the flexible, for they shall not get bent out of shape."

- **The "Perfect" Anniversary Gift**

For those of you who are married but haven't been married for very long, the ideas men and women have on gift-giving are

Nugget:

A strategy Kevin and I came up with is to treat ourselves to a night away for our anniversary in lieu of gifts (If you need to stay in a hotel in the same city you live in, it can still be special. The point is to get away.) We know that it is something we will both enjoy, and it is a wonderful way to enrich our marriage. Make sure to find something that works for you and your spouse and doesn't set either of you up for disappointment.

also different. Anniversary gifts are no exception. If you dream all day of a particular gift and instead you get a washing machine or a hair dryer, or a sweater or tie—again—disappointment strikes. You cannot enjoy that new washing machine or tie if you wanted something else. You can "help" your spouse or leave them hints about what you want as time goes by, but some spouses do not get hints even if you write it out and give them the phone number. And that's okay, because you are graced for *your* spouse, but you can forget you have a grace for that man or woman in your life if you do not keep your eyes on Lord (and off everyone else's gifts).

Keep in mind: Just because your spouse may not do amazing things on special events, it does not mean they are not really fantastic in other areas of life. Ladies, a man who does special events well may not have the same everyday strengths that your spouse has. Men, it goes the same for you. When you consider the qualities you tend to admire the most in women other than your spouse, remember those qualities have a flip side, too. You probably would not even like those women if you were married to them! No person is the whole package rolled up into one. If you could step back and view things objectively, you would most likely choose your spouse all over again. You chose your spouse for a reason.

On top of all this, we need to be creative to ensure that we really enjoy our loved ones to the fullest. So I am going to share with you one of the strategies that God gave me. At our church in Ireland, my husband is the senior pastor and I am the church administrator and events coordinator. (Most couples will never appreciate how much stress it takes off of their marriage to not work together 24/7.) My husband and I have completely different personality types. Though we have similar callings, they are expressed in very different ways. Our strengths and weaknesses complement each other perfectly. But just like anytime you work with someone of opposite gifts and temperament to your own, it can take finesse to find the balance. However, when those differences are embraced, you have a winning strategy every time. That is what Kevin and I have successfully learned to do. So, when there is a lot to be organized at the church or a big event looming ahead, I keep a wonderful, happy, smiling picture of Kevin on my laptop and desk to make sure that I remember that I am really happily married. It makes me think, "Oh yeah, I like him!" I have very fun pictures of my children everywhere so that on the days when I am tempted to feel overwhelmed or frustrated with them, I can remember how truly precious they are. Isaiah 49:16 says, "God writes us on the palm of His hand." I figured that was a good idea, and I decided to emulate that with photos. We need to do whatever it takes to remember that life is fun. Enjoy your life today!

In conclusion, we must remember that we did not make ourselves. God has blessed us all with different gifts, talents, capacities. We can show that we trust our Creator when we begin to enjoy His creation (us, our children, spouses, etc.). Remember, do not sweat the small stuff. Do not let the little things about life and people grate on your nerves. And above all, be on guard against dissatisfaction; it is a killer! Now go out there and start loving your life today.

Prayer

Dear Lord,

I pray You forgive me for the sin of dissatisfaction. Forgive me for allowing the Enemy to distract me from the truth. Forgive me for focusing on what I do not have instead of focusing on what I do have. Open my eyes, Lord, to see the many, many blessings around me. Forgive me for all the times

I have made details more important than people, and for sometimes forgetting that no one can be me as well as I can!

In Your Loving Name,
Amen.

Truth in Action:

1. The first step is to repent for the sin of dissatisfaction. We all need to do this.
   (Pray the above prayer or pray your own. Pray as long as you feel you need to.)

2. a) What do you like about yourself?

   ____

   ____

   ____

   b) What do you dislike about yourself?

   ____

   ____

3. Based on what you learned in the chapter, what can you work on changing?

   ____

   ____

   ____

   ____

4. What false expectations have you had that you are now going to be more realistic about?

____

____

____

____

Steps to Loving Your Journey

"For he that will love life, and see good days. . ." (1 Peter 3:10a KJV).

Make these simple steps a daily part of your life and see the blessings abound!

- **Repent from the sin of dissatisfaction.**

Chapter Two

The Mirage

Why do you set your eyes on that which is not?
For it certainly sprouts wings like an eagle and flies in the sky.
Proverbs 23:5 WEB

What an amazing gift we have been given: life! We are therefore only graced, or anointed, for our own life and not that of another. This is so very important, as our entire society today has an agenda to bend us toward a mold of another. Modern society sells an image enticing us to strive to be like someone else; "Then, you will really be happy." This image encourages us daily to walk a certain way, talk a certain way, dress a certain way, all with the promise that we will then discover fulfillment. If we allow ourselves to be fooled into living the life of another, we can never find significance in being ourselves. This is such an important point that God actually includes it as one of the Ten Commandments. He says we are to have *no* false images. (Deut. 5:8 NKJV).

As we launch into this next chapter, let's keep in mind that our number one enemy is dissatisfaction. To combat it properly we need to discover other sneaky, even crafty ways that dissatisfaction can enter our lives and thought processes. In fact, dissatisfaction is so insidious that it can creep in unawares. Let's look at one of the number one ways this happens.

Truth:

Most television shows, movies, magazines, and music prey off the human desire to be someone else or have something else. They encourage the fantasy, the dissatisfaction.

Many people experience disappointment and dissatisfaction because they live their lives wishing for someone else's life, or rather, how they perceive someone else's life to be. Far too often people live with tunnel vision, fantasizing about a life that is not theirs, so they are dissatisfied when this fantasy never materializes. Temptation lures all of us to keep our eyes on someone else and the perception of their perfect life. In reality, what you think that person has, the life you think they are living, is not even real so you've lost two things: the fantasy you will never apprehend and the God-given dream you have abandoned.

When people read magazines, particularly those about celebrities, it can become easy for them to fantasize about being someone else. Reading about the posh lifestyles of the rich and famous can make almost anyone feel unhappy with who they are. Further, it can make men and women alike, imagine that the celebrities they read about are all incredibly happy because of the wonderful things they have to enjoy. However, that's not true. Celebrities have their share of sorrow and disappointment just like we do, and often more than we do. Sadly, many people, even Christians, are taken in by this illusion, causing dissatisfaction with their lives. People waste precious time dreaming about having someone else's life; there are certainly enough magazines and tabloids to prove and cater to this fact.

My own, original definition of fantasy is:
A desire to live any life that is not currently yours, or, the constant dreaming of exactly how certain events are going to turn out. This can happen at any age. You cannot love your life while you're looking at someone else's life. Put a reminder note across your mirror that says, "I can only love *my* life."

Truth:

You will never be happy with a fantasy in your mind. (Remember, a fantasy is not a goal. It is an illusion that expunges the joy out of today.)

Wishing you were someone else, focusing on the lives of the rich and famous, or focusing on books and movies where the hero or heroine is flawless can make you very unhappy with who you are. Remember, this is the pied piper luring you into a life of dissatisfaction. Let me clarify, I am by no means saying that you should not watch movies or read magazines or books; I enjoy them as much as anyone. I am simply saying you should be aware of your weak spots and take note of what extra input makes you dislike your life most and filter it. Begin to challenge yourself to let some of those specific things go, and you may begin to see a marked difference in loving your life straight away. This is true of the believer as well as the unbeliever. The Enemy has the same trap for all of humanity. His tactics have worked so well, I don't know why he would change now. We must wise-up to love our lives and live a life of freedom and victory.

Nugget:

We also have to understand that we are not graced to carry someone else's life. We are only graced to carry our own lives. This is true whether there are days we feel like it or not. Remember, no one can be you as well as you! Let me also challenge you with this thought since we are on the subject: you are not graced to carry your yesterdays. If you are still hanging onto the hurt, the pain and misfortune of yesterday, you must realize that it is too heavy for you. Some people are carrying one hundred yesterdays all at the same time. We need to let go of the past. Your past cannot bring healing, but the Lord Jesus can and will if you let Him! The only grace you have in your life is the grace for today. We are not even graced to carry tomorrow; even it is too heavy. That's why the Lord says, "So do not worry about tomorrow; for tomorrow will care for itself. Each day has enough trouble of its own" (Matt. 6:34). Now let's go back to fantasy.

Esther

If we are not careful we can even begin to fantasize about the lives of those recorded in the Bible. Let's look at Esther, for example. Even our beloved Esther in the Bible, the one who was picked to be queen of the known world, had her heartache and challenges. Esther is one of those characters, those real life people in the Bible, who many little girls dream about becoming. If a young girl looks through her Bible role model options, she might think, "I do not really want to go to war like Deborah, and what Ruth did does not sound that fun—working in the field in the hot sun and marrying a really old man! Mary… well, there was only one of her; Elisabeth had to wait her whole life to have a baby, and I do not want to be Sarah—she was even older!" The list of women that overcame great obstacles goes on and on. So most little Christian girls dream of emulating Esther; the queen, the clothes, people waiting on you, the glamour, the jewelry! Every little girl wants to be a princess, so they think Esther's life is the perfect life they should dream of achieving. Even grown women can fall into this trap. Consider some sobering facts about our beloved Esther:

- Born: a captive in a foreign land.
- Family: orphaned and raised by a cousin.
- Home: harem of the king along with countless others.
- Married: to an alcoholic husband given to making rash decisions.
- Status: Queen to a pagan king.

That was the reality of Esther's life. That's not glamorous. She was allowed to talk to her husband once every six months *if* he called her; if not, it could have been longer. That does not seem to be a relationship, and yet people think her life looks so glamorous. Reality is never as glamorous as people think. That is true with modern dynasties as well.

Similarly, little boys dream of being the king, the champion, the giant killer! But who has taught them that the hero, David, spent a dozen years in a cave on the run from Saul? But in those critical years God transformed "the boy" who killed the giant into "the king" that led a nation back to God. Joseph, another example, ruled Egypt as second only to Pharaoh, yet who likes to focus on the many years he was in prison? Yet in his dark years God changed a slave into the savior of not only his people but also of the known world at the time. Reality can never live up to the fantasy or show how true character is forged.

Truth:

Fantasy leads people into a critical, back-biting spirit!

Do not kid yourself; complainers are unhappy people! If you have become critical and back-biting, stop and ask yourself, "Have I been envying other people's lives and allowing disappointment to set into my own?"

Fantasy is a life stealer!
Here are a few examples of how critical, back-biting people look:

- I have seen overweight people negatively comment on smaller people that just gain 5 lbs.
- I have seen people with bad marriages criticize those with average marriages.
- I have seen those with terrible children comment on other people's children.
- I have seen wrinkly people be critical of those just starting to get wrinkles, when their own could swallow you!
- I have heard others that cannot sing or act criticize those who can. They'll say, "I'd sing it this way."

Why does this happen? Why do these unhappy, critical people do this? Because they do not compare other people to themselves, or they'd give everyone a break. Instead, they compare others to their fantasy of perfection. And that is unfair. If they would stop complaining and enjoy people, then they might find that they'd start to admire the very person they were critical of.

I am not saying to compare everyone to yourself; I am saying love everyone and enjoy them. We're all going to get wrinkly, we're all going to gain weight, we're all going to have life happen to us, and it is great. It *is* great. Enjoy the state you're in. Enjoy the body you have. No matter what body you have now, it will not look that way in twenty years. Begin to enjoy what you have now and cut everyone some slack. It grieves the heart of God when we are critical. We need to make sure that we change.

"For he that will love life, and see good days, let him refrain his tongue from evil, and his lips that they speak no guile: Let him eschew evil, and do good; let him seek peace, and ensue it" (1 Peter 3:10–11 KJV).

The world does not need our comments if we desire to love our lives.

Truth:

Remember that whatever you are going through today is not the big picture; it is just today's picture.

Do not panic if your life is not exactly what you want it to be. Remember today is not the big picture; it is only today's picture. It is only a small piece in the puzzle of your life. However, please remember that each puzzle piece (day) is valuable in making a seamless picture. Be sure to treat each piece (day) as special and worthy. There is a bigger picture going on that deserves your care and attention. I love how one story in particular illustrates this idea:

> One night a man had a dream. In it he saw God weaving a tapestry. After a long while of gazing up at the tapestry, the man had a strange look on his face. The Father asked him, "Is something wrong?"
>
> His reply was, "Lord, I know you are the Mighty God and that You created the heavens and the earth. And I do not mean any disrespect, but that tapestry is really ugly."

The Father took a good look and agreed. He said, "Yes, there are knots and strings and threads that are all crossed in various ways." Then the loving hand of God tapped the young man on the shoulder and said, "Come up higher. Look from My view. You have only been seeing the back side."

The man was then overwhelmed. He began to weep. He said, "That is the most beautiful tapestry I have ever seen. Is this mine? Is this really for me?" The Father smiled, putting His arm on the man's shoulder.

When the man awoke, he began to get excited about his life. He began to live it with greater gusto, and he appreciated so much more all those that were in his life, looking to God in the hard times and learning as much as he could. Often with a wink toward Heaven he would say, "I cannot wait to see my finished tapestry."

-- Author Unknown (altered)

Truth:

No one's life is ever exactly what they think it is going to be.

This is not actually a negative statement. Different is not bad. It is just different. In fact, it can be wonderful. This truth is not meant to take your hopes away, but unless we understand this whole concept we will never learn to love our lives. I have never met anyone whose life ended up exactly like he or she thought it was going to, no matter who they were or how successful they were. When we get a fixed image of how we think our life should be, we can allow the image of that life to become an idol in our lives. This idol can be the very thing we stumble on. This carefully crafted idol, if permitted to stay an idol, will fill us with dissatisfaction.

Sometimes the reason our lives do not end up the way we expect is because our expectations are based on the wrong image; perhaps that of someone else's destiny or a dream that simply is not from God. Other times our dreams are just a starting point, a desire God puts in our hearts to get us on the right path or to meet the right people. However, once on this path we must keep our eye on the Master and stay very fluid and open to change. Some of the greatest blessings in life come from the most unexpected sources and from the most unexpected opportunities. Direction is good, but do not allow yourself to become so fixed on an idea that you are not open to change, or you will miss the joys and the adventure!

When children try to figure out what they want to be when they grow up, many begin to look at everyone else instead of looking at God for direction. Many years ago, after completing Henry Blackaby's well-known Bible study course, "Experiencing God", and Rick Warren's "The Purpose Driven Life", Kevin and I stopped asking our children and other children "What do you want to be when you grow up?" Why? Because they might aim for some suggested occupation even if it was never the plan of God for their life. We ask them instead, "What does God want you to be when you grow up, honey?" If they answer, "Gosh, I do not know." We say, "Just keep your eyes on the Lord and He will show you. Keep your eyes on the Lord and you will make it!" You do not need to know the end from the beginning; that's God's part. Your job is to enjoy the journey and discover it. That is what I want to help you with. Grasping this concept will help us enjoy all the changes, challenges, and detours in life.

What if you say, "I have already lived most of my life; have I missed it? I've never looked to God." The great news is that it is never too late to love your life and to find your purpose. Grandma Moses, the renowned American folk artist, didn't start painting until her seventies. She was a truly amazing woman. She was the mother of ten children, five of whom died at birth and one as an adult. If anyone could have given up on life, it should have been her. Yet we cannot find that reflected in her life. Not only did she not let that bring her down, she awed us with her beautiful works portraying happy everyday life. Grandma Moses told reporters that she turned to painting in order to create the postman's Christmas gift, seeing as it "was easier to make [a painting] than to bake a cake over a hot stove."[3] During the 1950s, Grandma Moses' exhibitions were so popular that they broke attendance records all over the world. A Mother's Day Feature in *True Confessions* (1947) noted how "Grandma Moses remains prouder of her preserves than of her paintings, and proudest of all of her four children, eleven grandchildren, and four great-grandchildren."[4]

Many know the story of good ol' Colonel Sanders. He went from steamboat pilot to insurance salesman to farmer to railroad fireman and on. He didn't start cooking chicken until he was forty. He didn't start franchising until age sixty-five. There are many such stories of people who made great strides later in life; even the thief on the cross. The bottom line is that it is never too late to look to God for direction, to take a chance, and to love your life!

Not everyone is called to be famous. However, do not think you are a failure because your life does not look significant enough to you. If you have loved God and loved your family, if you have helped the hurting and been a shoulder for those crying, if you have brought a smile and a laugh to another, if you have been faithful to your family and friends, you are a hero! Though earth may not give you the praise you are due, Heaven will! You are a hero to every life you have impacted and every person you have prayed for, cheered for, and fought for. Yours is a life that counts. You are living your destiny. "The King will answer and say to them, 'Truly I say to you, to the extent that you did it to one of these brothers of Mine, even the least of them, you did it to Me.'" (Matt. 25:40). If this does not describe you, it is never too late to become that person. That person's life is significant.

So how do we step into this?

Truth:

When we set our happiness on things of this earth, we will always be disappointed (2 Cor. 4:18, Col. 3:1–2).

"While we look not at the things which are seen, but at the things which are not seen; for the things which are seen are temporal, but the things which are not seen are eternal" (2 Cor. 4:18). "Therefore if you have been raised up with Christ, keep seeking the things above, where Christ is, seated at the right hand of God. Set your mind on the things above, not on the things that are on earth" (Col. 3:1–2).

When we set our happiness on the things above, life begins to change and happiness becomes attainable. You cannot *love your life* while looking at your life; you can only *love your life* while *looking at God.* So let's get started!

Prayer

Dear Lord and Savior,

I pray for the ability to see the difference between what I need to change in my life versus what is fantasy. I pray You begin to show me a very clear difference. Begin to "open the eyes of my understanding, so that I can know the hope of Your calling for me" (Eph. 1:18). Help me see the big picture and not get caught up in the mundane.

Also, Lord, please open my eyes to see all the wonderful things about my life. I choose to love my life and see it through Your eyes.

Please forgive me for all of the "false expectations" I have had.

In Your Precious Name,
Amen.

Truth in Action:

1. If you need to once again repent of the sin of dissatisfaction, now is a good time to do so.

2. What specific areas of your life have you been fantasizing about?

   ____
   ____
   ____
   ____

3. Write out how you can commit to pray over these areas and look to God, asking Him to open your eyes to what He has for *your* life. Now can you stop dreaming about someone else's life?

   ____
   ____
   ____
   ____

4. What are the influences that make you envious or unhappy with yourself, your life, and those in it? Can you commit to stop reading them or watching them?

   ____
   ____
   ____
   ____

Nugget:

Let me set you free from a lot of guilt. As one of my favorite ministers always says, "You cannot help which birds fly over your head, but you can keep them from building a nest in your hair." The negative thoughts you have been fighting are probably not your own. You cannot help which lies come to you, but you can keep them from settling into your mind and life. You can recognize them for what they are and refuse to believe them. Subtle lies, like, "Everyone is happy but you," or "You are never going to overcome that weak area" are like strong poison. Shoo those and other negative thoughts away just like you shoo a fly. (Remember, the devil is the lord of the flies and the lies!)

Steps to Loving Your Journey

"For he that will love life, and see good days. . ." (1 Peter 3:10a KJV).

Make these simple steps a daily part of your life and see the blessings abound!

- **Repent from the sin of dissatisfaction.**
- **Stop envying others and wishing you had someone else's life.**

Chapter Three

Love Your Life

"But the path of the righteous is like the light of dawn,
That shines brighter and brighter until the full day."
Proverbs 4:18

You must know with certainty that God is very excited about your life. Jeremiah 29:11 says, "'For I know the plans that I have for you,' declares the LORD, 'plans for welfare and not for calamity, to give you a future and a hope.'" The only question remaining is: "Can you be excited about your life?" The thought of loving our lives is actually foreign to most people. They either do not believe that God cares that they enjoy their lives or they do not know *how* to enjoy them. The reality is, the life that God intends for you and has planned for you should be getting better and better with every passing season, as Scripture says: "from glory to glory" (2 Cor. 3:18). But this requires a purposeful kind of living. It takes a simple but definite decision to love your life. Yes, it is possible to love *your* life!

Now that we are focused properly on reality versus fantasy, take a moment to ponder the following:
What could you do to make your current life happy just as it is? If you knew parts of your life would never change, how would you change and what would you do? What could you do to love it? What could you do to make it special?

Let me give you an example. Our pastor, Pastor Walter Hallam in La Marque, Texas, often teaches the following story in his marriage seminar. He tells of a man who reached the point in his marriage where things were difficult. The man was so frustrated that he thought there was no way out but out. One day he was looking out the sliding back door of his house and the Lord spoke to him. The Lord said, "Look at that tree out in the garden. If I told you that you had to live under that tree for the rest of your life, what would you do?" He answered, "That's easy. First I would fertilize the tree because I had to live under it forever. I would begin to take care of the tree. Then I would begin to make a house under the tree. I would put in an air conditioner under my tree, and I'd carpet everything." He began to make all these plans to make that tree wonderful. The Lord said, "Now do that with your wife." What God didn't say was, "You will be happy if you can change her, and this is how you change her ..." He said, "You change and accommodate her." Some of the spouses reading this may be thinking, *If my spouse only did that, I'd be happy!* But the point is not for them to do it, the point is for you to do it.

This example applies to all areas of our lives, not just marriage. The life you have now is your life. There are things you can do to change your future, and we will get into that later in the book, but what can you do to make it more comfortable now?

Whether you're single or whether you're married; if you knew your life may be the way it is for a while, what could you do to make your life special? How can you begin to love your life, embrace the hard things in your life and make them wonderful?

If you are single, how can you see your singleness as wonderful? How can you love it? How can you begin to cherish the extra time you get to spend on yourself? People that are married with families no longer have that special "me" time. You can make your own decisions without consulting anyone, from holidays to your home to how tidy you keep your room.

Instead of seeing alone time as lonely, begin to see it as "all yours." See it also as special time with the Lord.

If you are in a challenging marriage, how can you begin to make it special, valuable, and truly important to you? Can you learn to speak your spouse's "love language"? Gary Chapman has a great book that teaches the five basic languages of love. In it you learn that if you are letting someone know you love them through time or gifts or acts of service, etc. when that is not their "love language," they may never perceive that you love them. If a couple will take the time to read this one book, that bit of knowledge alone can cut down on much of the strife in many marriages.

Can you begin to say, "God, I love my life, including everyone all around me who is in it with their warts and all"? Why is it important to accept others even with their warts? Look in the mirror and you know what you'll find? Warts of your own that everyone else has to deal with. Learn to love your life and then God can do a miracle.

I cannot say it strongly enough: happiness does not come from each new thing, each new relationship, each new trip or job, but from the Lord (Ecc. 2:24–26). You must realize that lasting happiness is elusive outside of God, but with God anything and everything is possible! (Matthew 19:26) God is the ingredient that makes life special. In fact, God *is* life!

So how can you choose to love your life? For so many of us it is a simple choice. How? First, pray: begin to ask God to open your eyes to ideas to make your life special now while you are praying in the changes for tomorrow. Second, begin to put the ideas into practice. For example: if you do not like your house, what would you do? Begin to make changes. Put up some new curtains or pictures. If you cannot afford to buy anything, paint what you do have, bring in plants, rearrange what you already have and keep it clean! (Remember, this is only an example. This concept works with relationships, jobs, etc.)

Third, begin to take care of what you do have and bless it. Blessing what you already have opens the door for you getting more and better. For example: if you do not like your car, start treating your car like it's a Rolls Royce. Begin to wax it, begin to thank God for it and complement it. At least you don't have to walk everywhere! Anything worth having is worth taking care of, tune-ups and all. (If this analogy pertains to your marriage and not a car, then the tune-ups you need would be weekends away, marriage seminars, and having fun together.) You'd also need to bless your car with your words instead of cursing it every time you got into it. Begin to appreciate what you do have. Take care of what you do have. Nurture it. Be thankful for what you have today and watch a miracle begin in your life. In the case of things, if you are faithful with the small, I can promise you God will increase you and increase you, and you will not stay small long (Luke 16:10). In the case of relationships, if you will be faithful with what you have and nurture them as well, God can also begin to do a miracle. Stop complaining about your spouse, in-laws, boss, etc. I challenge you to stop trying to get your needs met and start meeting their needs with a whole heart. Hold on to your hat, you are about to see a lot of things change. Remember, praise can turn even a hard heart into a hero.

Here is a fun story I heard years ago and recently shared with a group!

> There was a lady who really hated her husband and went to her lawyer to divorce him. She told her lawyer, "I want to take this jerk for everything he is worth. I do not want him left with the shirt on his back. I hate him so much that I want this divorce to really hurt him as badly as he has hurt me emotionally."

Her lawyer said, "I have this great idea. If you really want to get him, not just financially but in every way, really devastate him where he cannot get up again, this is what you are going to have to do. I want you to go home and act like you love him. I want you to make all his favorite foods. Smile and drop what you're doing and celebrate him when he walks in the door. Whenever he wants intimacy, bless him and just act like you are head over heels in love with him for two to three months, and then unexpectedly we're going to rip the carpet out from under him and stick him for everything he's worth. This will devastate him. He won't be able to get up, he won't even know what to do." So the lady thought, "Yes, this is the perfect revenge." So the next day when her husband came home, she said, "Oh, honey! I am so glad you're home," but really she was thinking, "I really hate him! I cannot wait to get to the end." As days went on she was blessing him and talking to him, and over time she quit snickering to herself while she was doing it. Three months went by and her lawyer called and said, "Okay, are you ready?" And she said, "What are you talking about? I am married to the most wonderful, amazing man in the entire world! Why would I ever divorce him?".

> Is that possible? Absolutely. When you bless instead of curse, even if you do not feel "warm fuzzies," everything begins to change because love is an act. Her action of never speaking down to him, never being ugly to him, never being cross literally changed him and her. Disciplining what we say and when we say it is a sign of maturity.

Truth:

If we appreciate and take care of what we have, God will bless us with more and better. If we despise what we have, we risk losing it.

If we are faithful with the little (no matter how little), then the Lord tells us that is *all* He is looking for. He will then begin to bless us with more. "I tell you, that to everyone who has, more shall be given, but from the one who does not have, even what he does have shall be taken away" (Luke 19:26). Can we pass the character test?

What happens to most people is that as the morning breaks and the dawn rolls back they step into their day cursing it and they do not even know it. They open their day by saying with a sigh, "If my life were only different," instead of saying, "God, you gave me today, and I love it! I love my life. Now what can I do with my life and all its challenges to make it special?"

Each of our lives is like a coloring book that's not colored-in. People often do not like the page they were given, thinking they would rather turn to another page that will be colored-in for them. In life no page comes already colored-in. So even if you had a different life, that life too would not be colored-in. You would still have to color it in and make it beautiful. When you see people and think, "Gosh, maybe I can have their life," you do not realize that maybe they've been coloring. Realize also that we see other people through rose-colored glasses. We see their life in Technicolor, and we see our life in black and white. It is time for us to pick up our crayons and color with care! How do we color? By blessing our day, walking in love, starting it with God, praying for ways to make the mundane special. (We will be talking about all these things in detail in the chapters to come.) Get help for the broken areas of your life instead of throwing them away, and most importantly, get your crayons from the Lord. He has some colors that you have never even seen!

That is very good news! He only needs you to start to believe in the life He has prepared, get excited about it, and begin to move toward it today. Color in your life today. Wake up in the morning and say, "Thank you, God, for my life! How can I make my life beautiful? I will love it, I will honor it, I will thank you for it, and I will take care of it in Jesus' name." So I want to challenge you: Learn to love *your* life!

Prayer

Dearest Lord,

Thank you for this journey called life. I choose to love mine! Forgive me, Lord, for not loving my life today just like it is—my crazy life. Forgive me for wishing I had someone else's life. I pray for a new ability to embrace my unique and wonderful journey. I pray for the ability to see my life as You see it every day of my life. I do not want to miss even a minute of it.

I pray for the ability to see as precious and essential what You consider precious and essential. I pray I never throw away in haste that which is my whole reason for being here (i.e.: time with You, time with my family, time with my church, marriage, name your own).

Lord, I am so sorry, deep in my being, for envying. I repent for wishing I had someone else's life, or for wishing that certain things were so different. Holy Spirit, I give you permission to remind me when I allow dissatisfaction, fantasy, or a critical spirit to come in.

In Your loving Name,
Amen.

Truth in Action:

1. What permanent areas in your life are you struggling with (e.g., spouse, relatives, job, city you live in)?

   ____

   ____

   ____

   ____

2. Remember the story of "the tree"? How can you begin to nurture and prioritize these areas to make them special?

   ____

   ____

   ____

   ____

   ____

3. Can you begin to ask God daily for a genuine love in your heart for that person, situation, or location?

____

____

4. Can you commit to stop complaining and start blessing these areas and not let others complain about them to you?

____

____

Steps to Loving Your Journey

"For he that will love life, and see good days. . ." (1 Peter 3:10a KJV).

Make these simple steps a daily part of your life and see the blessings abound!

- **Repent from the sin of dissatisfaction.**
- **Stop envying others and wishing you had someone else's life.**
- **Learn to love your life:** Do not curse your day by starting it out saying, "If my life was only different," or "I hate my life." Instead say, "God, You gave my today, and I choose to love it! Now, what can I do to make it special?"

Chapter Four

Getting Rid of the "Ifs" and "Whens"

"Take therefore no thought for the morrow …"
Matthew 6:34 (NKJV)

The great chapter on the heroes of faith, Hebrews 11, starts off by saying, "Now faith is …." It does not say *then* faith or *one day* faith, it says *now* faith. Because God has a life for us now! The chapter then proceeds to list men, women, widows, fathers, mothers, and many more who lived a "now" life that was pleasing to God in the midst of adverse circumstances. Truly, it is then that the test comes. We must live in the "now" and not wait for the "ifs" and "whens" to blow favorably before we do something for God, for the world, etc. As I have said before, this book was birthed at the most difficult stage in my life, not when I had all my ducks in a row, but what a blessing the revelation God has given me during this time has all turned out to be! (In fact this book is a great example of not waiting for perfect circumstances. I would have never written this book had I waited for *when* I had time to write it.) As King Solomon instructs us, "He who watches the wind will not sow and he who looks at the clouds will not reap" (Eccl. 11:4). These important seasons in our lives cannot find us paralyzed waiting for better weather. Whether circumstances change or not, you still must act accordingly in each appropriate season with the corresponding action. God told Moses, "I Am that I Am," not "I am the Great I am Gonna' Be."

So what does that mean to us today? It means that God is a God that lives in the present and relates to us in the present. His blessings and tangibility are in the present, not the past or the future. Therefore we must take an honest look at our lives and ask, "What have we put on hold?" Too often we live our lives, consciously or subconsciously, in a holding pattern, waiting for the fulfillment of our dreams to suddenly happen and happiness to spring forth. Allow me to recount a story from author Jackie Kendall that really brings this point home:

> A former college friend remained single longer than any of us ever expected. She had dated incessantly in college, so we assumed if any of the girls would marry, it would be Donna. Ten years after her graduation from college, she was not married. Someone asked what helped her to be so satisfied as a single woman. Her immediate response was, "A full place setting." She had lived for several years eating her meals on paper plates while her good china and flatware were snugly stored in her hope chest. Then the Lord showed her that she did not have to wait for a "mate" to bring beauty to her private world. She unpacked her china and silver and began not only to entertain others in style, but also to daily set out china and crystal for herself. This satisfied single woman has someone sharing her china and crystal today, but her feelings of satisfaction did not come because of a husband. She found satisfaction by serving the Lord. Some women put their lives on hold, each waiting for some guy to come riding into her life on a white stallion. They have no china, no decent furniture, and no pictures on the walls—none of the little extras that make a house inviting. They make minimal investment in what they hope is a temporary condition. Their lives reflect a "paper plate" mentality.[5]

Is not that example true for so many of us (male or female)? How often do we hang our hope on "if this happens" and "when this finally happens"?

When in reality, if we want to love our lives, then it is up to us to get rid of the "ifs" and "whens." I will give you some examples.

Have you ever said ...?

- If I could have this or that I would finally be happy!
- If my husband/wife were saved, I'd be happy.
- If my husband/wife would change, I'd be really happy.
- If I had more money, I'd be happy.
- If I were thinner, I'd be happy.
- (For the very few) If I were fatter, I'd be happy.
- If I were prettier, I'd be happy.
- (For many married people) If I were single, I'd be happy.
- (For most singles) If I were married, I'd be happy.
- If I had a different job, I'd be happy.
- If I was smarter, I'd be happy.

OR

- When I finally get that raise, I will be really happy.
- When I finally get this or that, I will be happy.
- When so and so finally changes, I will be happy.

The if, if, if, or the when, when, when are life stealers! If we are going to love our lives, then we need to be happy now.

"He that has a glad heart has a continual feast [regardless of the circumstances]" (Proverbs 15:15 Amp). What a great way to live—from the inside out! This verse is teaching us that true happiness comes from the heart into the life, not the other way around. If we are waiting for things to change in order to be happy, happiness may never come. True happiness is a heart condition that is not circumstance based. Happiness that comes from things is only temporary, unstable and subject to change, but the God of the heart has designed life to be blessed and enjoyed despite circumstances. After all, we are not actually guaranteed tomorrow – we should start living today!

The final and ultimate "if" or "when":

- When this struggle (challenge in my life) is over, I can relax; I will be home free.

Life is far more of an epic battle than we realize. It is far more like *Lord of the Rings* than we think. Evil will always oppose good, and our carnal nature will always strive to overcome us. In this life there will always be some type of struggle. So if you don't know that and you are under the illusion that one day there will not be something you are working through, then let me destroy that concept once and for all so you can be happy. There will always be something you are praying for, standing in the gap for, believing God for!

I explained it this way to someone the other day. I explained that I used to think: *Once I overcome this struggle, or this weakness, I will be happy. I will have rest for my soul. I know this is the last big battle in my life.* I was then always surprised that immediately after I had overcome one issue, there was another issue in a totally different, unrelated area waiting for me. So it was hard to be happy and enjoy my life.

I would pray so hard, work so hard, and finally get the victory in an area and shortly there would be another situation. Have you ever felt that way? I would think, *Gosh, I am so tired! How can there be another situation?* In my mind I was thinking that never having another "situation" was the answer to happiness. I have since learned that cannot be the key to my happiness. That was a hard lesson to learn, but important since it has turned out that building a Christian church in a foreign country has certainly been one epic battle after another, some from within, some from without. I had to realize, that is life on this side of Heaven, but it does not have to be a place of unrest.

You can have *rest* in the middle of the storm and learn to have *victory* over the storm. Let's take a glimpse into the Lord's example. "And there arose a fierce gale of wind, and the waves were breaking over the boat so much that the boat was already filling up. Jesus Himself was in the stern, asleep on the cushion; and they woke Him and said to Him, 'Teacher, do You not care that we are perishing?' And He got up and rebuked the wind and said to the sea, 'Hush, be still.' And the wind died down and it became perfectly calm. And He said to them, 'Why are you afraid? Do you still have no faith?'" (Mark 4:37–40). Notice that even in the storm Jesus was at rest and expected the disciples to be, as well.

God expects us to not be afraid of the storm. He even expects us to learn to overcome our storms, but He does not expect us to *not* have storms. "These things I have spoken unto you, that in me ye might have peace. In the world ye shall have tribulation: but be of good cheer; I have overcome the world" (John 16:33, KJV).

Humanity so wants to think, *After this challenge, once this thing is worked through, there will not be any other problems.* But that is not the case. If you'll remember, history said that about World War I. It was to be the "war to end all wars"[6]. That generation truly believed that, but that sadly was not the case. Twenty-one short years later we were thrown into World War II.

You may have a weakness that you finally overcome, you finally break that bad habit, and then the Lord says, "Now that you've done that one, I want you to get going on the next area." You may think, "Cannot I enjoy what I just overcame, before I move on to the next issue?" Once you realize there will always be issues and challenges, then you can start learning how to relax and enjoy life and not always be battle weary. Then you can begin to really live life and not put it on hold.

I hear parents say, "I can finally stop worrying when my child leaves home." Then when their children do leave, they worry about them all the time. As parents we think that we will be at rest at the next stage of parenting, but we have to learn to be at rest at our current stages of parenting. We have to learn to love life in the middle of the challenges. When you get frustrated and think, "This is the last time I am going to have to discipline my child," you set both of you up for failure. As long as there is breath in your child, you will have another opportunity to discipline them. You need to be excited and think, *Great! This is great! I get to handle all sorts of issues today, and I am going to win on every front! Whether it is disciplining and instilling morality into my precious little child or winning a victory for the church, or winning a victory for me; whether it is overcoming a weakness in my life or a bad attitude, I am going to win this battle. I am a Christian and I love my life!*

David is one of my heroes in this area. The Bible says he would run to the battle (1 Sam. 17:48). Running to a battle means you are confident you are going to win. No one ever ran to a battle they thought they were going to lose. We must begin to see ourselves in Christ. "I can do *all* things through Christ which strengtheneth me." (Philippians 4:13, KJV). Let's take a page out of David's book and run to our battles.

> "For who is this uncircumcised Philistine, that he should taunt the armies of the living God?" (1 Samuel 17:26). "David said to Saul, 'Let no man's heart fail on account of him; your servant will go and fight with this Philistine.' Then Saul said to David, 'You are not able to go against this Philistine to fight with him; for you are but a youth while he has been a warrior from his youth'" (1 Samuel 17:32–33). "'Your servant has killed both the lion and the bear; and this uncircumcised Philistine will be like one of them, since he has taunted the armies of the living God.' And David said, 'The LORD who delivered me from the paw of the lion and from the paw of the bear, He will deliver me from the hand of this Philistine …' (1 Samuel 17:36–37). "The Philistine said to David, 'Am I a dog, that you come to me with sticks?' And the Philistine cursed David by his gods. Then David said to the Philistine, 'You come to me with a sword, a spear, and a javelin, but I come to you in the name of

> the LORD of hosts, the God of the armies of Israel, whom you have taunted" (1 Samuel 17:43–45). "Then it happened when the Philistine rose and came and drew near to meet David, that David ran quickly toward the battle line to meet the Philistine" (1 Samuel 17:48).

David's adversary was real; big, ugly, angry, and vocal. Yet David unflinchingly believed God was bigger and that God was on his side. He believed there was a cause and that good was supposed to prevail. There is nothing you cannot overcome with God on your side. As believers we need to have backbone, conviction and faith in the Living God! You are a hero! Let God's Spirit fill you, and you will begin to see yourself the way He does.

The other day I was watching the movie *The Rookie.* It is about a man who was the oldest rookie ever drafted to professional baseball. As he's going through the farm league, he begins to grow weary from the low pay and lack of respect. Then he sees something that makes him realize what he had forgotten—he loved baseball! The next morning when he woke up, though nothing had changed, he said to one of the other players, "Do you know what we get to do today? We get to play baseball!" [7] That is how we need to be as Christians. We need to wake up in the morning and say, "We get to win another battle!" We are anointed to win victory after victory. "But in all these things we overwhelmingly conquer through Him who loved us" (Romans 8:37).

The only time David, who loved to go to battle, got into trouble was when he *didn't* go to the battle.

> "Then it happened in the spring, at the time when kings go out to battle, that David sent Joab and his servants with him and all Israel, and they destroyed the sons of Ammon and besieged Rabbah. But David stayed at Jerusalem. Now when evening came David arose from his bed and walked around on the roof of the

> king's house, and from the roof he saw a woman bathing; and the woman was very beautiful in appearance" (2 Sam. 11:1–2).

Then proceeds what is likely the most famous account of adultery and murder in history. When we procrastinate by putting off the inevitable, when we refuse to face issues, or when we get so confident we feel we no longer need to deal with certain issues, that's when the troubles happen. Facing our problems in faith with God's direction creates a life of victory. Anything outside of that can open the door to chaos, deception, and even destruction. Be a giant killer. Do not let your problems intimidate you and mock you. Remember, in Christ the safest place to be is on the front lines.

Truth:

Your greatest trial is your greatest opportunity for promotion.

Let me share a profound truth with you that the Lord has been teaching me: many promotions only occur as a result of an adversity. In other words, your greatest opposition in life can catapult you to the next level of success. Look at history; heroes are only born during extreme conditions. Great men and women become great by overcoming impossible odds selflessly. Even countries are at their best in a time of sacrifice. The caldron of tests and trials creates unstoppable heroes. The only question is, will you let your challenges and trials crush you or turn you into a hero?

Each life has its battles, but if you know beyond a shadow of a doubt that God is with you, you can wake up happy. If the Enemy lies to you and tells you there is a day with no battles, do not believe it! I want you to hear me when I say that if you believe that lie, you will never be happy until you go home to be with the Lord. You need to settle it in your heart once and for all. You are anointed for victory on this side, and you are anointed to fight God's way! "Thanks be to God, who gives us the victory through our Lord Jesus Christ" (1 Cor. 15:57). "But thanks be to God, who always leads us in triumph in Christ, and manifests through us the sweet aroma of the knowledge of Him in every place" (2 Cor. 2:14).

Let's fight God's way and win.

Prayer

Dear Lord,

I now see how I have put off my happiness for the fantasy of tomorrow. I have let my "ifs" and "whens" stand in the way of my happiness today. Please forgive me. I choose to love today whether my "ifs" and "whens" ever take places or not.

I also pray for a heroic spirit. I pray for a renewed strength in my inner being, to run to the battle, to win victory after victory for You, Lord Jesus. I pray I am a winner, and I love my life.

In Jesus' Name,
Amen.

Truth in Action:

1. What "ifs" or "whens" can you think of straight away that you have placed as a barrier to your happiness?

   ____

   ____

   ____

   ____

2. Can you put those in God's hands, trust Him with them, let them go, and enjoy the day?

____

____

3. Commit to be happy today, whether these areas change or not. Write out your commitment.

____

____

____

____

____

____

____

____

4. Close your eyes and see yourself overcoming every challenge with grace and the love of God, never battle-weary! What does it look like?

____

____

Steps to Loving Your Journey

"For he that will love life, and see good days. . ." (1 Peter 3:10a KJV).

Make these simple steps a daily part of your life and see the blessings abound!

- **Repent from the sin of dissatisfaction.**
- **Stop envying others and wishing you had someone else's life.**
- **Learn to love your life:** Do not curse your day by starting it out saying, "If my life was only different," or "I hate my life." Instead say, "God, You gave my today, and I choose to love it! Now, what can I do to make it special?"
- **Get rid of the "ifs":** ("If this or that changed, I would be happy.") No! What are you enjoying now? Those who enjoy what they have receive more!

CHAPTER FIVE

Love the Process

"To everything there is a season, and a time to every purpose under the Heaven ..."
Ecclesiastes 3:1 (KJV)

The saying goes, "the devil is in the details".[8] But in reality, life is in the details. Life is in the everyday. Jesus taught this all-important lesson on process: "The Kingdom of God is like a man who casts seed upon the soil; and he goes to bed at night and gets up by day, and the seed sprouts and grows—how, he himself does not know. The soil produces crops by itself; first the blade, then the head, then the mature grain in the head. But when the crop permits, he immediately puts in the sickle, because the harvest has come" (Mark 4:26–29).

Real growth comes during the day by day, the going to bed and rising again. The harvest itself is a relatively small part of the cycle. Rewarding, to be sure, but it is short. To love our lives we have to begin to find joy in the process, and not just in the reward. We need to begin to see things eternally, and see the joy in the mundane of everyday of life. If we miss that, we miss life.

However, this principle of process is even further reaching than that. The problem is that when we do not thoroughly understand this process of time, we can give up too early, short circuit the system (the Kingdom) and abort the harvest. Galatians 6:9 tells us, "Let us not be weary in well doing: for in due season we shall reap, if we faint not" (Gal, 6:9, KJV).

If we understand that the harvest is appointed for a certain season, we do not mind waiting for it and working toward it. A simple understanding of this process will have a profound effect on the way we live each day. And guess what? As soon as the harvest is over, we turn the soil over and do it again in a new season. Life certainly is the process.

"Loving the process" is a vital part of loving your life. However, this can be a hard concept to grasp in its totality. So, here is an analogy to make it very clear and very simple.

Example of an Olympian

An Olympic athlete lives his or her life solely in pursuit of a gold medal. They often live years in pursuit of this goal, some starting as early as four or five years of age. Can you envision what it would be like to be in their place? If they were to win a gold medal, I would imagine they would be truly happy while they were receiving the medal and hearing their national anthem. Their joy might even last a few months to a year while their accomplishment was acknowledged by their country, but I would also imagine many of them will also spend the rest of their lives looking back at that Olympic achievement, living in the past and never in the present.

Suppose they do not win the gold (and only one person in the world does for that event!). I bet many would spend the rest of their lives wondering if they could have done something slightly differently on that day to change the outcome. Often, just that fraction of a second makes the difference between winning and losing. Many athletes spend their lives looking forward to a goal and the rest of their lives looking back at that same goal. Aren't we similar in so many ways? Isn't that how most of us live our lives; living for the future or the past, but never in the moment?

But if that Olympian loves training, loves the process, and then they win—great! If they don't, that's fine too, because they have loved the journey. And once the gold is achieved, it's on to the next thing in life. So they have won it; what's next? Wow! That would be a great way to live life. And we can live it that way. Yet most of us are living life for tomorrow, not loving the processes, not loving today, not enjoying today. Let me challenge you: Live today. Make loving the process your goal. If you do not, you might be amazed at what you miss.

Vacations:

If you are used to living in tomorrow, then even your vacations will not be fun. Constantly planning what you are doing the next day and every minute of that day can take the fun out of it all. If you wake up stressed, thinking, "I've got to get all the sandwiches made. I've got to get everyone out the door by eleven or we won't make it to the theme park on time. Then the baby's going to get cranky, and then everyone's going to be overheated. I've got to make sure we have our sun block ..." You get the picture. If you are trying to *hurry* so you can have fun doing everything you planned, and all of a sudden, nothing is fun, you missed the point. You can find a way to hurry and still get everyone to the theme park by eleven so that no one burns, but you can do it all and enjoy the day! And even though making sandwiches is not exciting, if you have saved up for two years for this vacation and nothing is fun about it, think about how much you have lost! Learn to enjoy even the daily mundane parts of life that find their way into your vacation. Make the process of the vacation fun. If the goal is being together even waiting in line can be fun.

Children:

Another area that's close to God's heart is our enjoyment of our children. Often if you talk to people with small children, they complain that the baby stage is so hard (and it is hard!) They think, "When this baby is a toddler, I will love that stage." Then their baby is a toddler and they think, "Gosh, this baby is pulling everything off the shelf. I am going to be so happy when this toddler is just a child running around." Then that child has so many activities and the parent becomes so very busy that they think, "Once this child becomes a teenager, then I will enjoy parenting." Then the child becomes a teenager with all these hormones around the house and the parent is left thinking, "Once the teenage years are over, parenting will be fun." And they turn around one day and their home is empty and they would give anything to have it back—anything; anything to have the sleepless nights, anything to have the unique conversations with their teenager, anything to be running those errands and left breathless.

We must learn that life is a process, a journey. What if you live your entire life for a goal that you do not reach until you're eighty? It would be sad to have wasted eighty years of your life when you could have enjoyed the journey. If you learn to enjoy the process of your goal, then reaching it is simply the icing on the cake. This is a very important lesson to master, because even the reward for reaching a goal can be something of a let down. Even the moment of joy, has the potential to be short-lived. Many people have thought, "All of *that* for *this?* Boy, if I had only known, I would have enjoyed the journey." How many have said with their last breath, "Had I known what I know now, I would have enjoyed life more and loved the people in it more!" I want to encourage you to wake up and say, "God, my life *is* the journey. I do not want to miss a minute of it!"

Life *is* the journey, not the arrival. Oh, how we need the ability to see it differently. When children go on any long trip in a car, they continually ask, "Are we there yet?" They hate the journey. Are we so different? We need to change our perspective and acquire God's heavenly one.

Prayer

Oh, my Precious Lord and Savior,

How I long for Your perspective! How I long to love the process! Forgive me for the time I have lost. You are the Restorer, and I pray You restore the time back to me.

Lord, I pray that I can see the process as the journey. I pray for a love of the process more than the goal. I pray I am not so focused on "my things" that I miss what You consider important. I pray my eyes are opened to today.

In Your loving Name,
Amen.

Truth in Action:

1. Are you living in the past or future? Are you living *only* for a goal?

   ____

   ____

2. If you are living *only* for a goal, what are you doing this at the expense of (i.e.: God, family time, relationships, etc.)?

   ____

   ____

   ____

   ____

3. What would it take for you to enjoy the process?

____

____

____

____

4. a) Can you enjoy the process of …
   - Waiting for a spouse?
   - Working on your marriage?
   - Waiting for that job promotion?
   - (Fill in the blank:) ___________________________
   - _______________________________________

   b) How will you enjoy the process? Be specific.

____

____

____

____

Steps to Loving Your Journey

"For he that will love life, and see good days. . ." (1 Peter 3:10a KJV).

Make these simple steps a daily part of your life and see the blessings abound!

- **Repent from the sin of dissatisfaction.**
- **Stop envying others and wishing you had someone else's life.**
- **Learn to love your life:** Do not curse your day by starting it out saying, "If my life was only different," or "I hate my life." Instead say, "God, You gave my today, and I choose to love it! Now, what can I do to make it special?"
- **Get rid of the "ifs":** ("If this or that changed, I would be happy.") No! What are you enjoying now? Those who enjoy what they have receive more!
- **Love the process:** Our lives are a constant journey. If we do not learn to love the process, we miss our entire lives!

Chapter Six

Contentment for the Journey

"But godliness with contentment is great gain."
1 Timothy 6:6 (KJV)

For life to be enjoyed, not to mention actually lived properly, one must maintain balance. Balance truly is, as the adage goes, the key to life. When we get off balance we can wobble, even fall. Even if we do not fall down, wobbling is uncomfortable, out of control, and down-right dangerous. If you have ever driven your car with a tire that was out of balance, you know what I am talking about. It is hard to handle. So it is with these two apparently opposing virtues: having contentment and pursuing goals. Yet these two are not contradictory and mutually exclusive. We must learn to balance the two. They work together for the glory of God to be produced in a life by maintaining tension, like a tightrope, suspending us while we traverse impasses. Let's dig in.

We have already learned:

- That dissatisfaction is a life-stealer
- How to love *your* life
- How to prevent the "ifs" and "whens" from postponing our happiness
- How to love the *process*

The next level of success to acquire is contentment. Why is contentment important? For one, it is actually Scriptural. In truth it is what we have already been talking about to some degree, but let's now look at it very specifically. Paul says in 1 Timothy 6:6 (KJV) "But godliness with contentment is great gain." Now let's look at the same Scripture in the Amplified version: "[And it is, indeed, a source of immense profit, for] godliness accompanied with contentment (that contentment which is a sense of *inward sufficiency)* is great and abundant gain" (1 Timothy 6:6, AMP; emphasis added). Amazingly, contentment is the source of great gain and inward sufficiency.

Do you want an abundant life? Learn contentment. It starts here. It starts deep inside, an inward sufficiency that you are enough. God is enough! What you have with God is enough! That is why Paul could say in Philippians 4:11, "Not that I speak from want, for I have learned to be content in whatever circumstances I am." Contentment is learned. It is an acquired skill.

Let's go back to dissatisfaction for a moment and focus in on the envying/coveting side of it. How are they the greatest rival to contentment? To begin with, they are life-stealers, not to mention being a violation of the tenth commandment: "Thou shalt not covet." Envy/covetousness are one in the same and are so powerful they have destroyed families, even nations.

Families have squandered inheritances on lawyer's fees because a certain member wanted more than their fair share. When one wants what does not belong to them, something terrible happens. As James says, "Where envying and strife is, there is confusion and every evil work" (James 3:16, KJV). Imagine, when you envy and begin to strive to obtain what belongs to another, you open the door to the Enemy himself to bring in every type of evil. People have killed for something that is not theirs, or destroyed a person's reputation so that the person would no longer have the coveted life either.

Truth:

You cannot be satisfied with what God has for you if you envy or covet what someone else has.

The same apostle Paul who taught "My God will supply all your needs according to His riches in glory in Christ Jesus" (Phil. 4:19); also wrote, "But godliness with contentment is great gain" (1 Tim. 6:6, KJV). God, speaking through the apostle Paul, said both of these things; therefore they do not contradict one another. On the contrary, they complement one another and are to be used together to provide balance between what you have and what you need. In other words, you do not have to be satisfied to *stay* where you are, but you need to be content in today and in the process. You need to be at peace on the inside. This is the last chapter on this point, but I want to show you how this all fits into our lives and how contentment was created to set you free from strife, controlling factors, other people, and the world's system. To set us free from a fallen system God has given us a powerful weapon: contentment.

My son, Matthew, was a great example of what not to do. In March 2009, he turned five and received a bicycle for his birthday. It was his first "real" bike. In July of that same year my middle daughter, Abbey, turned ten, and for her birthday she also got a new bicycle. As soon as Matthew saw her new bicycle, he said, "Where's my new bicycle?" I said, "You just got a new bicycle in March." To which he answered, "Aww, that?" I was frustrated with his response, but then I remembered that he was only five and I needed to teach him what the Bible says about contentment. Otherwise he would not be satisfied in life.

I didn't want Matthew to need the newest this or that to feel like a complete person, and I didn't want his identity wrapped up in a new bicycle. He needed to learn that he is more than a bicycle. He has a call on his life. God loves him and he needs to feel like he is enough just the way he is. That may sound funny, but we need to beware of the same trap, just on a bigger scale.

Just think, many years ago children often would only receive one toy. However, they loved that toy. And ironically, were so much happier than many of today's children who have so many toys that they just throw them to the side. Often the toys of today's children do not have any real value. The problem is that these people become adults and soon nothing in their life has value, including themselves. They need to have the newest and the best to feel important. "Things" are a blessing, and I am certainly not advocating going back to scarcity. "Things" can make life much easier, but they cannot become your identity. Our identity must be in Christ first, and then God can bless us abundantly. When we are content just the way we are, it is easy not to covet things, whether they are new things or things belonging to others.

"Make sure that your character is free from the love of money, being content with what you have; for He Himself has said, "I will never desert you, nor will I ever forsake you" (Heb. 13:5). Honestly, what makes most people discontent are things having to do with money.[9] I know there are other issues that cause discontentment, but I would say that at least 50 percent of people's discontentment comes from wanting something that they do not have. God calls this the love of money, and it truly is the root of all evils.

When we are discontent, we're not happy and we cannot thank God for what we have. Paul said, "In everything give thanks."[10] So don't be caught up in the love of money. It is possible to be totally content with what you have while at the same time you are believing God for something better; for the promises in God's Word to come to pass in your life. For example, you may be believing God for a better marriage, but you can actually expedite the process by thanking God for your spouse right now, by being content and thinking of ways to bless your spouse now even before the changes happen. Or, if you are believing God for a better job, begin to be content with the one you have even while you are praying God's promises for a better one. You will be amazed how your faith will grow, how much quicker you will get your answer to your prayer, and how you will not make a fool of yourself on your current job while waiting in a state of frustration. To be content where you are does not mean you cannot get "in faith" for something better. God answers prayer, and there are many things you should be praying over. Remember, God is *not* going to forget you; He knows you are there. In the meantime, be content!

In fact, Paul became so content that he could say:
"And He has said to me, 'My grace is sufficient for you, for power is perfected in weakness.' Most gladly, therefore, I will rather boast about my weaknesses, so that the power of Christ may dwell in me. Therefore I am well content with weaknesses, with insults, with distresses, with persecutions, with difficulties, for Christ's sake; for when I am weak, then I am strong" (2 Cor. 12:9–10).

Paul was expecting God's strength to work through his weaknesses, so God would get the glory! He didn't expect to stay weak. He *knew* God would come through! But can we be content with the process? Paul was! He was content being shipwrecked and left out to sea. He was content in all things, because he knew God would not leave him there or forsake him. He knew God was bigger than the problem and would come through every time!

Now let's bring this home. How does this pertain to us? The Bible says in 2 Corinthians 12:10 that Paul was content in "insults and distresses." I must stop right here and qualify this. This is insults and distresses *for Christ's sake.* If you experience insults and distresses because you are a difficult person, or contentious, or a gossip, or just plain rude, you should not be content with insults in this scenario. You should change. These persecutions are not because of Christ, but because of you. If this is the case, you have actually become a stumbling block for the cause of Christ, even if you didn't realize it. If that's you, then unless you change, you will never love your life.

However, if you are being kind and good to your neighbors and they still do not like you, can you be content? If people do not like you at work because you are a good worker, can you be content? If your relatives never accept the fact that you became a Christian, can you be content? Why would God ask such a thing? Because you cannot change other people. If you do not learn to be content emotionally, people will change you for the negative.

I was able to learn this first hand. To put this experience in context, it helps to understand that the Republic of Ireland is predominately Roman Catholic (over 90%). Therefore, only in recent years have they been exposed to any other expressions of Christianity. When most Irish people first met us, in the late 1990's, and found out that we were not Catholic, they were afraid of us; they assumed we belonged to some kind of sect or cult, instead of understanding we are just mainline Christians. (There was even one family who rented a house nearby who was terrified if their little child even touched our grass.)

Shortly after we moved to a new home in Ireland, we were going to build a landscaped shed/home workshop in the back yard, made out of timber. Kevin needed a place to work on household projects, putter, study, and pray. We checked and we didn't need planning permission from the city council for the size of the structure we wanted to build, so we began to build it.

One of the neighbors, however, didn't like that we were building this structure and we began to take a lot of heat for it. Letters were sent into the city council that were unfounded. Later we found out the fear was that we would turn this small, one-room shed into a church, which we would certainly never do. We have a nice sized church in Galway that definitely would not fit in one small room. It is amazing how irrational fears can push people to such lengths. Petitions were signed against us and harassment became intense. Finally, a man from the city council came to us and said we would have to take it down. Rather than taking it to court, we decided to simply tear it down.

I remember driving up to my house, crying and thinking, *I hate going home. I hate it. It's so miserable. I should feel happy about coming home, but I don't.* It was really tough. Kevin even looked at selling the house. We had only been in the house about a year when he said, "Look, let's just sell it and move somewhere else." We thought it was not right that we should hate driving home every day, but the Lord began to press on our hearts not to sell it.

You know what God taught me through it all? He taught me not to run. He taught me to keep my eyes on Him, because when my eyes were on Him, they weren't on the problem. The Lord taught me what true contentment was. It was hard a year, but by the end of it I realized that I didn't hate driving up to my house anymore. The people didn't change, the situation didn't change, but something changed in me. I was different!

Some of you may be in a similar situation today, and it might be very hard. You might be thinking, "Do I have to live by that person? Is my family ever going to accept me? Are things every going to change?" But the Lord wants you to be content in all things. He wants to be strong for you, where you are weak. Only then can you love your life in all its imperfections and all its challenges. I didn't have to love what the neighbor was doing, but I still had to love my neighbor. I didn't have to love the action, I didn't have to love the difficulty, but I had to learn to see God as my source. Ten years later, we actually get along well with them all. We just marked it off as a cultural difference and a misunderstanding. We truly care for them and pray for God's best blessings to be theirs. We never did get the shed. Though many years later we did receive planning permission to build an extension on the house should we ever decide to use it, but what we really received was far more valuable—contentment.

Contentment and Work

Truth:

Life is work and work is a blessing.

I think many people fantasize that life will not always be work on this side of Heaven. Many see work as a "have to" and would get out of it if they could, but that is not God's intention. We are missing God's perspective. In the Garden of Eden, a perfect environment, there was still work to be done. In Genesis chapter two, Adam worked before the serpent came into the garden, but it was not by the sweat of his brow. The earth willingly yielded its fruit to him.

I even believe that we are going to work in Heaven, only it will be free of all pain and all strife; free from what the Bible calls the curse. I don't believe we're going to lie around on clouds in Heaven and be bored, singing for ten thousand years at a time. I think we're going to be busy. We feel great when we accomplish something, and that's God's character in us. I don't think that is ever going to change. I believe we are going to have missions and goals in eternity. It is going to be great!

When Jesus came and died on our behalf, He did not come to rescue us from work, but from the curse! When we receive Christ as our Savior, we are not only set free from eternal death, separation from God and eternal despair, but also from the curse (Galatians 3:13a). By faith we can begin to tap into the blessing of Abraham, but we must first let go of the fantasy that life is free from work and be content with God's system. He has promised to bless the work of our hands, not give us life free from labor.

Nugget:

When Jesus Christ took our sin, He also took the curse (sickness, poverty, failure, misery, eternal death, etc.) into the grave through death. He then rose again victorious over it all and He promises a blessed life- an abundant life- for those who follow Him. For a better understanding of the blessings and the curses, you may want to read Deuteronomy chapter twenty-eight, where they are clearly contrasted. Even under the Old Covenant it was mankind's choice as to which they would receive. "I call Heaven and earth to witness against you today, that I have set before you life and death, the blessing and the curse. So choose life in order that you may live, you and your descendants" (Deut. 30:19). The choice is still ours today.

Here is a little story out of my six-year-old's reading book that helps us understand God's perspective on work.

How Thomas Learned to Work

Thomas was a very active little boy who liked to play. He enjoyed riding his new bicycle, running through the fields, and catching fireflies. Thomas had no little brothers or sisters to talk with, so he talked to the animals, the insects, and nature instead. He imagined that they all talked back to him.

One day his mother said, "Thomas, I think you are big enough to work a little more. You will find as you get older that everyone has some work to do; and it is better to learn to be industrious while you are young." "Oh, mom," he said, "Can't I ride my bike instead? I would rather play". Thomas' mother replied, "'If you have some work to do, do it. Do not sit and pout all day; naught was ever done that way.'[11] Yet since I have no work for you quite yet, you may play."

Thomas raced his bicycle through the green field into the cool woods nearby. As a gray squirrel ran across his path, Thomas called to it. "Mr. Squirrel! Mr. Squirrel! You do nothing but play and eat nuts, do you?" "My dear friend," chattered the squirrel, "you are very wrong! I have a large family, and I gather nuts for them. I work and work every day to store enough food to last all winter. I cannot stop now to talk with you," added the squirrel as he scampered away.

Just then a bee came buzzing by. "Little bee," Thomas called, "Do you have any work to do? I never see you do anything but get honey from all the pretty flowers." "Indeed," buzzed the bee, "it seems to me that I never have time for anything but work. After I have gathered honey from the flowers, I fly to my hive to fill the honeycomb with the honey." And away he flew to a sweet pink clover.

Thomas walked on a little farther. He saw some ants that seemed to be in a great hurry. As he watched them he saw one ant carry a very large crumb. "Is not that crumb too heavy for you? It makes me feel sorry to see you struggle so much. I wish you could play all the time like I do," said Thomas with compassion. "Oh," said the ant, dropping his burden. "It does weigh a lot, but I am so happy to get the crumb that I really enjoy carrying it." The little ant picked up the crumb and hurried away.

Thomas sat down on a rock to rest. "It seems to me," thought Thomas, "that God, our Creator, has given everything something to do. And it is very funny … they all seem to *like* their work."

Then Thomas slowly rode home. "Mom!" he called, "The squirrels, the bees, and the ants all have something to do. I am the only one who is not working. I would like to help you with the work after all!"[12]

Weekends

We truly need to learn to appreciate work and be careful of the trap of living only for the weekends. All week long people are waiting for the weekend to arrive. Therefore, many people are not truly living five out of seven days of the week. Their five working days are spent in drudgery instead of in contentment in their day. For this reason, I have included a list that I have found to help you love your life during your work days. Do not miss out on loving *all* of your life. Remember, at the end of the day, it is still your choice to love life and see good days. (Beware: living for vacations is no different.)

We would be wise to remember that it is work that finances weekends and vacations. Our jobs should be appreciated for that. Don't forget, what you are thankful for grows and is blessed. What you do not appreciate moves from you and diminishes; it is a matter of stewardship.

Here are a few practical tips on making your work week more efficient and enjoyable:

- o **Drop unimportant tasks**: Delegate or delete the non-essential items from your to-do list and always do your most important things first.
- o **Take everything in stride**: Do not make the challenges of the work (deadlines, tough bosses, rude clients) into dramas. Simply accept that they are there, and just keep moving forward.
- o **Face the tough stuff head on**: If there is something difficult that you must do, just bite the bullet and do it first thing in the day.
- o **Recreate your environment:** Try to make your work environment more colorful, neat, and clean. This will create a positive attitude and help you to relax and work.
- o **Learn from criticism**: Don't immediately reject critiques from others or take it personally. Listen, process, and then decide what positive action you might want to take.[13]
- o **Do not interfere:** Avoid any kind of interference in the business of other people. Interference only leads to unnecessary problems and makes you upset with your work and your colleagues.[14]
- o **Find something at work to get excited about:** Plan a company event, a lunch with co-workers, or get involved in some company activity. Increasing one's sense of belonging within a company will increase a person's happiness to be there.
- o **Avoid office politics and maintain good relationships with others:** Be friendly to everyone and it will make you avoid all politics. Work hard to maintain reasonable relationships with your work colleagues:
    - Do not harshly criticize others, even if they deserve it.
    - Do not take criticism too personally.
    - Avoid arguments with loud and obnoxious people.

    - Avoid gossip and backbiting. Backbiting leads to a lot of unwanted comments about other people and makes us more irritated. Rather, avoid talking about colleagues at work. It will get back around to them.
    - If you find it difficult to get along with someone, force yourself to remember a positive quality that person has. You may be surprised at how much the situation is improved.
- o **Take your lunch break away from work:** A change of scenery helps to put the workplace into perspective rather than causing you to feel claustrophobic.
- o **Do not think about work during non-work hours:** Do not let your work alone be the parameter of your happiness. People often become obsessed with work and let it dictate the terms of their whole lives to them (e.g., a failure at work translates to an overall failure for them.) To avoid this cycle of disappointment, think outside of the workplace; participate in activities that are radically different from your line of work, such as training for a marathon, volunteering at charity event, etc.
- o **Be a team player:** Working in an organization invariably means working within a team or leading one. Instead of being rigid and preferring individual work, reach out to your team members and be a good team player. If you find that you have plenty of free time left on your hands, offer help to a colleague who's seemingly bogged down with work.[15]

There are countless resources available in bookstores and online to help you maximize your work week and enjoy what you do more. Find simple tips that work for you and will help you find pleasure in your job.

Retirement

Please allow me to touch on a very taboo subject that often gets our eyes off of contentment—retirement. Please do not stone the author for mentioning this area. It is simply food for thought.

Are you ready for my big statement? I think retirement has stolen the older generation from this world. It has made them feel unimportant as if they do not have anything to contribute. If you are in that group, please do not allow the world to force you out of your greatest call; the call of bringing your wisdom and experience to the next generation. Some of the Bible's greatest leaders didn't even enter into service until retirement age or later. And we have certainly seen modern day examples of successful "over sixty-fives" earlier in this book. Youth is vibrant and wonderful, but it can also be hot-headed and overly idealistic. The distilled wisdom of over sixty-fives' tempers youthfulness and makes a winning combination. Experience is paramount to leading our families and our nations to the next level of growth and success.

It is my belief that retirement is a very sharp, two-edged sword: one side makes companies and society at large disrespectful to those over sixty-five. The other side can make the over sixty-fives more self-absorbed, and less giving.

Don't get me wrong; retirement can be a huge blessing. It can provide the time a person has desired to live a life of purpose, a life of service, but many people spend their time and resources after retirement only on themselves. I have even overheard modern grandparents say, "I cannot believe my son is bringing those children over to my house again. I paid my dues and now it is their turn." Their concept appears to be that life should no longer be an effort, a selfless act of giving. That is not God's way of thinking. Retirement has stolen from some grandparents the desire to help with their grandchildren. Their grown children need to earn a living, and it would be a blessing if they all worked together as a team.

My Grandfather

During World War II my grandfather, along with many Americans, went to war. As the commanding officer in Manila, my grandfather had to stay three additional years and close down all the bases in the Philippines for General MacArthur when the war was finally over. During the seven years while he was gone, my grandmother needed to work, as so many American women did. So my father was raised in the country by his grandparents in the meantime. His mom (my grandmother) would only get to visit him on the weekends. It was a life-changing time for my dad. His grandfather told him stories of adventure and family heritage. My dad learned life lessons of courage, character, and godly living. Instead of spending that time in a daycare, he learned what it meant to be a hero and a man. How sad that most of today's families have no other options available to them. This generation may never know what it has missed. I know beyond a shadow of a doubt that my dad would not be the man he is today without that time and influence from his grandfather. (And what a wonderful man he turned out to be. He is twice fellowed in nuclear medicine and radiology. He was also "America's Radiologist of the Year" for 2007 and 2008.)

There are valuable lessons that grandchildren will never learn from their parents; they will only learn them from their grandparents. It does something special within the soul of a child when children hear the stories from their grandparents. It gives them sense of heritage. "What was Ireland or Texas or Nigeria like when you were a little girl or boy?" There's a sense of wonder for children in these stories. "Wow!" or "That really happened?" or "That's what it was like?" There's a history there.

Though society today is becoming more and more globalized, most family units still appear to be isolated. Even though we may have more "friends" than ever with Facebook, Twitter, texting, and e-mails, the connections between family members, even friends, can still be distant. The truth is, we need each other. As far as it depends on you, keep reaching out, and showing love to those around you. It does take effort to be a blessing to others and to develop healthy relationships. However, people and family are truly worth the effort.

The impact of a more self absorbed and disconnected society is reflected in growing trends that older people as well as younger people no longer want to be inconvenienced. Church statistics emphasize this fact. Only 20 percent of the congregation volunteer to do all of the work. But it should not be that way. The more time you have, the more you should volunteer. Life is too short to only spend it on ourselves. Real living is in the giving of ourselves to another.

Nugget:
Several studies have shown that significant numbers of men die within two years of retirement.[16] *God created us to be productive.*

A great example of a lady who understands this is our stateside ministry secretary. Marcia Edelstein is in her seventies and still works full time. She is full of life, vitality, and passion for the ministry. She completes every project given to her with a whole heart and more energy than most college kids! Her experience and drive have been invaluable to us. I only wish we could have a hundred more just like her. If you are a senior citizen, you have such a rich resource of wisdom to offer. Do not miss out on sharing this precious treasure with your own family as well as the Body of Christ!

God wants us to learn to be content just where we are! We need to know the truth of what God's Word says about contentment. As believers we need to receive the whole Word of God over our lives, not just parts. The contentment message is not always the most popular, but it is a key component in learning to love our lives. The apostle Paul had a word from God, a dream: he would go before Caesar. However, for most of his ministry, he was not in Rome. But because he was on the road to Rome, and not all roads actually lead there, he was blessed, happy, and satisfied where he was.

Contentment and a love for the journey are paramount for you to be the best you that you can be!

Prayer

Dear God,

Forgive me for the many areas I haven't been content in my life. Forgive me for blaming You for the many difficulties I've had that were of my own making, my own bad choices. Lord, with You by my side I am more than enough. Forgive me for the many times I have taken my identity from "things," and please forgive me for envying other people's lives.

"God grant me the serenity to accept the things I cannot change, courage to change the things I can. and wisdom to know the difference." (Serenity Prayer, Author Unknown)

In Your precious Name,
Amen.

Truth in Action:

1. Have you found the balance between practicing contentment and pursuing goals? If not, reread the chapter and come up with an action plan. Write it here.

____

____

____

____

____

____

____

2. Have you slipped into finding your identity from things? How can you change that?

____

____

____

____

3. What steps can you take to be content where you are and stop coveting what other people have?

____

____

____

____

4. What areas of contentment do you need to work on most and how are you going to accomplish that?

____

____

____

____

____

Steps to Loving Your Journey

"For he that will love life, and see good days. . ." (1 Peter 3:10a KJV).

Make these simple steps a daily part of your life and see the blessings abound!

- **Repent from the sin of dissatisfaction.**
- **Stop envying others and wishing you had someone else's life.**
- **Learn to love your life:** Do not curse your day by starting it out saying, "If my life was only different," or "I hate my life." Instead say, "God, You gave my today, and I choose to love it! Now, what can I do to make it special?"
- **Get rid of the "ifs":** ("If this or that changed, I would be happy.") No! What are you enjoying now? Those who enjoy what they have receive more!
- **Love the process:** Our lives are a constant journey. If we do not learn to love the process, we miss our entire lives!
- **Contentment for the journey:** "But Godliness with contentment is great gain" (1 Tim. 6:6). Remember that whatever you are going through is not the big picture; it is just today's picture! Enjoy life today!

Chapter Seven

Peace for the Journey

"Peace I leave with you; My peace I give to you; not as the world gives do I give to you. Do not let your heart be troubled, nor let it be fearful."
John 14:27

How many of you need peace for the journey? That would be all of us, I would say! Peace is an amazing commodity! It cannot be bought or sold, although it is very valuable! The world clamors for it, yet the world can only offer counterfeits, never lasting peace. There is One, however, who gives peace. In fact, He is known as the Prince of Peace. Who is He and how do you invite Him in?

First thing's first. Let's settle the issue. Some people struggle with the question: Is there is a God? Creation, however, makes the answer simple and testifies of a glorious Creator. "For ever since the world was created, people have seen the earth and sky. Through everything God made, they can clearly see his invisible qualities—his eternal power and divine nature. So they have no excuse for not knowing God" (Romans 1:20, NLT).

Have you ever noticed that when you are out in nature, in a field, the woods, or on the water, that you can "feel" God's presence? And it always brings peace. When we get away from the clamor and clutter of city life, when we get rid of the distractions, the Creator of the universe is present.

Many have misinterpreted His presence and thought the trees or nature were God instead of the Creator being God. I was talking once to a gentleman who was telling me how he worshiped creation. I explained to him how that must leave a void in his life, for he worships what he must protect and take care of, but I worship what takes care of me. Don't get me wrong, it is our job to take care of creation, but it is also my job to take care of my children, and I do not worship my children. It is not their job to take care of me, but for me to take care of them. For centuries mankind has tried to worship what their own hands have created or what they were born to nurture. However, that would mean we were greater and superior than what we are worshipping. Doesn't something seem amiss with that? That's because there is. The great news is God does not need our protection; He is so much bigger than us and deeply loves and cares for us.

We recently used a very simple example of a cell phone when explaining this concept to our children. The fact that the cell phone was developed with such intricate detail and for a specific purpose vouches for the fact that there must have been a designer behind it. It could not have created itself or simply appeared from nothingness. The creation proves the Creator. How much more can we see God's design when we look at the world around us and at ourselves, His creation.

God is real. At the end of your life—and that day comes for every human—you will not want to have ignorantly denied your Creator. The evidence that He is real is beyond dispute. If that is an area you struggle with, may I suggest reading Josh McDowell's *More than a Carpenter* [17] or *Evidence that Demands a Verdict.*[18]

The most amazing attribute of our Creator is that He is loving and good. God could have been indifferent, but He is not! He loves us so much that He desires a relationship with us. Imagine the God of the Universe wants to spend time with you and me! He loves us and desires us to have a journey of peace.

What is peace? The Hebrew word for peace is *shalom.* The English word leaves much lacking for a biblical understanding. It leaves us with the thought that we are not in a war. The Hebrew word, however, leaves a much deeper and more powerful impression. Any concordance will teach that the full meaning of the word shalom is very full indeed. It means safe, well, happy, friendly, welfare, health, prosperity, peace[19]. One Hebrew scholar paints a picture of the meaning of shalom as being, "nothing missing, nothing broken"[20]. It is full of promise. It denotes a life of safety, blessing, health, and prosperity where you are not anxious and fretting bad news when the phone rings. All is well. Praise God forevermore! Isn't that what we all want? But we cannot do it without Him.

The Prince of Peace wants to walk into your life today. Will you let Him in?

I. Settle Salvation

If you are reading this and you have never "settled salvation," then I can confidently say you will never have peace for the journey. The Lord Jesus came to create peace between God and man, to reconcile us, the Bible says, to God. Why did we need this? What happened? Let's look at four simple concepts.

First, God is good and He never created man to sin nor to live a hard life. God placed Adam and Eve in a perfect environment full of love and joy, where all their needs were met and they never knew pain or lack. What they chose instead was never God's plan for us. Adam and Eve's decision affected all of humanity. The Bible states in Romans 5:12, "Therefore, just as through *one* man *sin* entered into the world, and death through sin, and so death spread to *all* men, because *all* sinned." Just as we carry forward our natural father's traits, mannerisms, habits, and characteristics, we also carry our spiritual father's traits—sin and death passed to all. There are no exceptions.

Second, we must understand that God is perfect and Heaven is perfect. This can be hard for our modern mind to understand. In a world with no absolutes, absolutes can seem very threatening and rigid. However, if something is perfect and sin (envy, evil, harm, etc.) enters, then it is no longer perfect. Since Heaven is perfect, we cannot go there with our sinful nature or it would no longer be Heaven.

Third, God loved us so much He sent Jesus, who was without sin, the "express image of God," the "Word made flesh … the only begotten of the Father," to die on our behalf and give us a new Spiritual Father with a new bloodline and new traits! "But God demonstrates His own love toward us, in that while we were yet sinners, Christ died for us." Why? Sin and death came to all mankind through one act of rebellion. Conversely, through one selfless act of obedience, righteousness and life became available to all men. Jesus, the perfect sacrifice, carried the sin and the punishment of all mankind on Himself and thus paid the penalty that we should have paid but no longer have to (Heb. 1:3; John 1:14; Rom. 5:8; Rom. 5:18–19).

> Surely our griefs He Himself bore,
> And our sorrows He carried;
> Yet we ourselves esteemed Him stricken,
> Smitten of God, and afflicted.
> But He was pierced through for our transgressions,
> He was crushed for our iniquities;
> The chastening for our well-being fell upon Him,
> And by His scourging we are healed.
> (Isa. 53:4–5)

Fourth, for those who will receive His free gift of grace, He will wash them of all sin and make Heaven their home. Once you have received Christ as your Savior, when God sees you He no longer sees your mistakes, He sees the righteous of Christ through Jesus' sacrifice. The Bible clearly states, "If you confess with your mouth Jesus as Lord, and believe in your heart that God raised Him from the dead, you will be saved; for with the heart a person believes, resulting in righteousness, and with the mouth he confesses, resulting in salvation. For the Scripture says, 'Whoever believes in Him will not be disappointed'" (Rom. 10:9–11).

What to do:

1. Admit your need (I have sinned).
2. Be willing to turn from your sins (repent).
3. Believe that Jesus Christ died for you and rose from the grave (faith).
4. Through prayer, invite Jesus Christ to come into your heart and give Him your life. Receive Him as your Savior (Confess Him as Lord).

Prayer

Heavenly Father,

I come to You in the name of Jesus. Your Word says, "Whoever shall call on the name of the Lord shall be saved." I am calling on You. I pray and ask You, Lord Jesus, to come into my heart and be Lord over my life. Your Word says, "If I confess with my mouth that Jesus is Lord, and believe in my heart that God raised Him from the dead, I will be saved." I now confess that Jesus Christ is Lord and I believe God raised Him from the dead, and I give my entire self to You, Lord Jesus, now and forever. Heal me, change me, strengthen me in my body, soul, and spirit. Cleanse my sin by Your precious blood and fill me with your Holy Spirit. I ask You to go before me today and prepare the way. I will do my utmost to follow you every day of my life. (Acts 2:21; Romans 10:9–10)

In Jesus' Name,
Amen.

Now when you are out and people say, "Oh, you look so peaceful today," let them know you have given your heart to the Lord and that you are confident that Heaven is your home! You have more opportunities than you realize to help other people. People are looking! Do not withhold what they are looking for!

II. Never Be at Odds with God

This seems simple, but it is far more difficult than most people think, depending on where they come from. If you are at odds with God, you will never find peace. This is a different issue than salvation. Can a Christian find his or herself at odds with God? Yes! What do I mean? If you are hurt and say, "God, I've been praying and praying over this, why didn't that happen?", then you are not going to have peace that day. You are not going to find peace with God if you are blaming God for things not happening the way you expected. "'For My thoughts are not your thoughts, nor are your ways My ways,' declares the LORD. For as the Heavens are higher than the earth, so are My ways higher than your ways and My thoughts than your thoughts" (Isa. 55:8–9). God's timing is always perfect. If you have put your plans in His capable hands, let Him establish them. The well-known country song, "Unanswered Prayers," tells the story of a grown man looking at his beautiful wife and children, thinking how grateful he was to God that God never answered his prayer to marry his high school sweetheart. The song always brings tears to my eyes, because it makes me think of the different things in my own life that I thought for sure were right for me, only to gratefully find out later that God's "delay" protected me from some of the biggest mistakes of my life. God sees further down the road than we do, and if we will put our plans squarely in His hands, He will perfect those things that pertain to us (Ps. 138:8). Let's not be caught acting like a toddler who throws a fit when they do not get what they want when they want it. Part of maturity is learning the wisdom of waiting. Just like some things are dangerous to a toddler, some things are dangerous for us if they come to us too soon.

Some people have a more complicated situation. They are not hurt with God because of a delay or because they didn't get what they wanted, but because they have had a very tragic childhood or incident. They have understandably asked God, "How could this or that have happened to me?" Or if someone loses a loved one, they might say, "God, why did that happen?" If that is you, please hear me. The tragedy was not God's doing! There is an answer to your question and it is clear in Scripture (though I do not understand why many denominations do not teach this. I heard a Christian comedian say once, "It takes a theologian to misinterpret simple Scriptures"). John 10:10 says, "The thief comes to kill and to steal and to destroy, but I (Jesus) came that you may have life and have it more abundantly." Who is the thief? Satan, our Enemy. The question should not be "Why did it happen?" but, "Who did it?" The thief did it! Jesus came that you might have life and have it in abundance. God gives us the measuring stick of John 10:10 so that we can know where evil comes from. It comes from Satan and he is cruel. If you can find the strength to trust God, despite any injustices in life, knowing that He is just and the injustice could not have come from Him; then you can pray, "I know that it is the Devil that has wreaked havoc in my life. So God, I choose to love You and I know the pain from my past is not from You. You are my answer! Even though I am working through the anger toward the one(s) that caused my pain, I refuse to allow a railing accusation against my God to come from my heart! God, You loved me so much you sent Your only Son to take my place and to set me free from a miserable life. I need Your help today!" Now that's a prayer that will begin to flood you with peace.

Accusing God will not bring you freedom. He is such a good Father that your accusations will not make Him mad at you, but they will not bring you peace either. Your pain or tragedy is not of God's making (Jas. 1:13). We all need to settle the argument once and for all that God is good. It is very difficult to win any war if you do not know which side you are on. Many Christians try to push their hurt toward God far enough away so that they can get on with their day, but in truth they cannot. You may not have understood how bad things came into your life, but I can promise you it was not from God. Your heart can deceive you in many,

many different ways, and so can your adversary. You have to understand that. You heart needs to begin to be healed. Ask God to begin to heal it. Give it to Him anew. Trust that your Creator is good!

God cares so deeply about your pain that He has kept every one of your tears in a bottle (Ps. 56:8). I think I am a good parent because I kept my child's first tooth and a lock from the first haircut. I even kept the plastic clamps the hospital put on their umbilical cords—gross, I know. But imagine, the God of the Universe is such a loving Father that He keeps all of our tears for all of our lives. That is something far more precious than a tooth. God is tender and He hurts when we hurt.

Numbers 21:9 tells the story of the Children of Israel grumbling and complaining about anything and everything. As they did, deadly serpents (snakes) from all over the desert came and began to bite the Israelites. They began to cry to Moses for help. He interceded for them and God told him to place a bronze serpent on a pole and lift it up high, and all who looked at it would be healed. What did they have to do? They had to look at the serpent on the pole. This was a foreshadowing of the coming Christ. The interpretation is that we have to look at Jesus on the cross, Who became sin for us. If the Israelites kept looking at their bites or pain they would not have been healed. They had to look up. It is the same for us. If we keep looking to our past hurts and pains we will never get healed. We have to look to Calvary, to the Lord. If you will begin to look at the Lord, He will heal the places where the serpent has come in and stolen your life. Also you must know that it is the serpent that bit you, or you are going to keep looking at the situation and feeling anger toward your answer—God!

Anytime we complain and grumble instead of looking to God for help, it always opens the door to pain, problems, and confusion in our lives. Our grumbling gives the Enemy permission to go to work in our lives. Grumbling is one of the deadly sins that kept the children of Israel from going into the Promised Land. "Nor grumble, as some of them did, and were destroyed by the destroyer" (1 Cor. 10:10). Wow! Grumbling calls the destroyer! And grumbling was the tool the Enemy used to destroy them. Grumbling has, in many cases, become such a part of our culture that we do not even notice it anymore. We grumble about the boss. We grumble about the job. We grumble about the spouse and the children. We grumble about the church and about the pastors and about the services. We even dare to grumble about God. Grumbling is what stopped the children of Israel from entering into their Promised Land, and grumbling will stop you, too, if you do not stop it first.

We are all growing in this walk of faith, but we can do that only if we decide once and for all not to struggle with God. Do not be at odds with God. Let me say this too, even if you are still struggling with something, don't give up. When Jacob struggled with the angel he did not let go until he got his blessing (Gen. 32:24). Hang in there until you feel peace in your relationship with God. Remember, when you wrestle with God, God does not change; you change! Hang in there until you feel peace. Do not let go until you receive the blessing! This is an important step to having peace on the journey.

Let me end the second step in "Peace for the Journey" by reassuring you how fathomless and enormous God's love is for you. He is the God you can trust with every ounce of your being! Be assured, He cares only for your welfare.

"The LORD appeared to him from afar, saying, 'I have loved you with an everlasting love; Therefore I have drawn you with loving kindness'" (Jer. 31:3).

"'So I have sworn that I will not be angry with you nor will I rebuke you. For the mountains may be removed and the hills may shake, but my lovingkindness will not be removed from you, And My covenant of peace will not be shaken,' says the LORD who has compassion on you" (Isa. 54:9–10).

"Consider the lilies, how they grow: they neither toil nor spin; but I tell you, not even Solomon in all his glory clothed himself like one of these. But if God so clothes the grass in the field, which is alive today and tomorrow is thrown into the furnace, how much more will He clothe you? You men of little faith!" (Luke 12:27–28).

"How precious also are Your thoughts to me, O God! How vast is the sum of them! If I should count them, they would outnumber the sand" (Ps. 139:17–18).

Prayer

Dear God,

I have really thought it was You that caused and/or allowed all this pain into my life. But Your Word says in John 10:10 "The thief comes only to steal and kill and destroy; I came that they may have life, and have it abundantly." I understand, Lord, there is a real thief and You are not him. "Your lovingkindness is better than life" (Psalm 63:3).

I desire peace with You. Forgive me for all of the times I have thought it was You and not the serpent. I choose right now to put my eyes on the cross and be healed from all the bites from the serpent, the bites from my past, and the bites from my present, and I pray that You show me how to close the hedge.

Lord, You loved me enough to let Your Son die on my behalf. I have misjudged You and now I let go of my anger toward You. I am excited about being free and being on Your team again. Please be quick to remind me when I forget that You are my biggest cheerleader and advocate.

In Jesus' Name,
Amen.

III. Be at Peace with Yourself

That is very important.

- It is just as wrong to hold a grudge against yourself as it is to hold one against someone else.
- It is just as wrong to be bitter against yourself as it is to be bitter with someone else.
- It is just as wrong to hate yourself as it is to hate someone else.
- Learn to love who God made you to be.

This truth became a reality to me in the early spring of 2009. During a very difficult delivery with our youngest child, Elisabeth, my hip and my knee were dislocated. For an extended time, I didn't have much use in my hip or knee. I was on crutches for the first couple of weeks, but even after that I was still having a lot of problems with them both. I began to be dissatisfied and not like myself because I couldn't bend down and get things from the cupboard without pain. The simple things hurt so badly. I felt the Lord challenging me, saying, "You need to be at peace with who you are right now, even if that's not the hip or the knee you are praying for; be grateful they still work to some degree. Be grateful for the knee you have!" He impressed strongly on me that my healing would come, but that it would be a process, and the first step of the process was for me to be at peace with myself. We need to begin to be grateful for who we are. This was an invaluable lesson for me. I didn't realize how little it took not to like myself, to be disappointed with who I was.

We must learn to be at peace with who we are (height, looks, abilities, I.Q., etc.), and this is a process. It can take a while, but we must persevere and practice. The way we can conquer these things and finish our races is by keeping our eyes on the Lord Jesus and not ourselves (Heb. 12:12). As Isaiah 26:3a (KJV) says, "Thou wilt keep him in perfect peace, whose mind is stayed on Thee."

To powerfully illustrate this, let me share with you a story about a man who is possibly the most amazing individual I have ever seen. His name is Nick Vujicic. Nick was born without any arms or legs (www.lifewithoutlimbs.org.). Think of his parents; his dad a pastor and his mom a nurse.[21] They had a lot of choices to make. They probably thought, "What am I going to do with an infant with no arms and no legs?" What the "thief" meant to destroy this family God was able to use to set many people free. "And we know that God causes all things to work together for good to those who love God, to those who are called according to His purpose" (Rom. 8:28).

Nick has clearly overcome discouragement, depression, and many other obstacles through the power of the Lord Jesus Christ. This incredible man leads a powerful ministry and is one of the happiest people I have ever seen. Few have ever had to overcome what he has overcome. He has embraced life and now teaches a message of hope and faith. There are few things as humbling as watching this man encourage people who have gone through less. He loves God and believes God loves him. He is at peace with God and at peace with himself. When he preaches it is a sign and a wonder. No one has overcome those kinds of obstacles without a fight, but he has fought the fight and won. This young man has an amazing ministry because he is at peace with God first and amazingly at peace with himself. Wow! What an inspiration. If you have never seen anything like it, you need to watch the videos on his website. His story really puts life into perspective.[22]

All people have challenges, and yet we still have to learn to love who we are that day. It may not be who we want to be, but it still needs to be who we embrace. You may not have overcome all the obstacles, and you do not have to settle for where you currently are, but you need to love who you are in the process. You need to say, "This is everything I can do in Christ today, and I am going to do my very best, change whatever I can, and trust God with the rest. I am fearfully and wonderfully made, whether my mind tells me that or not!"

There are times in everyone's life when we think, "My life is of no use to anyone! I am doing such a bad job living my life!" Everyone goes through those points of discouragement, and when it happens, you have to realize you are not at peace with yourself. Shake yourself and realize that you have been letting the "thief" dump his thoughts right into your ear with a funnel and you're taking it. Remove the funnel. Pull yourself up by your bootstraps and say, "Thief, you're a liar! I am fearfully and wonderfully made!" (Ps. 139:14). Even if you may have made the same mistake over and over, the Lord understands how you feel. The Bible says that "a righteous man falls seven times but he gets up again ..." (Proverbs 24:16). You may be thinking, "If only I could fall just seven times, it would be great!" But seven is the number of perfection. That means who knows how many times he fell. He fell a perfect number of times, it was never ending, it went on and on and on, yet because he is righteous, he got up again. And you must get up again too, take out the negative funnel, and put in God's funnel. You say, "I will be at peace with who God made me to be, even right now, I am going to be at peace with me."

Let me say one more thing about that. In order to be at peace with yourself, you must keep your eyes on the Lord Jesus. You need to spend daily time in the Word of God. If you keep your eyes on yourself, you will either think more of yourself than you ought, or you will only see all the warts, all the problems, and all the failures. If you keep your eyes on God, it makes peace with yourself attainable.

Truth:

If you keep your eyes on the Lord Jesus, then it is easy to remember that you are fearfully and wonderfully made.

- It is a sin to wish to be someone else.
- Acknowledge what is good about yourself. "She perceiveth that her merchandise is good" (Prov. 31:18).
- Work on the things that are not good about yourself.
- See yourself the way God sees you and agree with Him! He sees you through Christ!

Prayer

Dear Lord,

Help me! Help me love myself no matter what I look like on the outside, because that's not who I really am. You only look at the heart and that is the real me. Help me to not dislike myself while I am changing. Help me to feel Your love while I am changing and making mistakes. Help me to separate what I have done from who I am. Help me to realize that I am a *new creation in Christ* (1 Cor. 5:17) and the things I dislike the most about myself belong to the old me. Help me to no longer see them as who I am during this process of change.

Lord Jesus, forgive me for not believing I am fearfully and wonderfully made. I receive myself just as I am. It may not be where I am going, but it is me today.

In Your Holy Name,
Amen.

Truth in Action:

I. Settle Salvation

1. If you have not settled the issue of giving your heart to the Lord, there is no time like the present. There is no greater place to put your life than in the hands of a loving Savior. If that's you, please go back and pray the "Salvation Prayer" as the start of this chapter.

2. Let a Christian know that you have just asked the Lord Jesus into your life.

3. Find a great, Bible-believing church that you can attend.

II. Peace with God

4. Write John 10:10 "The thief comes only to steal and kill and destroy; I came that they may have life, and have it abundantly" on a sheet of paper and put it somewhere you can see it every day.

5. Remind yourself daily that God is not the thief; that He is for you and loves you!

III. Peace with Yourself

6. Are you at peace with yourself? Take a close look at who you are and ask yourself, "What areas in my life do I still beat myself up about?" Write them down and give them to God.

____

____

____

____

____

____

____

____

(We all have areas in our lives where we desire to be different, where we think, "I wish I could just get this right." And that's okay … but while you are growing you must still love who God made you to be today. Don't be so hard on yourself.)

Steps to Loving Your Journey

"For he that will love life, and see good days. . ." (1 Peter 3:10a KJV).

Make these simple steps a daily part of your life and see the blessings abound!

- **Repent from the sin of dissatisfaction.**
- **Stop envying others and wishing you had someone else's life.**
- **Learn to love your life:** Do not curse your day by starting it out saying, "If my life was only different," or "I hate my life." Instead say, "God, You gave my today, and I choose to love it! Now, what can I do to make it special?"
- **Get rid of the "ifs":** ("If this or that changed, I would be happy.") No! What are you enjoying now? Those who enjoy what they have receive more!
- **Love the process:** Our lives are a constant journey. If we do not learn to love the process, we miss our entire lives!
- **Contentment for the journey:** "But Godliness with contentment is great gain" (1 Tim. 6:6). Remember that whatever you are going through is not the big picture; it is just today's picture! Enjoy life today!
- **Peace for the journey:**

  a) Settle Salvation b) Never be at odds with God

  c) Be at peace with yourself

Chapter Eight

More Peace for the Journey

If possible, so far as it depends on you,
be at peace with all men.
Romans 12:18

The most amazing Bible story comes to mind that illustrates the importance of people in the scheme of life. It is very important to the Lord how we treat others. Luke chapter 16 tells us the story of the rich man and Lazarus. The latter was a beggar who was placed at the rich man's gate every day hoping for crumbs from his table. The rich man "fared sumptuously every day and was clothed with purple and fine linen." The record shows that the dogs would come and lick Lazarus' sores, but it never shows the rich man helping him in any way. I can imagine this wealthy man passing his gate at least twice every day, going and coming, and being bothered by this "eyesore" at his front door; the only exception to a perfect life. Since Lazarus was a beggar, I am sure he begged every time he saw the man or saw any of his friends. Surely the rich man was embarrassed by the situation. However, if he would have had God's perspective, he would have seen Lazarus as a "gift" from the Almighty specially delivered to him every day. He had an opportunity to show kindness and love to a fellow traveler so very often—and never did. A friend of mine always says, "God does not expect you to go out of your way to help anyone. He simply wants you to help those that are 'in the way.'" The most wonderful opportunities are hidden in the most unlikely packages. God has sovereignly placed people (packages) along your journey to help develop your character into the image of His Son. How you treat them will directly affect your eternal reward. Read Luke 16 for the rest of the story. I know the rich man has regrets. I hope we will not.

IV. Be at Peace with Others

Wow! That is a big statement. Someone once said, "The only thing I hate about life is people." People can make life wonderful, but they can also make life very complicated. One famous Proverb says, "Where no oxen are, the crib is clean: but much increase is by the strength of the ox" (Prov. 14:4). That means when no oxen were there you had a spotless barn and never had to clean up, but you also didn't accomplish much. However, when it was full of oxen, you had manure galore to clean, but the work you were able to accomplish made it well worth it.

Well, life is like that. If you shut everyone out of your life, your life is tidy but nonproductive, fruitless and lonely. However, if you are willing to step over poo and clean up after the quirks, attitudes, etc., other people leave behind, your life will be strong, healthy, incredibly productive, full and wonderful!

We are not shocked or mad when oxen, cattle, or sheep poo. We should not be mad when people do the same verbally, emotionally, etc. If we are wise we can actually turn it into fertilizer and grow from it! I promise … people are worth the effort. The Lord Jesus said to "love your neighbor as yourself" (Mark 12:31). If it was easy, it would not be a commandment. You need to decide once and for all that you love people or you will never be at peace with them.

You also need to realize you will only reap what you sow (Galatians 6:7). So if you are kind to others you will begin to reap kindness. Proverbs 18:24 (KJV) says, "A man that hath friends must shew himself friendly:

and there is a friend that sticketh closer than a brother." And Proverbs 17:17, "A friend loves at all times." Be that friend!

A Few Do's and Don'ts

One:

Be at peace with all men.

"As much as depends on you be at peace with all men" (Rom. 12:18). How do we do this? Well, 2 Timothy 2:23–24 says, "But refuse foolish and ignorant speculations, knowing that they produce quarrels. The Lord's bond-servant must not be quarrelsome, but be kind to all, able to teach, patient when wronged."

If you have not decided how you are going to act, you will be forced to *react* all of the days of your life. You will be living on the defense all of the time, because life (and people) can be challenging. You will be invited into many contentions throughout the day, but you must not be unwisely drawn into such traps. Simply, as this verse instructs us, decline to. Just kindly refuse to quarrel. Many of the debates that fill our days are not winnable because they are initiated by people who are not interested in Truth. They merely wish to argue their own point and will never be convinced. The only way to win is to not play. Be gracious and do not participate, because once you do, you will be drawn off target, off center. And once the door is opened to strife, many evil things will come through that door (James 3:16). So shut the door on the Enemy and stay at peace with your friend.

You can also be proactive and begin to implement strategies that are revealed in Scripture into targeted relationships or scenarios. For example, the Bible says, "A soft answer turns away wrath" (Prov. 15:1). While dealing with certain people or going into problematic situations, determine ahead of time to "do" this Word. You will be amazed at the results of the wisdom and power of God's Word.

Again, "As much as depends on you be at peace with all men!" (Rom. 12:18). Let me tell you what this Scripture is not saying. It is not saying that you must compromise your convictions to please people.

Some people take this Scripture out of context. They say, "I know God has given me a conviction not to do certain things or not to watch certain things; however, this Scripture says I am to be at peace with all people. If I tell them I do not want to participate in X, Y, Z then they will not be at peace with me." This Scripture does not say to make all people at peace with you, it says, "As far as it depends on you, be at peace with all people." That does not mean you cannot have conviction or a backbone. It does mean that you love people unconditionally anyway, not judging them, yet still not participating with their sin. They could be mad as a hornet at you, but you are not mad at them. Do not let "the thief" use this Scripture to make you compromise what God has told you specifically to stay away from because it is life or death for you. The thief will use that Scripture to get you right back in the same situation that God rescued you from. Make sure that does not happen. Do not be fooled. "For even Satan disguises himself as an angel of light" (2 Cor. 11:14).

Two:

Return good for evil.

"Never pay back evil for evil to anyone. Respect what is right in the sight of all men" (Rom. 12:17).

Now, that can be hard. It is easy to return good for good, but how often do we return evil for evil? When someone is ugly to us, do we feel like we have a right to give them a piece of our mind, thinking, "That will set them straight"? That's not what the Bible says. It says to return good for evil. "Do not be overcome by evil, but overcome evil with good" (Rom. 12:21). Why? Because Romans 2:4 says, "The goodness of God leads us to repentance." You cannot be at peace and be angry at the same time.

You cannot hold on to the pain that person has caused you and still be at peace. You have to be quick to forgive, quick to love, and quick to be able to do what God requires you to do. Keep in mind, it says, "overcome evil with good." It does not say overcome evil by ignoring it or not reacting to it. So what good can you begin to do today in the face of evil?

Three:

Do not judge others.

You only need an opinion on your own actions! A well grounded minister of fifty years asked God in his prayer life, "What is the biggest problem facing Christians?" God's response: "It is their dogged determination to correct one another."[23] We must stop trying to correct everyone and begin to correct ourselves instead. Love must win the day! We need to ask the Lord to show us the "beam" in our own eye and leave others alone. Often Christians feel like it is their duty to have an "opinion" on everything. Being critical or being opinionated is actually a sign of spiritual immaturity. What other people, churches or Christians do is really none of our business. "We are not called to be the Holy Spirit policemen for the body of Christ!"[24]

Truth:

If it does not pertain to you, close the door on it.

You do not have to judge or have an opinion on anyone but yourself. God is a good Judge all by Himself.

Human nature loves to judge someone else. However, once again, God's ways are not our ways. Instead of judging others, the Bible tells us to judge ourselves, lest we be judged. If we judge ourselves, God does not have to judge us. If we will humble ourselves daily and say, "God, where am I missing it?" He will faithfully begin to open our eyes, to where we need to judge ourselves.

A form of being judgmental is gossip. We should never go around gossiping, saying, "I saw so-and-so the other day and they should not have been where they were." That does not impress God, and it does not make you full of peace with other people. If you see something like that, just pray for the person and love them. It is not your job to correct them. You only need an opinion on your own actions.

We also do not need an opinion on the other churches in town either, except to love them. And while we are on the subject, another related area that receives a lot of criticism is Christian television. True, not every program caters to *every* personality or taste, but that is okay, because it does cater to *someone's* personality and taste. People are as varied as their fingerprints. You will not find two alike. Do not be threatened by variety, enjoy it. What one person sees as beautiful another sees as tacky. What you may see as tasteful another may see as bland and boring. What leads one person to the Lord is very different from what leads another to the Lord. Be careful of the trap of saying, "Did you see their media? Their lighting was not very good." Why say those things and have those conversations? God cannot bless our lives if we have a critical spirit, and He cannot give us peace with others if we're tearing others down instead of building them up. Whether you enjoy Christian television or not, the truth is that it has blessed many people.

Truth:

You are not responsible for other people's decisions, only for yours.

Keith Moore, a pastor in Branson, Missouri, was asked about a big public scandal that was currently going on in America. When asked what he thought about that scandal, his response was, "I really haven't given it any thought." They didn't believe him.[25] How sad!

Be on guard against craving details about another person's life or conversations. It is not healthy. A hunger for details about the lives of people around us can open the door to gossip and constant crisis in your own life. The Bible says "The words of a whisperer are like dainty morsels, And they go down into the innermost parts of the body" (Proverbs 18:8). There is something about gossip that can seem very delicious, but in truth it is dangerous and goes down deep inside of us. Besides, how do you know you would not have made the same mistake if you were in the same situation? Be careful what you judge. It can actually come back to you. Luke 6:37 says, "Judge not, and ye shall not be judged: condemn not, and ye shall not be condemned: forgive, and ye shall be forgiven." The "bad" you "perceive" in someone else's life is none of your business. You are not responsible for other people's decisions.

We have another friend who also pastors in Missouri. Years ago, a veteran minister came to preach in his church. At that time a lot of gossip was going around about a high-profile ministry that had fallen into sin. Everyone was talking about it. The pastor asked the elder minister, "What did you think about that?" The minister just continued doing whatever he was doing without answering. The pastor thought he didn't hear him, so he asked again, "What do you think about that situation? What's your take on that?" The minister still continued doing what he was doing and didn't say a word, and then the pastor understood. It didn't matter to this minister whether the person was really in sin or whether he was not in sin, it was not his business; it was God's. And God is well able to deal with His children.

Other people's mistakes, even ministers' mistakes, cannot be an excuse for us to *not* follow God. We must all run our own race. We are responsible before God for following Him, not someone else. Disappointment is natural when leaders we love fall, but we cannot let this pull us off course. Their human failure does not disqualify God's Word or His Truths. "God is not a man, that He should lie." (Num 23:19). Praise God for that!

As we honor and love leaders and mentors that are in our lives, make sure it is God in them we are following, not their personalities. Then if something unthinkable happens, you may be sad but you refuse to be moved away form God or His presence. Let *no* human be as big as God in your life. Also remember, the more we judge others' mistakes the more we will make our own.

So unless God has spoken to you about it, you need to close that door having to do with other people's lives. To be at peace with other people, you need to shut out gossip and "opinionism."

Four:

Turn the other cheek.

Someone came up to a pastor and said, "I don't like you." It is hard to believe people say things like that to other people. You know what his response was? It was not just to walk away, because that could still be seen as offensive. He just smiled and said, "Brother, it's because you don't know me," with a smile.[26] Isn't that amazing? That is turning the other check. How we need to become experts at this! To bring this further home, let the following truth sink in. . .

Truth:

Others should not determine (or control) our ability to be at peace with them.

T.L. Osborn

T.L. Osborn, a renowned evangelist to the nations, was walking up to preach in front of hundreds of thousands of people at one of his crusades. Just then a lady said to him, "You look more like Satan than anyone I've ever seen." (For, you see, T.L. Osborn had fuzzy red hair and a red beard.) You cannot imagine how a statement like that can affect someone's focus and ability to minister the love of God to hurting people. Our ability to carry God's anointing can be as fragile as the vessel that bears it. If you are grieved on the inside and step on the platform, it is very difficult to be anointed. It is paramount that as Christians we do not let those things get to us. They destroy our entire day, and then we cannot effectively minister on whatever level it is that we minister.

Osborn's response was: "Bless you, dear lady." He didn't allow it to affect him. About two feet down was another lady who didn't hear what the first lady had said, and she said, "Brother Osborn, you look more like Jesus than anyone I've ever seen." But that didn't faze him either, because that also would have placed his eyes on himself. His response to both was, "Bless you, dear lady."[27] I am equally impressed with each response! It is important that we grow to this level of maturity. Without it, it is very difficult to be at peace with others.

We need to learn not to take exception to what people say. It is funny how we can say something about ourselves such as, "I am not a very good singer," but if someone else says, "You are not a very good singer," we think, "What do you mean I am not a good singer?" Or you could have just said that you need to lose weight, but if someone tells you that you need to lose weight, you're ready to fight. You know you need to lose weight. You've told hundreds of people that, but it is the fact that someone would have the nerve to tell you so that makes you mad. We need to be unoffendable. It will go a long way in helping us love our lives.

Let's go even one step further. Sometimes people say ugly things, and sometimes what they are saying is 100 percent true, but they are just not saying it correctly or in a way that we can hear it. So you must ask yourself: Is it true? If it is, deal with it. If it is not, do not worry about it.

Five:

Barbs

Finally, don't notice "barbs." Do you know what I mean by barbs? Barbs are digs, when someone is saying one thing, but they really mean something else. This most often happens when a person is in public and they want to poke at you, or say something to make fun of you, or ridicule you in front of others; usually in front of people whose opinions really matter to you. Some people do it constantly, over and over and over. We need to stop responding to them until we reach the place where we don't notice them. Usually when someone digs and pokes us enough, we react, and guess who looks the fool in public? We do. It is a lose-lose scenario. We have no peace and we look like a jerk. No one ever sees the person who was poking you and causing you to react the way you did, but at the end of the day, you still have a choice whether or not to receive the barbs. You need to extend the benefit of the doubt. Refuse the temptation to simply want to show people how sharp you are by never missing an innuendo, barb, or dig. Overlook it.[28] If you hear a barb, think, "That's not really what they meant." You need to do it to the point where people say, "I can't believe he/she didn't get that! Doesn't he/she know?"[29]

Romans16:19b says "But I want you to be wise in what is good and innocent in what is evil." God actually wants us to be innocent of evil. Why is it such a challenge then to let a barb go unreturned? For some, it is the desire to let others know that they are smart enough not to *miss* a barb or innuendo. For others, it is the desire to show that they are well able to *defend* themselves from such barbs. Human nature, left unchecked, will defend itself at the expense of anyone and anything. Rather, we need to reign in those destructive tendencies, be pure-hearted, and let love win the day. When we let love win, we keep our peace and our health. Many people lose their health because they are so consumed with bitterness about the things other people do to them. The more bitter they become, the easier it is to poke at them and the easier it is to say negative things about them. We really have to choose when someone is bitter or mean, to say kind things to and about that person. "But I say to you who hear, love your enemies, do good to those who hate you, bless those who curse you, pray for those who mistreat you" (Luke 6:27–28). God's ways are not our ways, but they are the right way. If we learn to consistently walk in this Scripture, we will begin to walk in peace unspeakable! Also, if we learn to overlook pettiness, people will begin to actually bless us in return. But whether they do or they don't, we still win.

Nugget:

Joking can often be hurtful, that's why Ephesians 5:4 says we should not "coarse jest". The Greek word means "well-turned with a witticism", like parrying in a (verbal) tussle or sarcastically poking at each other under the guise of joking. Don't do that. It will not give you peace with others. And by all means, do not return evil for evil, or critical joking for critical joking. If we do, we will only stir up more trouble.

Six:

Learn to genuinely love people.

This topic is so significant that it has its own chapter later in the book: Chapter Thirteen. But until then, I am going to end with this last thought. The late Dr. Sumrall, the world-renowned pastor and evangelist, said, "Other people's heads are *no* place to find your happiness!"[30] Boy, don't we all need to write that out and put that up on our mirrors? You cannot control what other people think about you, no matter how hard you try. If your happiness hinges on what they think about you, you will never be happy. If we can be free of the need for people's approval, then we are free to love people unconditionally and be at peace with them because we do not need something from them.

God designed our life's journey to be peaceful. Most people have not realized that God meant for that peace to come first from within. God did this to benefit us. As we truly learn to have peace from the inside out, then circumstances will not steal our peace and we will have attained something far more valuable. "Peace I leave with you; My peace I give to you; not as the world gives do I give to you. Do not let your heart be troubled, nor let it be fearful" (John 14:27). Take heart, you do not have to do everything perfectly, but as you make strides toward peace in all these six areas, you will not be walking alone; the Prince of Peace will join you and help you the rest of the way.

Prayer

Lord Jesus,

I release all of the people in my life that have wronged me or despitefully used me (name them). Your Word says that if I forgive them their sins, then I will be forgiven my sins. Lord, I let them go and put them squarely in Your hands. Lord, I pray now for Your healing to come into my heart. I give you permission to heal all those memories. I let them go.

Lord, I also pray for a grace for people that get on my nerves. I pray that Your love is shed abroad in my heart by the Holy Spirit (Romans 5:5) toward those people. I choose to act in kindness toward them.

Lastly, Lord, forgive me for all gossip. Love covers and I have uncovered. I am sorry, and I will change the way I do things and not share information about someone else.

And, Lord Jesus, forgive me for being at odds with others. Forgive me for a critical spirit, for being quick to answer, quick to anger and slow to hear; I repent Lord. I choose to be quick to hear, slow to speak and slow to wrath (James 1:19). I pray for the grace and the love to love the unlovable. Forgive me for all of my opinions, and right now I let go of all anger and all bitterness. I choose to stop being critical and judgmental of other people. My only measuring stick for others and myself will be the grace of the Lord Jesus, the blood of Jesus, and the mercy of Jesus. Lord, without Your blood, none of us measure up.

In Jesus Name,
Amen.

Truth in Action:

IV. Peace with Others

1. How do you react when someone wrongs you? Do you return evil for evil, or do you reply with a soft answer that diffuses the situation, even if you know you are right?

____

____

____

____

____

2. How can you respond differently? What will you say?

____

____

____

____

____

3. When you meet other Christians do you encourage each other or argue about doctrine? (If your answer is "argue," commit how you are not going to become involved in doctrinal debates again.)

____

____

____

____

4. Think about the "barbs." Who do you need to forgive? How can you respond differently?

____

____

____

____

Forgive them today and experience God's supernatural peace in your life.

Steps to Loving Your Journey

"For he that will love life, and see good days. . ." (1 Peter 3:10a KJV).

Make these simple steps a daily part of your life and see the blessings abound!

- **Repent from the sin of dissatisfaction.**
- **Stop envying others and wishing you had someone else's life.**
- **Learn to love your life:** Do not curse your day by starting it out saying, "If my life was only different," or "I hate my life." Instead say, "God, You gave my today, and I choose to love it! Now, what can I do to make it special?"
- **Get rid of the "ifs":** ("If this or that changed, I would be happy.") No! What are you enjoying now? Those who enjoy what they have receive more!
- **Love the process:** Our lives are a constant journey. If we do not learn to love the process, we miss our entire lives!
- **Contentment for the journey:** "But Godliness with contentment is great gain" (1 Tim. 6:6). Remember that whatever you are going through is not the big picture; it is just today's picture! Enjoy life today!
- **Peace for the journey:**

  a) Settle Salvation
  b) Never be at odds with God
  c) Be at peace with yourself
  d) Be at peace with others

Chapter Nine

Grace for the Journey

"And He said to me, 'My grace is sufficient for you, for My strength is made perfect in weakness.'"
2 Cor. 12:9 (NKJV)

Amazing Grace! Anyone who has experienced the grace of God will immediately tell you it is truly amazing. Many are in the dark, though, as to what it actually is. Simply put, it is God's favor, benefit, and assistance ... His help. Imagine the Greatest Being in the universe, the Most High, Most Exalted One, is willing to also be your Helper. Wow! Who in their right mind would not request the assistance of such a One, but sadly many do not, or do not know how to. Ephesians 2:8 says, "For by grace are you saved through faith; and that not of yourselves, it is the gift of God." We see here that we are saved by this amazing grace. The original word for "saved" also means to protect, preserve, heal, to do well, and to make whole[31]. This is what grace will do for you and infinitely more, and best of all, it is a free gift and a promise from the Almighty. The only hitch is that this amazing "gift" can only be "opened" one way—by faith. What is the faith the Scripture is talking about? It is being fully persuaded that what God said He will do. It is the assurance that if you look to the Lord Jesus for grace, you will receive it. Another beautiful definition of grace is found in Luke 1:30 (AMP): God's free, spontaneous, absolute favor and loving-kindness. Let's learn how to receive this precious gift.

Grace for the journey is so important, yet most people underestimate its necessity and value in literally opening up the floodgates for us to love our lives. Grace is the oil in your life that keeps everything from squeaking and causing sparks. Grace is the very special ingredient that all of our lives need. People often think that if they are Christians, the grace is automatic in their lives, or if they have a "calling" or purpose (like being a doctor, teacher, parent, minister, spouse, etc,), the grace for it is automatic. However, that is not true. We must learn to tap into the grace that God has for us.

This really hit home in the summer of 2009. Elisabeth, our youngest, was just about to turn one. I still had health issues from the delivery and it had been such a very, very hard year. That August, Kevin went to America, and Hannah (our twelve-year-old then) had the privilege of travelling with her daddy and going to a two-week summer camp for girls in Texas. When Hannah and Kevin left, all of a sudden I felt relief. (Follow me in this for a moment.) I said in my prayer time, "Lord, what is it?" And the Lord very clearly impressed on my heart that it had to do with the children. Then I realized "Wow! I am comfortable with three children, but now I have four." Kevin and I knew in our hearts that God called us to have four children. We had no doubt about that! We even called this baby our "extra mile baby," but the transition to four had been hard. When Hannah left with Kevin for the two weeks, one would think it would have been harder without her since she was older and could help a lot, but it was not. It was easier to go back to three children. As I asked the Lord in prayer, He clearly showed me, "You managed three children naturally. It was easy for you. You didn't need Me. Now you need My grace."

Let me rewind time for a moment. You have to understand that Kevin and I had three children almost straight away. In 1998, when Hannah was one and a half, we filed to foster Samuel, a little boy from Nicaragua (where we used to pastor a church). Samuel came to us within a month. Then, by the time Hannah was two and a half, I gave birth to Abigail. So we had three children in two and a half years. After having Samuel for almost five years, he returned to Nicaragua. We helped him return to his native land and to a safe family environment. It was an incredibly sorrowful time for us, but through God's amazing love, Kevin and I discovered I was pregnant again, this time with a boy. So within six months of Samuel leaving, we were back to three children again, back to the exact dynamics—two girls and a boy, and for me that was "normally" quite easy. For some people three is a stretch, but for whatever reason it usually was not for me (unless, of course, I was very pregnant!).

I didn't know that I had never truly depended on the grace of God to parent three children. All of a sudden I had four and I thought, *"This is really hard!"* I didn't know how to do four different schedules, four different everything. In fact, that previous spring, because it was so hard for me to adjust from three children to four, I had one of those horribly, embarrassing parenting moments. Kevin and I were hosting a conference in Galway, so I made arrangements for all the children. The girls had a special day out, the baby was with me, and Matthew had a play date arranged. About 10:30p.m. I got this very sweet phone call from the mother of Matthew's friend on my mobile saying, "Are you going to come pick up Matthew at any point, or do we need to put him to bed over here?" I had totally forgotten him! We had meetings all day and I was not actually home. I would not have forgotten him if I had been home (I promise!) He was with a good family, praise the Lord! I hadn't realized that I had arranged a way for him to get there, but I hadn't arranged a way for him to get back from there. So the family had Matthew 'till late at night. They gave him pajamas, dinner, … everything. They said they were ready if they had to put him to bed, but I said, "No, no! I am really sorry, and I am really embarrassed!" I was so embarrassed because I hadn't tapped into the grace God had for me.

Let's return to the revelation God was showing me that August in 2009. I began to pray and the Lord clearly spoke to my heart, "If you pray for grace, I will parent the four children through you. Up until now you have parented the three children, but I will parent the four children!" And I began to pray, "Lord, I am so sorry. I thought when You told me to go the extra mile that the grace was automatic." From that point on I began to not only pray for God's grace, but also to lean on His grace. Since that day managing four schedules and parenting four children has been a pure delight.

The Bible says that people perish for lack of knowledge. People might obediently go the extra mile and yet they often struggle and die in their last mile, but it is not meant to be that way.

Nugget:

The thought of "the extra mile" comes from Jesus' teaching in the Sermon on the Mount in Matthew 5:41. He was dealing with character and with heart. He instructed His followers that if someone "should compel you to go a mile, go with him two." The Romans had a law for their conquered lands that allowed any Roman authority to commandeer the labor of a local citizen for an official task. A soldier, for example, could grab a bystander and require him to carry something for him anywhere. In an effort to be reasonable, the injunction had a limit—one thousand paces. The Jews would certainly have despised being hijacked by a foreigner in their own country and being required to immediately evacuate their own life and day in order to serve Rome's pleasure. A soldier would have cared less if they were on their way to synagogue, a family meal, or even if Sabbath was rapidly approaching. The local would have acquiesced to the order, but would have expressed disdain with every step. They were required to go a thousand steps (mil-ia, where "mile" comes from), but not to be happy about it! You can be sure that any self-respecting Jew would have faithfully counted every single step, and then dropped the load with a sneer and returned to his life. Likewise the soldier, hating these rebellious Jews, was not about to let them off a single step. They would have both been counting, together.

But Jesus' standard is not the standard of men. It is greater. Can you imagine the Christian? Having been nabbed by a soldier he walks alongside the soldier testifying of the loving Servant Christ. The skeptic authority would have been counting: "997–998–999–1,000 ....1001–1002 ... what?" The Christian keeps smiling as he finishes the story while going an "extra mile." What could be more convincing? What could show more love, more of God to a soldier just trying to do his duty? Only the "extra mile" could!

Truth:

When you go the extra mile the grace is not automatic!

You must humble yourself and ask for grace! Do not try life in your own strength. You were never meant to live it alone and were not designed to.

A good analogy would be the parable Jesus told of the ten virgins (Matthew 25:1–13). Besides the obvious interpretation, the Lord began to have me look at this parable in relation to grace! In this parable there were ten virgins waiting for the bridegroom with their lamps trimmed. Five of the girls had the extra oil (grace) for their lamps in case the night went long and five did not. The five that did not have the extra *grace* were still virgins! In other words, they were still pure hearted. They had some *grace*, so they had some anointing. But they needed to go the "extra mile" to wait for the bridegroom to arrive, and they found themselves without the extra *grace* needed to wait. The others, however, did have the extra *grace* to wait. As soon as the five without the *grace* left, they missed the bridegroom. And the Lord spoke to my heart, "When I call you to go the extra mile, whether it is with your family, with your husband, with the ministry, or whatever it is, you're going to have to pray for My *grace* in order to succeed. Without enough *grace*, there are many wonderful opportunities of loving your life that you are going to miss." So I began to realize, when you get the extra *grace* (oil) from the Father, the Bridegroom will always arrive and show up on the scene for you!

> "He said to me, My grace (My favor and loving-kindness and mercy) is enough for you [sufficient against any danger and enables you to bear the trouble manfully or strongly]; for My strength and power are made perfect (fulfilled and completed) and show themselves most effective in [your] weakness.' Therefore, I will all the more gladly glory in my weaknesses and infirmities, that the strength and power of Christ (the

> Messiah) may rest (yes, may pitch a tent over and dwell) upon me!" (2 Cor. 12:9 Amp.)

In my weakness! "Therefore, I will all the more gladly glory in my weaknesses" (2 Cor. 12:9). I am not embarrassed to tell you my weaknesses. Paul gloried in his weakness. I glory in the fact that, naturally, I cannot do everything. I stand in awe of those who have twelve children; I couldn't manage four without God. I glory in my weakness, that the strength and power of Christ (the Messiah) may rest (yes, may pitch a tent over and dwell) upon me!

It does not mean I stay weak or sick. It means that now God's glory can come through me in the area of my parenting if I lean on Him. It means I can be anointed on a level that I never have been. I was doing what I could with my children, but it was not anointed. Once I leaned on God I realized I didn't have to be weak and I didn't have to do it all by myself! I couldn't wait for Hannah to get back from camp so that I could go to four children and step into the grace that God had for me. Because I tapped into His grace, I was able to properly implement the knowledge He had given me through books and other materials. Without His grace, I may have had the same facts, but I wasn't able to walk them out in love.

Work:
Do you need a grace for your work schedule? Many do! So many people think, "I am in such a busy season of life! There are so many things pulling on me. I am needed here or there. I never have enough time. I cannot wait for this season of my life to be over!" That's not Scriptural because, again, you are waiting for something else in order to be happy, and you are not using faith for what you are doing today.

What if you prayed for a grace for your schedule and for your job. You could say, "God, I cannot do it all. I have too much going on! I do not know how to do it all, and I need help!" What if you prayed, instead of waiting for a magical time when life will not be hectic (which I do not know will ever happen in this time period in history)? What if instead you step into the grace God has for you? God would begin to multiply your time, show you creative ideas and short cuts. When you have grace for the day, instead of making twenty phone calls to get a hold of one person, you get a hold of the first person the first time, and your time is multiplied. What if we had grace for our jobs, grace for our students if we are teachers? What would life look like if we weren't praying for our life to change, but if we changed? What if we called our life beautiful? If we "decree a thing, and it shall be established" (Job 22:28)? (To decree a thing means to speak God's Word authoritatively over a situation and with confidence instead of speaking out the negative circumstances.) If we did this, we would begin to see the grace of the Lord and the anointing of God on a level the world has never seen, all to the glory of God!

I am convinced that when people take the glory or credit for themselves, they are still operating in their own talent. They could be outrageously talented. They could even have a great gift from God, but the greatest day of their lives is when they reach the end of their gift. Perhaps one who can minister to thousands God calls to go the extra mile and minister to *hundreds* of thousands. That person will finally get to a point where they say, "Oh my gosh, I cannot!" and God's response will be, "I was waiting for you to finally get to that point!" Humility then enters the person and God can take over. "It is no longer I that live, it is Christ that lives in me" (Gal. 2:20). In the process, God gets the glory.

I can honestly say that few of my natural strengths are in the areas I work in the most, and I have grown to love it that way. I have learned to lean on God instead of on my talent. From children's ministry, to public speaking, to fund-raising, to drama, to camp director, designer and more—none of these are my natural abilities. Yet God has used me in these areas and He gets the glory, not me! Our children's camp, for example, has been voted one of the best in the nation. Our women's conferences now draw ladies from all parts of Ireland as well as other countries. It was so exciting for me to see all that God could do when I stop using my weaknesses as an excuse. Even in the areas of church where I use my natural strengths, I've learned even in those to lean on God. But when I forget to do that, life all of a sudden gets hard.

It is good to know where you are talented and where you are not, but do not let that limit you. One of our interns said, "Gosh, your church staff does everything! They are so talented! I do not have any of those talents." I thought, *"That was me a few years back."* But I told God, "I am available. I may not be the most talented person I know, but I am available." And God said, "That's great; I just get to use you faster." I was quicker to invite God into my work than my parenting because I saw my deficiencies more clearly, but now that has all changed. Glory to God! In my weaknesses, He is making me stronger!

Stop asking for everything to be different and step into the grace God has for you. When you are in His grace, you are not carrying the burden of your job, your marriage, your children, your parents, etc. God is. It all becomes His burden. It may be what you are dealing with, but you are still not the Savior; He is. And when you begin to step into this grace, then you can hear Him say, "Do not do that," or "Do this," or "This is how you do this." At this point life gets easier.

Nugget:

And for you comfort eaters out there… there is a Scripture just for you: "Do not be carried away by varied and strange teachings; for it is good for the heart to be strengthened by grace, not by foods, through which those who were so occupied were not benefited" (Heb 13:9). Did you see that? "Not by foods"! God is so smart! We can't get anything by Him. God wants us to turn to Him in times of need. Comfort eating will never give us the grace we need for life and will only hurt our waistlines. It may feel great at the time but the guilt that follows is seldom worth it.

Prayer

Heavenly Father,

According to 2 Corinthians 12:9, "You said Your grace (Your favor and loving-kindness and mercy) is enough for me [sufficient against any danger and enables me to bear the trouble manfully or strongly]; for Your strength and power are made perfect (fulfilled and completed) and show themselves most effective in [my] weakness."

So I whole-heartedly invite You into my life and all my weak areas (list them in prayer). I rest in Your grace today! I pray I remember to lean on You and Your grace every time I am tempted to give up or get discouraged.

In Jesus' Name,
Amen.

Truth in Action:

1. What is the extra mile that God has put on your heart to do?

____

____

____

____

____

____

____

____

2. Do you find it difficult to acknowledge your own strengths and weaknesses and to ask the Lord for help?

____

____

3. What burdens can you commit today to the Lord?

____

____

____

____

____

____

4. Now that you know that His grace is available, what adjustments will you make to step into it?

____

____

____

____

____

____

Steps to Loving Your Journey

"For he that will love life, and see good days. . ." (1 Peter 3:10a KJV).

Make these simple steps a daily part of your life and see the blessings abound!

- **Repent from the sin of dissatisfaction.**
- **Stop envying others and wishing you had someone else's life.**
- **Learn to love your life:** Do not curse your day by starting it out saying, "If my life was only different," or "I hate my life." Instead say, "God, You gave my today, and I choose to love it! Now, what can I do to make it special?"
- **Get rid of the "ifs":** ("If this or that changed, I would be happy.") No! What are you enjoying now? Those who enjoy what they have receive more!
- **Love the process:** Our lives are a constant journey. If we do not learn to love the process, we miss our entire lives!
- **Contentment for the journey:** "But Godliness with contentment is great gain" (1 Tim. 6:6). Remember that whatever you are going through is not the big picture; it is just today's picture! Enjoy life today!
- **Peace for the journey:**

  a) Settle Salvation
  b) Never be at odds with God
  c) Be at peace with yourself
  d) Be at peace with others
- **Grace for the journey**: "My grace is sufficient for you, for My power is perfected in weakness" (2 Cor. 12:9). Daily ask God for His grace to help you love your life, complete your journey, and go the extra mile.

Chapter Ten

A Daily Journey with God

But He answered and said, "It is written, 'Man shall not live by bread alone, but by every word that proceeds from the mouth of God.'"
Matthew 4:4 (NKJV)

We all want to find out what our destiny is and fulfill it, right? We want to do that not only in the long term, but on a daily basis too. God has a daily destiny for each of us. There are people that God will send your way that only you can bless and touch with the love of God. I believe God has a daily destiny, a weekly destiny, an annual destiny, and a lifetime destiny for each of us. In order to find this we need a daily time with God, our Creator. It is very important! It is key in fulfilling our destiny and discovering why we were born. As a pastor's wife, many people ask me, "How do you do a morning devotional and what is it? How do you spend time with the Creator of the universe?"

In this chapter I am going to go over some basics on how to spend a daily quiet time with God (time you set aside to get to know God by reading His Word, praying, and worshipping Him each day). Regular church attendance is also an important part of the Christian life, however, it is only a part of the Christian life. Many Christians only go to church and never spend private, individual time with God. But imagine if I never spent alone time with my husband. We would not have our four beautiful children. It is in our alone time with God that He births His dreams into our hearts, helps us bring them to pass, and raises them to maturity. Therefore, I am going to share how I do my quiet time and hopefully share some new insight.

If you are a well-versed believer who has had a regular quiet time for years, I encourage you to still finish this chapter. I believe there are many things in this chapter that will bless you, as well. My hope is to stir you up in your love and passion for God. If our daily time with God is not fresh and if it is not real, then what are we here for? What's the difference between true Christianity and dead religion if what we're doing is just out of obligation instead of out of love? Jesus' commandment is to love God and one another. We need to spend time with God because of our love for Him. No one enjoys being loved purely out of obligation.

Every believer desperately needs to spend daily time in God's Word and in His presence. As you do this faithfully, it will develop into an absolutely vital part of your life. If you are a new believer, this may be the first time you have been taught to have a quiet time. You may not always understand everything you read in the Bible the first time around, but as you are faithful to keep reading God's Word, the Holy Spirit will open your eyes to new things. Do not give up!

Truth:

No success in life is ever achieved without a plan!

Before we go much further, please allow me to paint a picture of what a basic quiet time ideally looks like. Please do not think this is the only way to spend time with God! This is simply the most fundamental way to spend time with God on a daily basis and to grow in your Christian life.

The Basics

- **Set a goal.** I highly recommend that you allow at least thirty minutes per day for your devotional time with God. You will soon find that this is not enough!

- **Choose a specific time and place.** Make a plan so you can be with God when and where you know you will not be interrupted or distracted. The goal is to be able to open your heart up to Him, allow yourself to feel His love, and respond to what His Word says. You will have a hard time listening or responding correctly if the children are running around the kitchen table as you read, or if the news is blaring in the background.

- **Do not split up your devotional time.** You will miss much of what God wants to show you if you only spend a few minutes praying, and then hours later spend a few minutes reading the Word. Just like with any person you wish to show your love and respect for, nothing replaces undivided attention with God!

- **Time in the morning is best.** Have your quiet time in the morning, before the day begins. The Scriptures tell us that, "the Lord's mercies … they are new every morning" (Lamentations 3:22–23 KJV). There is mercy available to you for each new day. You need to spend time in God's Word to find the mercies afforded you for that day. Only He knows what is ahead and what you will need to get through the challenges successfully. If you have your quiet time only at night, you may often read the Bible and think, "If only I had read that Proverb or Bible verse earlier, it would have saved me a lot of trouble and I would have known how to respond more effectively today."

  Having your Bible study first thing in the morning also sets your day and your heart on the right course. Having your quiet time in the morning does not make God like you any more, nor does it make you more holy. It is just a practical way to love your life. If you want to love your life for that day, then do not miss the mercy and the Word that God has waiting for you to discover. However, additional Bible reading at night is a lovely way to end your day. I also highly recommend nightly additional Bible reading as the very last thing you do if you suffer from bad dreams or insomnia. The living Word of God will minister peace to your soul and to your sleep whereas a TV drama or even the news as your last thoughts of the day can actually stir you up.

- **Find a well balanced reading plan.** I will recommend a few reading plans. First, I want to recommend the *One Year Bible* in whatever translation you prefer. It has a reading for each day from the Old Testament and the New Testament, as well as daily readings from Psalms and Proverbs. Also, it is dated. If you get behind, just jump to the current day. There is no condemnation! Your quiet time with God is a joy! The *One Year Bible* website offers downloadable versions of this and other reading plans (see the list of recommended resources at the back of this book for details). One of the reading plans also available is *The Chronological Bible Reading Plan.* This takes you through the Bible in the order in which biblical events occurred historically. If you want to take a bit longer than one year to read through the Bible, several websites offer two and three year reading plans.

  However, if you are a brand new believer, you may enjoy just reading through the New Testament first. If that's you, be sure to read through a full chapter per day.

- **Prayer List.** One great way to consistently pray over areas is to create a prayer list. This is a wonderful tool to remember who and what to pray over. It also serves as a list of inspiration and a "thank you" list.

As you begin to pray over the areas on your list, check them off as they get answered. As you check off the answers always be sure to say, "Thank You", by praising the Lord and rejoicing in the victories He has given you! Do not move on to the next problem until you take a moment to say thank you and really savor the victory over the last problem. When you go to God, go in the posture of actually believing He is going to answer your prayer. If you do, you will see incredible change in your prayer life. "This is the confidence which we have before Him, that, if we ask anything according to His will, He hears us. And if we know that He hears us in whatever we ask, we *know* that we have the requests which we have asked from Him" (John 5:14–15). God takes pleasure in answering your prayers! He is glorified when He can show Himself strong in our lives. He also answers us so that our joy may be full. "If you abide in Me, and My words abide in you, ask whatever you wish, and it will be done for you. My Father is glorified by this, that you bear much fruit … These things I have spoken to you so that My joy may be in you, and that your joy may be made full" (John 15:7, 8, 11).

All quiet times ideally consist of four basic components:

1. Reading the Bible
2. Prayer (conversation with God from your heart)
3. Praying God's Scriptures over your life
4. Worship with song ("God inhabits the praises of His people" [Psalm 22:3]. This is the part of your daily devotional where you will feel God's presence the strongest).

Thirty minutes may sound like a long time to some of you, however, if you are fitting in all the areas above, it really goes fast! For instance, if you are setting aside thirty minutes per day for your quiet time with God, you might want to plan something like this:

Bible reading	15 minutes
Prayer	5 minutes
Praying God's promises	5 minutes
Worship	5 minutes

Here is an example of a single day on the devotional chart at the end of the chapter:

Sample:

Bible Reading						Prayer, Worship Times				Overview
	Old Testament		New Testament		Proverbs	Reading	Prayer	Praying Gods Promises	Worship	
Day	*Book*	*Chp*	*Book*	*Chp*	*Chp/Vs.*	*Time Spent*	*Time Spent*	*Time Spent*	*Time Spent*	*Total*
Sun	*Genesis*	1	*Matthew*	1		15	5	5	5	30

You may want to change up the plan from time to time. You could start with worship or finish with it. Variety makes your quiet time interesting.

One fun way for new believers to accomplish devotional goals is to use a timer. You may enjoy setting the timer to keep yourself on track and keep you from constantly checking your watch for those five-, ten-, or fifteen-minute intervals. Once the timer sounds, you realize, "Wow! I am already finished with that part? That went so fast!" It makes hitting your goals a bit more attainable, and we all love that! (It may sound silly, but try it.) You eventually will not need this.

However, for those experienced in having a morning Bible study, there is one time in particular that a timer still comes in handy. On those very hectic days when I do not feel like I have time to do my morning quiet time, or on the days I seem very distracted, I have to make a bit more of an effort to not only have my quiet time, but to make it *quality* quiet time. It is on those days that I like to set my phone alarm for the full length of my quiet time. When I do this I am then able to let "time" go and the pressures of life go and feel great peace during that thirty minutes or hour. By confidently knowing that that alarm will go off at that thirty-minute or hour marker, I do not have to worry about time or distractions or pressures. I make sure all my ringers are off, and it is as though time stops and eternity enters. When that timer goes off, I am able to take the peace and joy I received from my time with the Lord into my day, and what a difference that makes!

On the devotional chart I have included at the end of this chapter you will see that there is space to record what God "spoke" to you through each day's time with Him. As you spend time in God's Word, expect Him to "speak" to you. It may be something as simple as a verse jumping out at you. Don't think that it's just your mind. It may be an impression given as you sing a certain worship song to the Lord. The important thing is to be with Him and receive what He has to say. If it ministers to you, it was the Holy Spirit, your Teacher.

Truth:

Nothing else can substitute for God's Word and His presence.

We are so blessed to live in a day where countless Christian resources are at our fingertips. However, Christian television, magazines, books, or radio are no substitute for the Bible. Do not deceive yourself into thinking those things qualify as your devotional time with God. Yes, they are a tremendous blessing and God uses them to speak to us, but each of those things should only be an "extra," (i.e.: something you read or listen to throughout the day, after you have already spent your private time with the Lord.)

Along the same lines, Christian television cannot substitute for attending a local church. In order to be a well-rounded believer, you need both personal times with God and corporate (or group) times with God (Heb.

10:25). Christians that are not connected to a local church are more easily overcome by the trials of life and even by the Enemy. Jesus compared us to a flock of sheep. There is safety in a flock that is being overseen by godly pastors. Sheep out on their own usually do not last for long; they need a shepherd.

Truth:

Who you spend time with is the voice you know the best.

Anytime I am away and need to phone my children, I have noticed something: they always recognize my voice over the phone. They know that it is really me because they have spent time with me. When the children speak with others on the phone, they often do not recognize the person to whom they are speaking. Why? Because they have not been with the person regularly. Similarly, we will only recognize God's voice above our own voice (or the world's voice) as we spend more time with Him. There are many voices calling out to us each day. The voice we listen to the most shows where we have invested our time.

As you faithfully continue to study God's Word, you will develop a beautiful relationship with Him, far richer than you ever imagined possible. Hang in there! Don't give up. This is the greatest treasure we can have in this life!

Truth:

Those you run to when you are happy or sad are those you are truly closest to.

How do you face disappointment, obstacles, and discouragement? By spending time with God.

Now, how do *you* normally respond to adversity? The way we are *supposed* to respond is not how we always respond, and that is true for everyone. We need to learn to run to the Word of God before we run to a person or the telephone. It is in His presence we will find what we need. We have to learn to believe He is really God not only in our words, but also in our actions. If we really believed God is God and God is for us, He would always be the first person we run to. For example, if you are having a problem at work, excuse yourself and go to a quiet place, and for a moment be quiet in God's presence. Take a deep breath, relax, and let go of the situation and put it squarely into God's hands. Remind yourself that God loves you; He will not leave your or forsake you. But it is your choice whether or not you get God involved in the situation or you try to handle it yourself. When you give it to God, it gives you a chance to clear your head and tackle the difficult problem with a fresh perspective. God loves you and He's there for you to call on!

In addition to that, how do you spend your time when you're full of hope, when you're full of excitement, when you're full of joy and you know exactly what your day is going to look like? Most Christians do not know how to share their joy with God. They do not know how to stop and say thank you. They do not know how to say, "God, this is working out so well. I am so excited!" When people are really happy, they can even forget to spend time in the Word of God. Do not just go to Him when everything is sorrowful, but go to Him also when everything is good. If you do that, then your whole life will begin to change. So whether you are discouraged or whether you are happy, you need to begin to spend time in God's Word. Learn to share your joys as well as your sorrows with God. Your house will get sweeter, your life will become more joyful, and your relationships will become more meaningful simply by going to God in those times as well.

In this chapter, I am going to focus on two of the four basic components mentioned above, though they are all equally important. I will focus on reading God's Word and speaking (or praying) God's promises.

I. Reading God's Word

Truth:

Ninety percent of all you hear from God will be through His written Word.

Therefore, it is imperative that you spend time in the Word and find a Bible translation that you can understand. There are several incredible translations available, all of which present the same Gospel, just in a different vernacular. In the back of this book I have included an appendix of recommended resources, including Bible translations. Popular translations include: the New King James Version, the New American Standard, The Amplified Bible, the New International Version, and God's Word Translation (a translation that is easy to read for children and teenagers). My personal favorite is the New American Standard Version. My husband's favorite is the King James Version for its poetic nature.

From my Personal Quiet Time

I cannot stress enough how important your personal quiet time is. To endeavor to show its importance, I have included a few personal examples.

For instance, I have August 20 marked in my *One Year Bible.* I refer to it often in addition to my normal daily reading, because it encourages me so much. This particular day has been such a huge blessing! God had so much waiting for me. I am certainly glad I didn't miss reading on that day. August 20 has readings from I Corinthians 13, Psalm 37 and Proverbs 21:23–24.

Wow! 1 Corinthians 13, the great love chapter: being patient, being kind, not irritable, etc. I do not know about you, but I can fall so short in these areas so I read it and read it and read it so that I can begin to mirror God. I may not mirror Him today as well as I would like, but if I keep speaking His Word over my life I will mirror Him more and more every day of my life.

Then, Psalm 37:1–11. This Psalm means more to me than I can ever tell you. Since Kevin and I are living in a foreign country, sharing the Gospel, this Scripture speaks to my heart in such a special way. It says, "Trust in the LORD and do good; Dwell in the land and cultivate faithfulness" (Psa. 37:3). That's an important Scripture no matter who you are.

> "Delight yourself in the LORD; And He will give you the desires of your heart. Commit your way to the LORD, Trust also in Him, and He will do it. He will bring forth your righteousness as the light. And your judgment as the noonday. Rest in the LORD and wait patiently for Him; Do not fret … Cease from anger and forsake wrath; Do not fret; it leads only to evildoing. For evildoers will be cut off, But those who wait for the LORD, they will inherit the land … But the humble will inherit the land And will delight themselves in abundant prosperity." (Psa. 37:4–9, 11)

This portion of Scripture always encourages me. There is so much in it. In life, there are so many opportunities to fret and worry, but this verse says, "do not fret, trust God, He will do it." Do you know what the Proverbs for the end of that day is? The proverb is "he who guards his mouth and his tongue guards his soul from trouble." So you can see why I enjoy re-reading this whole page often. What great reminders it has!

Also, as you do your Bible study, begin to write in your Bible! God will not mind. It means you are using it; valuing it. Having it on a shelf does you no good. As someone once said, "A dirty Bible leads to a clean life!" Mark those pages that you need to go back to every single day of your life to remind you to put yourself in that posture. This way you can learn to love your life. I am a different person when I read Scriptures than I am when I do not read them, and that is up to me. God gave me the Word. He did everything He could, and I have to do my part to love my life. One of my priorities is to spend daily time in the Word of God.

I recommend you read the whole Bible. A preacher friend of ours always says, "God sent His Son, but left His Book." If you are only picking your favorite parts, you have no idea what the Bible says in context. At the Passover, for example, the Children of Israel were told that they must eat the whole lamb. This was a type of Christ. We must receive and accept all that Jesus offered and all the truth in His Word. To be a healthy, growing, well-rounded Christian you will want to read your Bible from Genesis to Revelation. But wait; don't stop! Do it again and the amount of new revelations and deeper understanding you will get will astound you. Amazingly, no matter how many times you read through the Bible it will always seem new! The Word is alive and living like nothing else written on this earth!

This daily time with God will send you out with joy and strength for the day, a heart for your responsibilities and a passion to glorify God in all you do. If you start your day with the Word of God, you will walk, not in your own strength, but in God's strength, and live to the glory of God.

I hope these Scriptures have helped to illustrate the point that spending time with God is very vital. No matter who you are there are times when your day gets busy and you think, "If I could just spend a couple of minutes in the Word, it would all be okay." But I can guarantee you that on those busy days a couple of minutes will not be enough. The busier your day is the more you need your full time with God, because in those busy times there are more opportunities for a wrench to be thrown in the works. You want to make sure that does not happen.

II. Speaking God's Promises over Your Life

There is nothing more powerful than the spoken Word of God. The Word of God spoken from your mouth is the most powerful agent of change in your life. We were created in the image of God. We were created to speak things with authority. However, our own words are not an agent of change. It is God's Word spoken from our mouths that can move mountains, sometimes dramatically; other times one rock at a time. Isaiah 55:11 tells us that "God's Word will not return void without accomplishing what it was sent to do."

God's Word in your mouth will always produce a landslide of change and blessing. As you begin to speak God's promises over your life in the midst of impossible circumstances, you begin to change. You become God-minded and not problem-minded. You begin to see God as bigger than your problems. You will begin to run to Him quicker, lean on Him more, and see Him as the true and only God. "Is not My word like fire?" declares the LORD, "and like a hammer which shatters a rock?" (Jer. 23:29). Just as a rock may not break with just one swing of the hammer, your mountain may not move the first time you quote a verse. But keep on swinging, keep on speaking, and God's powerful Word will work for you!

Truth:

Find Scriptures that speak God's promises over your life. Pray them over yourself daily, and everything will change!

If you are having trouble in a certain area of your life, find a Scripture that pertains to that area. Take time to search for verses specific to the areas in need of change. (I recommend a concordance or topical search. You can also find this in the back of most Bibles. In the back of this book you will find a list of recommended resources). Write the verse(s) on a card, stick it in your pocket, and throughout the day pray it. For example, if you are quick tempered, then pray, "I am quick to hear, slow to speak and slow to anger" (Jas. 1:19). It may help to put the verse into first person, like in the example above. If you are in a difficult situation, pray "I will not lose heart in doing good, for in due time I *will* reap, if I do not grow weary" (Gal. 6:9, emphasis added). Speak it over yourself as part of your devotional time, and again throughout the day. When you are tempted to get angry, complain, or give way to fear or self-pity, instead build yourself up by speaking God's Word. Say it until you believe it. Believe it when you say it (Mark 11:23). It will change you!

One Scripture that I pray all the time is:

> "I let no unwholesome word proceed from my mouth, but only such a word as is good for edification according to the need of the moment, so that it will give grace to those who hear, that I do not grieve the Holy Spirit of God … I let all bitterness and wrath and anger and clamour and slander be put away from me, along with all malice. I am kind to one another, tender-hearted, forgiving each other, just as God in Christ also has forgiven me" (Eph. 4:29 changed to first person by author).

Do you need to be renewed in the likeness of God every day? We all do. Eph. 4:22–24 says, "Lay aside the old self … put on the new self, which in the likeness of God …" There are so many promises that God gave to us as a treasure, it just makes you want to dig in!

When Mark Hankins, a minister in Louisiana, was a young man, a minister came to his dad's church and encouraged the congregation to pray Ephesians 1:17–22 at least once a day, every day, for six months. He said to pray it over and over and stick with it until something happened. When Mark was a teenager he decided to do this. He began to pray Ephesians 1. He prayed it without fail morning, noon, and night, day after day, week after week for a long time and the day came when the spirit of wisdom and revelation kicked in. The revelation God gave to him of who he was "in Christ" changed his life forever and set him on the road to ministry.[32] Mark Hankins has taken the revelation of who we are "in Christ" all around the world. He has been a successful minister for over thirty years and has impacted the lives of many people, including me, all as a result of praying this prayer.

So, three years ago I felt lead to begin to pray this same portion of Scriptures. "That the Father of our Lord Jesus Christ may give to me a spirit of wisdom and revelation in the knowledge of Him. I pray that the eyes of my heart may be enlightened so that I may know what is the hope of His calling, the riches of His glory of the inheritance of the saints, and what is the surpassing greatness of His power that is toward us who believe" (Eph. 1:17–19 changed to first person by author).

As I began to pray this I have to say that I was thinking God would give me a really amazing, earth shattering revelation that was going to change my life and ministry! I was expecting an incredible revelation like Mark Hankins had, but that is not what happened. God gave me a revelation of today. Plain ole' today! I have to admit I was not excited about it at first. I felt a bit like a remedial student. I thought, *"Is that it?"* But then as I began to study and be faithful with my "nugget," He opened my eyes to today. When I was asking for a spirit of wisdom and revelation, what God showed me was the importance of each day, the actual day. This is not an earth shattering revelation, I know, but it was something I was missing!

For those who do not know me, I work on projects in our church, and I work way ahead of time. For example: It is December, and we are already working on the *next year's* Halloween outreach. We are working on our National Women's Conference in May, St. Patrick's Day outreach, our annual April 5k Fun Run, our annual Golf Classic, and our summer Christian Camp of the Arts simultaneously, not to mention all of the regular church events and courses. When we planned our summer camp God gave me a seven-year plan…seven years of themes. People look at me strangely sometimes when I am writing a check and I have to stop and think of the year, but it is because I am working on so many years simultaneously and I tend to have those years on my mind. I may begin to write a date on a check and someone will say, "Hey, wait, it's…" That can happen to anyone working on annual projects. What I was clearly missing was a revelation of today. My actual day didn't change, but this new revelation changed the way I view today. The gift of God is today. I still have to plan for the future for the church to have our big events, but today is a gift. That's why, as they say, it is called "the present!"

I was also always looking at my future goals and where the church was going to be. I would say, "Lord, I am so excited about what's going to be happening as the church grows," or "When we get more people we can do this or that," instead of enjoying our church at the size it is. In all of its different capacities, life can be fun. At the time when I started writing this book, our church had just moved from a wonderful 10,000 square-foot facility back into a hotel for services, after fourteen years of having a beautiful, rented building. The Irish economy took a big downturn and we needed to adjust our overhead expenses accordingly, to only having rented office spaces and not a full building. So services were back in a hotel, just like when we first started the church! We all had the choice to make the "hotel adventure" fun, to enjoy today. We had to remember: it will not be this way forever, but we cannot live for tomorrow. It was a choice to make moving sound systems twice a week fun. The praise and worship team did not have a regular place to practice, but they could actually make that fun too! All our office staff were cramped into one small office, but that could be fun, too! Even my husband got the adventure of leaving behind a beautiful, spacious office and turning a small guest bedroom at our house into a study. Everyone was a sport and had a great attitude. Thankfully, we are now back into a new rented facility and are believing God that we will soon be able to build our own. But during the year in the hotel, we all learned that even in the midst of change, today can be fun!

I would like to think that I am not the only one in the world who needed a revelation of today. You may pray the Ephesians 1:17–19 Scriptures and get an amazing revelation like Mark Hankins did, but as for me, it has set me on the path of learning how to love my life today. And in truth, this was all born out of my daily quiet time with God. Please do not miss yours!

Prayer

Dear Lord,

I am excited about spending time with You. I didn't fully realize how vital and life changing it really is. As I step more accurately into this adventure called life, I want to do it with You by my side and with You leading the way. I choose to trust in You with all my heart, lean not unto my own understanding, in all my ways acknowledge You, and let You direct my paths (Prov. 3:5–6).

Lord, I commit to starting a real and consistent devotional time with You.

In Jesus' Name,
Amen

Truth in Action:

1. What time commitment can you make (and keep) to have your daily quiet time? Where can you meet God daily without distractions?

   ____

   ____

   ____

   ____

   ____

2. If you are already in the habit of a regular quiet time, is it still alive? What can you do to fan the flames again?

____

____

____

3. What areas do you need to find target Scriptures for? (Promises that speak directly to those areas of need, weakness, or sin [e.g., anger, oversensitivity, etc.]) Write out those areas and the scriptures you find.

____

____

____

____

____

____

4. What areas do you need to find target scriptures for to encourage you, to lift you up, and to make you feel good about yourself? Write out the scriptures that you find that minister to you in those areas.

____

____

____

____

____

____

____

Nugget:

How do I know if what I'm hearing is God speaking to me? Few Christians are confident that God wants to speak to them today and that they can actually hear Him. If you believe God has spoken something to you (for yourself or to share with someone else), it is wise to first stop and consider where it's coming from: yourself, the Enemy, or God. Each of these has its own characteristics. Here are a few very simple guidelines to aid you in discerning what you may be "hearing."

- *If you will remember, ninety percent of all you hear from God will be from His written Word, the Bible. (This usually happens as you are studying His Word; a verse or phrase may simply stand out to you or speak to the situation you are currently in. This is a word He is giving you for your correction, instruction, encouragement, or victory.) It is important to know that the words or directives He speaks to you in other ways will never contradict the Bible.*
- *God's voice is seldom audible to our natural ear. It is usually a "knowing" deep on the inside of you, a subtle unction or a "still, small voice."*
- *God's Word will flood your heart with peace, even if His instruction is contrary to your natural mind.*
- *When God speaks something to you, the carnal nature in us seldom wants to begin to say it over and over. However, if God speaks something to you, then the power is in returning God's Word to Him by speaking it out. If you do, you will create a good life around you.*
- *On the contrary, if you have a driving desire to say something, it is probably not God. (How funny human nature is.) The words or thoughts from the Enemy are often pushy or compulsive; they bring tremendous pressure. When it is pushy, you need to find a way to give it to God and to not give voice to those words. If you speak them anyway, it could set you up to look like a fool.*
- *If we have a negative thought, it is natural to want to speak it out loud, but do not. It is not from God. E.g.: "I cannot believe I did that. I am so stupid." Human nature loves to speak the negative. However, this is self-destructive. Do not get into agreement with the Enemy. He knows the power of words and wants you to repeat his thoughts out loud over and over. If you will notice, they are often easier to believe than God's thoughts.*
- *Racing thoughts or replaying conversations are never the voice of God. They never bring peace and they keep your mind focused on yourself or on pressures.*

I have included a sample devotional chart that may be helpful to you. Feel free to photocopy this page or download a digital copy on our website (listed in the back).

Let's recap the four parts of a quiet time (listed on the chart below):

1. Reading: time spent reading the Bible
2. Prayer: conversation with God from your heart
3. Praying God's Promises: speaking His Word over your life through Scriptural promises
4. Worship: singing to the Lord (If you cannot remember songs well, you may want to sing along with a worship CD).

Note: Please see the list of recommended resources at the back of this book for materials to help in your daily quiet time. I've included favorite musicians, worship cds, books with Scriptures to confess, and more.

Daily Devotions (30 minutes of undivided attention with God)

Name: ______________ Month: ______________ Week: ______________

Bible Reading						Prayer, Worship Times				Overview
	Old Testament		New Testament		Proverbs	Reading	Prayer	Praying Gods Promises	Worship	
Day	*Book*	*Chp*	*Book*	*Chp*	*Chp/Vs.*	*Time Spent*	*Time Spent*	*Time Spent*	*Time Spent*	*Total*
Sun	*Genesis*	1	*Matthew*	1	1	15	5	5	5	30
Mon										
Tues										
Wed										
Thurs										
Fri										
Sat										

What stood out to you/ What spoke to You...	
Sun	
Mon	
Tues	
Wed	
Thurs	
Fri	
Sat	

Other Notes:

Steps to Loving Your Journey

"For he that will love life, and see good days. . ." (1 Peter 3:10a KJV).

Make these simple steps a daily part of your life and see the blessings abound!

- **Repent from the sin of dissatisfaction.**
- **Stop envying others and wishing you had someone else's life.**
- **Learn to love your life:** Do not curse your day by starting it out saying, "If my life was only different," or "I hate my life." Instead say, "God, You gave my today, and I choose to love it! Now, what can I do to make it special?"
- **Get rid of the "ifs":** ("If this or that changed, I would be happy.") No! What are you enjoying now? Those who enjoy what they have receive more!
- **Love the process:** Our lives are a constant journey. If we do not learn to love the process, we miss our entire lives!
- **Contentment for the journey:** "But Godliness with contentment is great gain" (1 Tim. 6:6). Remember that whatever you are going through is not the big picture; it is just today's picture! Enjoy life today!
- **Peace for the journey:**

  a) Settle Salvation
  b) Never be at odds with God
  c) Be at peace with yourself
  d) Be at peace with others
- **Grace for the journey**: "My grace is sufficient for you, for My power is perfected in weakness" (2 Cor. 12:9). Daily ask God for His grace to help you love your life, complete your journey, and go the extra mile.
- **Spend time with God:** This daily time with God will send you out with joy and strength for the day, a heart for your responsibilities, and a passion to glorify God in all you do.

Chapter Eleven

Rest for the Journey

"Come to Me, all who are weary and heavy-laden,
and I will give you rest."
Matthew 11:28

Rest is not what most people think it is. It is not really even physical, as can be proven by many Scriptures. But its need is profound and proven by the very fact that God Himself rested on the seventh day. God is a spirit and had no flesh to rest; yet He rested, for true rest is from the soul. His form of rest was to enjoy His creation. We see from this, one of the highest forms of rest is enjoyment. We also see that God was very satisfied after the creation of man, the Scripture testifying that it was all "very good" (Gen. 1:31). Yet after their creation, He wasn't actually through. He had one more thing to create, and that was rest! The crowning act of creation was not man, but His creation of rest. God has placed such a high premium on this requirement to rest that He has included it in the Ten Commandments (Ex. 20:7–17). It is not only listed at number four (Ex. 20:8–11), ahead of all the greats like "thou shalt not kill," "thou shalt not steal," and such, but He has also given us another clue as to how important this is to Him. These two egregious violations of human behavior, killing and stealing, which are the sixth and eighth commandments, are only expressed in four meager words; actually only two words in the Hebrew. Do you know how many words are in the Commandments about remembering the Sabbath day? There are ninety-four words that God has weighted this command with. How little we have heeded it, to our own detriment. Buckle up! You are going to enjoy the revelation you are about to receive on rest.

"Come to Me, all who are weary and heavy-laden, and I will give you rest. Take My yoke upon you and learn from Me, for I am gentle and humble in heart, and *you will find rest for your souls.* For My yoke is easy and My burden is light" (Matt. 11:28–30; emphasis added).

"My presence shall go with you, and I will give you rest: (Ex. 33:14).

The above Scriptures are referring to rest of the soul. This type of rest is of utmost importance and impacts so many areas of our lives. When you find rest for your soul, you will find physical rest. In this restful state you will even sleep better; your sleep will be so sound that you will wake up refreshed, with more energy regardless of the amount of hours you slept. Also, when you take a short break, you will be so relaxed you actually *feel refreshed.* Rest for your soul has a profound impact on your physical body, and we'll talk about that in just a minute.

In the Psalms, we see King David actually speaking to his soul!

- "Bless the LORD, O my soul, And all that is within me, bless His holy name.
  Bless the LORD, O my soul, And forget none of His benefits;
  Who pardons all your iniquities, Who heals all your diseases;
  Who redeems your life from the pit, Who crowns you with loving kindness and compassion;
  Who satisfies your years with good things, So that your youth is renewed like the eagle." (Ps. 103:1–5).
  (David is telling his soul to bless the Lord. He is telling his soul to remember God's goodness.)

- "Why are you cast down, O my soul? And why are you disquieted within me? Hope in God, for I shall yet praise Him, For the help of His countenance" (Ps. 42:5, NKJV).

- (Before David was a king he knew how to speak to his soul. And we see he never stopped.) "Return to your rest, O my soul For the LORD has dealt bountifully with you. For You have rescued my soul from death, My eyes from tears, My feet from stumbling. I shall walk before the LORD In the land of the living." (Ps. 116:7–9).

This is one of my favorite portions of Scripture in the entire Bible: "You have rescued my soul from death, my eyes from tears and my feet from stumbling." To me, that is the definition of rest. The neatest part of it is that David expected to see this in the "land of the living"! He was not waiting for the sweet bye and bye for the rest and the success. He was anticipating it here on this side of eternity. He had a real revelation of this. In fact, David wrote, "I would have despaired unless I had believed that I would see the goodness of the LORD In the land of the living" (Ps. 27:13). We need to aim no lower!

If you are crying, you're not at rest. If you are fighting death on every front, you're not at rest. If you are stumbling and thinking, "No matter what I do I keep making the same mistake, one after another …" you are not at rest!

Have you ever been hiking? Some hiking paths are so full of rocks that they make you stumble the entire path. After a while you can grow weary. It is not that there were any huge rocks; you didn't fall, you were just constantly stumbling. Maybe you are struggling with sin in a certain area of your life. Maybe they are even small sins, but if you are constantly repeating them and stumbling, you will not have rest for your soul. That is why David said, "For You have rescued … my feet from stumbling" (Psalm 116:8). God has a way of escape. Luke 3:5 says that He makes the crooked palaces straight and the rough road smooth. "With weeping they will come, And by supplication I will lead them; I will make them walk by streams of waters, On a straight path in which they will not stumble;" (Jer. 31:9). We need to learn how to stay on the Heavenly path; it is a smooth path full of refreshing.

Marriage

Another example of rest is seen in the first chapter of Ruth. The story tells of Naomi and her two daughters-in-law, Ruth and Orpah; all three of whom had lost their husbands. In this famous story of love and loyalty, we see Naomi counseled the two young ladies to remarry and move on with their lives. "May the Lord grant that you may find rest, each in the house of her husband. Then she kissed them, and they lifted up their voices and wept" (Ruth 1:9).

What kind of rest is she talking about here? Emotional rest. She is certainly not talking about physical rest. Few people get married and then go sit down. Once you're married you will have more laundry to do, more food to cook, more financial responsibilities. After marriage usually comes the baby carriage, so most have a lot to do after they get married. Therefore, she's talking about an emotional rest. What a blessing! I love to give this blessing to young brides who are getting married; "that they find rest in the house of their husband," never having a troubled marriage, and always communicating well!

The Physical Body

Truth:

There is no true physical rest without spiritual rest.

"For David speaketh concerning Him, 'I foresaw the Lord always before my face, for He is on my right hand, that I should not be moved: Therefore did my heart rejoice, and my tongue was glad; moreover also *my flesh* shall *rest in* hope'" (Acts 2:25–26, KJV).

Another translation for the word "in" in the above Scripture is "because of." So David is saying, "my flesh shall rest, because of hope." When you rest in hope, it provides rest for your flesh. What caused David to hope? The Lord was always before him. That is our job—to keep the Lord always before our face. To do that is far easier than you think. You do not have to be a theologian or a spiritual giant to have God ever before your face, but you do have to put Him first; do not neglect your quiet time. Develop a life style of worship, always thanking God in your heart, always thinking of God, and looking to God throughout your day. In other words, keeping God before your face instead of keeping your problems ever before you. Through spending time with the Lord, David became so convinced that God was for him that he was confident he would not be moved! That is a real place of rest. So real rest for your body starts in your spirit and moves to your soul (mind, will, emotions) and lastly goes to your physical body.

"For even when we came into Macedonia our flesh had no rest, but we were afflicted on every side: conflicts without, fears within" (2 Cor. 7:5).

Let me restate, there is no true physical rest without spiritual rest. People often think, "If I could just get away for a few days, I could be at rest." But really they go away for a few days and often come back as tired as when they left. They could get the rest they need right where they are in their hectic schedule if they could find that place of peace.

If there is fighting going on all around you and there is fear inside of you, there is no rest for your flesh. Even Paul was struggling at times with this area. He said there was conflict all around them and fear within them, and "our flesh had no rest." In other words, "we were bone tired and so weary." However, we need to be like Jesus who was able to sleep in the bow of the boat in the middle of the storm. (You may remember in the "If's and When's" Chapter, we read this account in detail.) There were conflicts all around the disciples and fear within them, yet when they woke the Lord up, He calmed the storm (Mark 4:36–39). If we will begin to look to the Lord in our storms instead of panicking over our situations,

He will show us how to safely get through them or instantly calm them. How do we look to Him? Again, through reading our Bible, meditating on His promises and *not* the problem, and through praise and worship. Nothing bolsters faith and gets your eyes back on God like praising God in song. Acts 16:23–26 is a great illustration of this. It shows that once Paul changed his focus, his circumstances changed.

> "When they had struck them (Paul and Silas) with many blows, they threw them into prison, commanding the jailer to guard them securely; and he, having received such a command, threw them into the inner prison and fastened their feet in the stocks. But about midnight Paul and Silas were praying and singing hymns of praise to God, and the prisoners were listening to them; and suddenly there came a great earthquake, so that the foundations of the prison house were shaken; and immediately all the doors were opened and everyone's chains were unfastened."

Paul and Silas' breakthrough came when they began to sing! You cannot sing God's praises and feel sorrow for yourself at the same time. God was their solution, not their problem so they looked to Him instead of to their problems and found their deliverance.

Exercise

Let's now look at exercise in relationship to rest. I think you will enjoy the following story: Pastor Joseph Prince, from Singapore, tells how he was filled with anxiety one particular year. He was worried about his body, and his doctor had given him a bad report. He began to eat flawlessly and exercise, but the exercise did not benefit him because he was worrying the whole time he was exercising. Pastor Prince really got his breakthrough when a man from his church shared this story with him, how he too had very high blood pressure and the doctor also said to him that he was going to have to be very strict with his diet and run every day. The man did, and it brought his blood pressure down some, but only some. Then that man began to learn about rest in his soul and began to put it into practice. So he didn't worry about what he ate that week (I am not recommending this), and he didn't exercise that week (I am not recommending that either), but he wanted to prove the point of rest for his soul. The man went back to the doctor after two weeks and the doctor said his blood pressure was flawless! The doctor said, "Whatever you're doing, keep doing it!" All the man did was get peace on the inside, no fears from within. He had rest on the inside and it completely changed his physical body. Physical exercise is a blessing, but for maximum benefit it must be combined with rest on the inside.[33]

Rest and health go hand in hand. In fact, someone once said "Disease is made up of two words: *Dis* and *ease*." When you are not at ease, you are uncomfortable so you have disease! In the United States, the number one killer is heart disease. We can now say based on our new definition that heart *dis/ease* is the number one killer. People are dying all over the world because their hearts are not at ease. This is something we need to conquer.

The other day I was captivated by a certain portion of Scripture. I was reading and studying Jesus' words to the woman with the issue of blood. After the woman was healed, Jesus said to her, "Be whole of your disease." I felt led to look up the word *disease* in that Scripture. This is what I found: the Greek word is *mastix* meaning "scourging." Anyone who has ever had a serious physical illness, understands what this powerful definition is talking about. Physical ailments are like a scourging on your body, a torment; "a relentless beating." It is hard on you physically, and it can be a vicious cycle. It may start out as sickness, but it causes such turmoil emotionally that it keeps the cycle going. So if rest and health truly go hand in hand, we need to find that place of perfect rest in the Lord Jesus.

Which leads us straight into the next part of rest …

Rest for Your Mind

When your mind is not at rest, you live in torment. Tormenting thoughts come from thinking of things that could happen, that haven't happened, long before they ever happen. Sometimes they never happen at all, and other times they happen only because you have been working yourself up, tormenting yourself, and obsessing over a thought, even giving "birth" to the problem.

Truth:

We often cause a bad situation to happen by worrying or obsessing over it.[34]

This leads one away from rest. It is important that we begin to understand how to get our minds at rest in order to get our souls at rest. Rest in our minds is what God wants for every single one of us. God wants us to put everything in His hands and let our minds stop racing! Have you ever had your mind racing from one thought to another, and another, and another? We have to be able to quiet our minds in God. We need to stop thinking of outcomes. We need to stop re-living conversations. We need to stop thinking of failures.

The other day I was asleep and a little uncomfortable so I rolled over, and for whatever reason I remembered one of those dumb moments from when I was eighteen years old! I had to laugh and think, "Mind, stop it!" Even something as ridiculous as that will make you anxious, especially if you're too sleepy to realize how ridiculous it is that you had that thought. You have to get on top of it. The Bible calls Satan "The accuser of the brethren" (Rev. 12:10). He is the one that reminds us of our failures, no matter how silly they are! Whatever you did in the past is in the past. God does not remember your failures! They are under the blood of Jesus if you have asked Him to forgive you. The Enemy is the one who wants our minds to race. If we're not at rest, we are full of anxiety and we are not keeping our eyes on God. We are then thinking on the wrong things.

Phil 4:6-8, a very familiar portion of Scripture, teaches us:

"Be anxious for nothing, but in everything by prayer and

> supplication with thanksgiving let your requests be made known to God. And the peace of God, which surpasses all comprehension, will guard your hearts and your minds in Christ Jesus. Finally, brethren, whatever is true, whatever is honorable, whatever is right, whatever is pure, whatever is lovely, whatever is of good repute, if there is any excellence and if anything worthy of praise, dwell on these things."

The reality of what you are thinking about may be true. It may not be fabricated in your mind; it may not be exaggerated. You may really have a bill that you have to pay that is looming in your mind, trying to torment you and take peace from you. And you know, we tend to think that we are doing our part if we worry about it. (As though worrying will get the bill paid!) If you do not have the money to pay the bill, the best thing you can do is rest in God's Word, quote His Word, and be at peace. Begin to look to Him for a solution. God gives the power to attain wealth (Deut. 8:18). Partner with God. He can show you how to become more valuable at work so you can get a raise. He can give you creative ideas so you can earn extra money, and He can give you favor if you look to Him with your creditors. It takes faith and confidence to move toward the solution. Use wisdom. Worrying is actually the worst thing you can do.

This principle works the same in relationships. If you are tempted to worry and worry over a broken relationship, you must stop and begin to look to God. Or perhaps you are being mistreated or gossiped about at work or among relatives. Again, worry and replaying the injustice of it all in your mind will not help. It will only make it worse. And the saddest part is you lose twice; every time you are in the situation and then in your thought-life afterward. Worry amplifies your suffering. If you begin to look to God and rest in Him for the answer, things will begin to change and you will not lose your health.

Worrying is not noble. Some moms think they are really good moms if they worry the entire time their children are away from home. As if that earns them a special "Mom badge"! It's not noble to worry about your family. It isn't noble or healthy to constantly try to be the savior of your grown children or your spouse, or to constantly try to fix and worry about everything. There is only One Savior … and we are not Him.

One day the Lord spoke to a particular minister and said to him: "Do you know what's worse than cancer on the brain?" And he thought, "I cannot think of anything worse than cancer on the brain!" And the Lord said, "Cancer on the mind!" The Lord said, "If they will not get cancer off their mind, I am unable to get it off their brain."[35] Now that is a life-changing principle!

So … what areas in your life are so on-your-mind that God cannot go in and heal them? Work? Spouse? Children? Health? Maybe it is fear of what your future holds. Until you let it go into God's hands, really give it to Him and no longer worry over it, He cannot restore the damaged area. God's desire is for you to have total restoration in every needed area. Will you let go of the fear and look to Him?

"Take no thought for tomorrow, because we do not really know what tomorrow holds" (Matt. 6:34). We need to live one day at a time not worrying about tomorrow; handling one problem at a time, loving one person at a time. When problems are overwhelming, try writing them down and begin to whittle away at them one by one. God will give you the grace you need if you look to Him. Often when we refuse to worry some problems even sort themselves out. True rest only comes when we focus our minds on God's love and God's Word and let go of fear.

Truth:

Dreading little things makes us not love our lives.

And that is so true. We have talked about some of the big areas of our lives that cause unrest and anguish, but let's not forget the little areas of dread. Because they are so subtle, these areas can be easily overlooked. Their impact on us, however, must not be. "Take us the foxes, the little foxes, that spoil the vines: for our vines have tender grapes" (Son. 2:15). When your life is full of potential the "little foxes," as Solomon called them, can actually ruin it. Dread is one of those little foxes. Dreading little things is so subtle that most people underestimate how much of a life-stealer it is.

There is a grace for you to do whatever must be done for each day. Remember, the compassions and mercies of the Lord are new every morning (Lamentations 3:22–23). If you think back to times when you have dreaded something, it usually didn't turn out as bad as you expected. Once you arrive at the event, there is grace available for you if you just tap into it. That grace is not present a day early or a day later … that is why you do not feel it beforehand.

If you have to mow the lawn tomorrow and you hate doing that, do not think about it until tomorrow. If you know Thursday is laundry day, and you hate doing laundry, do not notice there is over five feet of laundry in your house until you get to Thursday. If you are nervous about going to the dentist, do not let your mind "go there" until the day of your appointment. Do not think about whatever it is that you need to do. "Roll the care of it over to the Lord. Trust Him to give you the grace you will need, then spend today rejoicing in the Lord."[36]

A lady minister said she had a ministry opportunity that was not a big deal, but it was something she dreaded. She would have to get up very early in the morning, get on a plane, and fly to another state to meet another ministry couple and fly back. She said she started to dread it.

It is funny that so often the people that God has placed in the pulpit are not actually extroverts. Since they are in public, however, everyone wants to meet them. It can be hard for them. This lady minister didn't really know these people she had to visit. She became negative and thought, "I really don't want to do this. I will do anything else, Lord, just not this." She realized that it was stealing her today, and her appointment was not until tomorrow so she decided she would trust God and deal with it tomorrow. Tomorrow came, and as it worked out, her daughter and granddaughter were able to go with her. They had a wonderful day and enjoyed meeting the people. The minister even had a lovely lunch with her daughter and her granddaughter. God provided her with a grace, even though it was not her natural inclination to meet new people.[37]

We all have things we do not want to do, but we have to do them anyway. There are things we are not talented at or that are out of our comfort zones, but they are directly in our paths. To not do them is dysfunctional. Life often forces us to live outside of our comfort zones. We just need to choose to not think about it today! But do not go blindly into tomorrow; go into tomorrow by faith saying, "God, I receive Your rest. I trust that tomorrow is going to be great. You have provision for tomorrow and I will not be at all afraid of it. It is going to be exceedingly, abundantly beyond anything I can ask for or think of." The proof of your faith in God is that you are not worried about tomorrow. A great compliment to give to God is to not sweat the little things.

The renowned pastor and leader of the great South African Revival of 1860, Andrew Murray, said, "I am going to do the will of God today without thinking of tomorrow."[38]

"Commit your works to the Lord, and your plans will be established" (Prov. 16:3). The Bible also says, "Cast all your care upon him, for he cares for you" (1 Peter 5:7 KJV).

May these verses guide your tomorrow.

Prayer

Dear Lord,

I pray for true rest to come into my life. Flood my heart and my mind Lord, with peace that passes all understanding.

I choose from this day forward to have a mind that is stayed on You. I commit to stop all racing thoughts and to stop replaying conversations. I also realize that unless I am at peace, all the exercise and nutrition in the world cannot protect me from disease. So I, therefore, commit to "be anxious for nothing, but in everything by prayer and supplication with thanksgiving let my request be made known to You".

I love You, dearly.
Amen.

Truth in Action:

1. Consider all of the areas in your life that bring stress or anxiety. Write them down.

____

____

____

____

____

____

____

____

2. Remember, there is no physical rest outside of spiritual rest. What can you spiritually do about these problems to bring rest?

____

____

____

____

____

3. The Bible says to "take your thoughts captive to the obedience of Christ" (2 Cor. 10:5). From now on, whenever you start thinking of a failure, a conversation that didn't go well, or an argument you had with someone, stop and let it go into God's hands, and then make the mental choice not to revisit it.

4. Are you a worrier? Repeat point number two every time you begin to worry, because the Bible says, "Be anxious for nothing, but by prayer and supplication, with thanksgiving, let your requests be made known unto God" (Phil 4:6, NKJV). It also says, "Take no thought for tomorrow …" (Matt. 6:34).

Nugget:

Sometimes you may not know which areas of life you should let go of and which things you should focus on in prayer. Believers often "release" areas of personal weakness instead of working on them. We then frequently pour ourselves into outside problem areas we cannot change. So, how do you know which things to focus your prayers on and which things to release to God? Here's a simple guide:

- *Release into God's hands all of your problems as well as circumstances outside your control.*
- *Pray consistently over areas of personal weakness, temptation, or character flaws.*

Steps to Loving Your Journey

"For he that will love life, and see good days. . ." (1 Peter 3:10a KJV).

Make these simple steps a daily part of your life and see the blessings abound!

- **Repent from the sin of dissatisfaction.**
- **Stop envying others and wishing you had someone else's life.**
- **Learn to love your life:** Do not curse your day by starting it out saying, "If my life was only different," or "I hate my life." Instead say, "God, You gave my today, and I choose to love it! Now, what can I do to make it special?"
- **Get rid of the "ifs":** ("If this or that changed, I would be happy.") No! What are you enjoying now? Those who enjoy what they have receive more!
- **Love the process:** Our lives are a constant journey. If we do not learn to love the process, we miss our entire lives!
- **Contentment for the journey:** "But Godliness with contentment is great gain" (1 Tim. 6:6). Remember that whatever you are going through is not the big picture; it is just today's picture! Enjoy life today!
- **Peace for the journey:**

  a) Settle Salvation
  b) Never be at odds with God
  c) Be at peace with yourself
  d) Be at peace with others
- **Grace for the journey**: "My grace is sufficient for you, for My power is perfected in weakness" (2 Cor. 12:9). Daily ask God for His grace to help you love your life, complete your journey, and go the extra mile.
- **Spend time with God:** This daily time with God will send you out with joy and strength for the day, a heart for your responsibilities, and a passion to glorify God in all you do.
- **Rest for the journey:** "And He said, 'My presence shall go with you and I will give you rest'" (Ex. 33:14). "Therefore let us be diligent to enter that rest …"(Heb. 4:11).
- **Learn not to dread:** Pray, "I am going to do the will of God today without thinking about tomorrow."[39] "Casting *all* your cares upon Him, for He cares for you" (1 Peter 5:7).

Chapter Twelve

The Ultimate Rest Stop

"Keep thy heart with all diligence; for out of it are the issues of life."
Proverbs 4:23 (KJV)

How would you like to find the ultimate "Rest Stop"? As you are driving down the highway on those long trips, it is always so great to see "rest stop" signs. It is great to pull over, get out of the car, stretch and get something to eat. Well, God has a "Rest Stop" for us and our food is God's Word. This is no ordinary rest stop. It is all-inclusive. It comes with direction as well as warnings to avoid detours. This Rest Stop comes with the Ultimate Mechanic that can "fix" your heart and has complete body repair. All of it is free to the customer, but it cost the Owner everything. And the greatest part is that instead of leaving His "Rest Stop" behind we get to take it with us and really enjoy the journey. So, let's quickly turn our cars, called "life", into this "Ultimate Rest Stop" and get those all important directions and warnings.

Let's look at the first direction and warning on the map of life: "Keep thy heart with all diligence; for out of it are the issues of life" (Prov. 4:23 KJV). Just as your car needs a good engine, our bodies and lives need a good heart. To understand this more fully note that the word "issues" in the Hebrew in this verse means *boundaries*. Guard your heart, it sets the boundaries for your life and makes rest a reality.

In order to enjoy *rest* for our lives, we must learn to protect our boundaries. Remember back in the Garden, God gave Adam the responsibility of developing his new domain for the Glory of God. The Lord put a border, a hedge, around it, perhaps like a garden wall. But it was Adam's job to protect it. However, the next thing you know, Eve was speaking to a serpent which Adam, knowingly or unknowingly, had allowed in. Well, our lives are no different. We are responsible for what we allow into our "gardens". The garden, for us, is the heart. It must be guarded above all else. It must be manned by a vigilant guard – us! If it is contaminated, it will sour our entire life and cause great unrest, resulting in great loss. Our hearts, the well we draw from daily must be kept pure. As scripture says, "Blessed are the pure in heart, they shall see God" (Matt 5:8). If we are to see Him, we must protect our hearts. Do not let anyone move the boundaries that God has given you.

Let's learn how to diligently guard our hearts and set the right boundaries. Boundaries, *not* to keep people out, but to keep fear, guile, and turmoil out. Boundaries that keep health, blessing, provision, and goodness in! Boundaries that makes it possible to have rest in difficulties and that equip you not only to love the unlovely, but to love your life!

In order to learn how to set healthy boundaries around our hearts, keeping the good in and the bad out, we need to learn how our spiritual heart (garden) works. To do that let's look at key analogies for clarification. Our hearts are so essential to our lives, our rest, our health and our destinies. It is good to look at several different types of analogies to understand its importance and its function.

Rest for Your Heart

Truth:

Supply only flows through an untroubled heart.

The hard part in life is not trying to get healing, provision, and blessing *to* us, the hard part is getting it *through* us! When Jesus died on Calvary, He carried all of our sin, sickness, and loss. Once we have received Christ as our Savior, everything redemption provides is available to us. The issue is not God's willingness to release it to us, but our ability to receive it. Teaching our hearts to be untroubled is key in our ability to receive. Let me explain it like this. Imagine that you have only one glass and it is filled to the brim with water. Now if you change your mind and decide to have cranberry juice instead, you would not begin to pour the cranberry juice into the full glass of water. You would first dump out the water and then the glass would have room for your juice. It is the same with our ability to receive from God. If we are full of worry, fear, and unrest, we are not able to hold God's Word or His peace. He is giving it to us, but we are already full of other things so we do not seem to hold it. When we begin to hand the worry and anxieties of our lives completely to Him (not picking them back up again), then we find we are amazingly able to hold on to His peace and rest.

Your heart is likened unto a door.

Our heart is a door, a door that God needs open in order for Him to supply our needs emotionally, physically, and relationally.

I heard this the other day and I thought it was interesting: If you are a Christian, God's Promised Land is already inside you. "No one will say, 'Look, here it is!' or, 'There it is!'; because the Kingdom of God is within you" (Luke 17:21 GNB). It is inside your spirit, because the Spirit of God lives within you, but you need to begin to let the Spirit of God flow out of you! We think that God's provision is out there, somewhere externally, but God has given us all the ability we need. I am not talking about New Age beliefs that say you are god, and you are self sufficient. The Bible teaches that everything you need is within *God*. However, if Jesus is your Lord, God lives within you. And when God speaks to you, He does not speak as a voice out there somewhere, He speaks as a voice inside. Your provision is in His voice, in His Word, in His speaking. As you spend time in His Word, if your heart is untroubled, His Word will come out of your heart, and that is where your provision will be. That is your seed (Mark 4:14). You then sow that "seed" back into your untroubled heart, for a great harvest, by speaking God's Word back to Him and by doing what He spoke to you. The Bible says His Word will come to pass which leads us to the next important analogy or concept.

Your heart is your soil.

It is vital that we do not wait until circumstances are in order for us to enjoy an untroubled heart! Do not let circumstances dictate if you are going to be good soil and if you are going to be at rest. Be good soil now! We see that God does not even wait for circumstances to be resolved before He begins to bless us. "You prepare a table before me in the presence of my enemies; You have anointed my head with oil; My cup overflows" (Ps. 23:5). With enemies all around, God still puts a banquet before you (Ps. 23:5). He expects you to dine with Him, to enjoy Him and sit with Him at a lavish table no matter what is going on around you. When you keep your focus on the Lord it will not bother you who is around you or who does not like you; nothing will steal the enjoyment of the banquet the Lord has prepared for you. I am sure we will be amazed at the end of our lives to see how many "banquets" we missed that the Lord had prepared for us, because we were so distracted by our enemies, be it people or circumstances. In the book of Esther, chapters 1–10, we find an incredible example of this.

> In the days of the Ahaserus, king of Persia, there lived an Agagite named Haman. The Agagites had been enemies of the Israelites for generations. But Haman's hatred centered on one Jewish man in particular: Mordecai. Little did he know that Queen Esther was a Jew and this same Mordecai was none other than her first cousin. In the course of time, Queen Esther held an elaborate banquet for the king. Haman was the only other invited guest. Haman bragged incessantly to his family and friends about his position within the palace, the honor bestowed upon him and

> being invited to the queen's banquet. However, Haman could not enjoy the glory of the moment, or the fact that he was invited to another banquet, simply because Mordecai, his enemy, was alive. Despite the great honor shown him, it meant nothing unless Mordecai was dead. His wife and friends urged him "Have a gallows fifty cubits high made and in the morning ask the king to have Mordecai hanged on it; then go joyfully with the king to the banquet" (Est. 5:14). And the advice pleased Haman, so he had the gallows made.
>
> Haman's obsession with his enemy consumed him mentally and very soon consumed him physically. Not only did it cause him to not enjoy his banquet, but his compulsive desire to have *no* enemies around to enjoy his life went too far. The irony of the whole situation was that Haman was hanged by the king on the very gallows he had made for his enemy.

The moral of this story is that when we become fixated on our enemy, it does not destroy them, it destroys us! If this principle worked in the life of evil Haman, how much more can we see it in our own lives? God does not wait for everything in our lives to be settled to bless us; He wants to bless us all the time. It is our finite minds that seem to think the blessings can only be enjoyed once the problems are resolved. Let us learn to be good receivers all the time, always ready to receive the blessings and banquets, never distracted by negative circumstances or our enemies. That is a real heart at rest, a heart that's good soil.

We might as well understand now that problems never stop. For example: There are all kinds of new illnesses. There was mad cow, bird flu, and now swine flu (who knew?); so you never know what's next. But it doesn't matter. There is economic depression; the world market is failing, the housing market is falling, and there are wars as well as natural disasters on a large scale everywhere. And according to the Bible, it is not going to get any better. At what point do we decide to have untroubled hearts?

I think we need to decide now, when things are not as bad as they could be. No matter how bad it looks, it is not as bad as it could be. Conversely our lives will not ever be as wonderful as they can be unless we choose to have untroubled hearts.

Do you remember the famous plagues God put on Egypt during the time of Moses? Well, the children of Israel were living in Egypt in a land called Goshen. The Hebrews were slaves, and God was setting them free. As the plagues grew worse, God saw to it that the plagues did not enter the land of Goshen. God will provide a Goshen for us. In the middle of everything, God always has a land of Goshen for His people; a land where He has provision in the midst of chaos and a light in the darkness. God has that place for you. But how do you find it? Only an untroubled heart can hear His voice.

Truth:

Fear is the presence of the Enemy.

The Devil cannot work apart from your restless heart! He has to have us restless to be able to work through us. When you worry, you open the door to him and you allow him to begin working in your life.

Let's go back to the door analogy: Your heart is like a door, but it has two-way hinges. When we are at rest, it is automatically open to God. His blessings flow through us, His words speak through us, and we hear His voice. In those peaceful moments, we understand the Lord and we have a calm, quiet spirit that is of great value to God (1 Peter 3:4). But as soon as *restlessness* comes in, the hinge swings the door the other way. The door then snaps closed to God, but opens to the Enemy. In this restless state, nothing from God in Heaven gets through to us and we have opened a door to the Enemy. Our door is sprung open the wrong direction as long as we are fearful, restless, and not at peace. Then whatever chaos the Enemy wants to bring into your life just walks straight through. Fear will bring doubt and confusion, which will open the door to every evil thing (James 3:16). This will continue until you stop it and close the door by refocusing on the Lord. Being at peace in God's presence slams that door shut again. Just as light dispels the dark, the presence of God will drive away your fears and flood you with joy.

We need to remember that the entrance of fear is so subtle. People hear news and they begin to fear. They see their bank accounts and they begin to fear. When something breaks they begin to fear. They get symptoms of an illness and they begin to fear. They talk to their relatives and they begin to fear. The phone rings and they are afraid. Subtly, subtly, all day long, the Enemy is trying to get us to have a restless heart so that the hinge on our doors is constantly open to him. That is his goal.

When the Enemy throws worry at you, throw it back. The Enemy wants you to live in fear and confusion. When we are not resting in God, confusion, fear, depression, even anger, come in every time.

"Let not your heart be troubled, neither let it be afraid" (John 14:27). A heart free from fear is very important and it is our job to get rid of fear. "For God hath not given us the spirit of fear; but of power, and of love, and of a sound mind" (2 Tim. 1:7). But how do we do that? *First,* by seeing the *necessity* to get it out of your heart, and seeing that it is not from God. *Second,* by pressing into God and His Word until you begin to have His love envelope you and restore you to that place of "power, love, and a sound mind." "There is no fear in love; but perfect love casts out fear, because fear involves punishment, and the one who fears is not perfected in love" (1 John 4:18).

Let's look at a more subtle side of fear: guilt and/or an over concern of what other people think. This too is fear. The other day, Kevin and I were taking a parenting course called "Growing Kids God's Way" by the Ezzos. We took one of their tests to see whether we had a healthy conscience or a guilty conscience. This test teaches about positive vs. prohibitive thinking processes. Do you make decisions for the love of your virtue because it is right, or do you make decisions because you're worried about what other people think? One of the examples the course gives is if someone needed you to do something, and you genuinely couldn't do it; would you feel guilty that you couldn't? That is actually a prohibitive conscience; but I thought it was caring about the person. So Kevin scored great on his test, and I didn't score that great on mine. If Kevin genuinely couldn't do something and he didn't feel guilty about it, I thought he didn't care as much as I did. I thought he just didn't have the same amount of compassion that I had. How funny to find out it was him wearing the halo, not me! God's ways are not our ways, but God's ways produce life.

Before you throw stones at me, I want you to think about yourself. How would you score? Guilt and fear of disapproval swing our heart doors the wrong way. If you cannot do something for someone, you can pray for that person, give them someone they can call, and be proactive, but worrying and rubbing your hands together about it leads to restlessness. It does not make us virtuous. It is a bill of goods that the Enemy has sold (particularly to women) for centuries.

"The Ultimate Rest Stop"

Now, why else do we want Rest?

1. "Rest in the LORD and wait patiently for Him; Do not fret because of him who prospers in his way, Because of the man who carries out wicked schemes" (Ps. 37:7–8).

   "Cease from anger and forsake wrath; Do not fret; it leads only to evildoing" (Ps. 37:8).

   Why? Because anger, fear and fret lead to bad decisions! Straight away, it will put you on the wrong path.

2. The second reason that we want rest in our lives is because when we are not resting in our souls and emotions, it makes us mean and irritable. When we are not at rest in our minds, everyone knows it.
3. Not being at rest also makes us hate our lives, and the purpose of this entire book is to learn how to love your life. God wants you to love your life. "All the days of the desponding and afflicted are made evil [by anxious thoughts and forebodings], but he who has a glad heart has a continual feast" [regardless of circumstances] (Prov. 15:15, AMP).
4. Not being at rest affects our health. "Watch over your heart with all diligence, for from it flow the springs of life" (Prov. 4:23). Life flows from within. We must, therefore, guard our hearts. It is the garden that produces the harvest of health. We must keep it free from thorns and weeds.
5. And lastly, it makes us poor soil. In poor soil it is hard to produce anything and even what you do manage to produce is weak and small. I don't know about you, but I want to be good soil so that the promises of God will bloom and flourish in my life. (In the Promised Land one cluster of grapes was so big and juicy it took two men to carry it on a pole [Num. 13:23]. That's how fertile I want my heart to be! What kind of soil do you want to be? Are you willing to make the necessary changes?)

How do we hinder rest?

"To whom he said, This is the rest wherewith ye may cause the weary to rest; and this is the refreshing …" (Isa. 28:12, KJV). Isn't that what we all want? "Yet they would not hear." God is trying to refresh all of us. We are no different than they were then. God desires us to live in a refreshing way, the ultimate "Rest Stop". It is us who hinder it, not God.

And how do we hinder it? *First,* by not hearing. Things enter our hearts through our ears. Romans 10:17 says, "So faith comes from hearing, and hearing by the word of Christ." Then faith in turn brings strength, light, healing, and dispels fear and darkness. When we will not hear God's voice—His Word—and let it calm us, we are condemned to live with unrest in our hearts.

Thus says the LORD, "Stand by the ways and see and ask for the ancient paths, Where the good way is, and walk in it; And you will find rest for your souls. But they said, 'We will not walk in it'" (Jer. 6:16).

What were the ancient ways? "You shall love the LORD your God with all your heart and with all your soul and with all your might" (Deut. 6:5). "Man doth not live by bread only, but by every word that proceedeth out of the mouth of the LORD" (Deut. 8:3 KJV). The "ancient ways" are simple things: put God first, do not covet, do not gossip about your neighbor, do not commit adultery, do not steal, do not lie, do not cheat, etc.

A *second* way we hinder rest then, is sin. If we are truly honest with ourselves, we can acknowledge that in most of our lives, there is some area which the Lord has convicted us about. Great or small, these all qualify as sin. Simply put: sin hinders rest. Rest cannot enter a life with willful disobedience. It is not that God is angry at us and withholding rest, but rather, sin hindering rest is another spiritual law like those we discussed earlier. Often, we find ourselves doing a great many things to seek rest and love our lives, yet without this simple step, we are merely spinning our wheels. Until we let go of those areas and change our ways, rest will never enter.

We must go back to the way that God meant it to be. Jesus sums it up in two commandments: love God and love your neighbor. If you put God first, you will not want the sin; that is the first step to finding rest for your soul. Even if you are not yet completely free from that sin, if you sincerely desire freedom from it and are pressing into the Lord to be free from it, you open your heart up to receive rest bit by bit. The more you let go of the weaknesses, the more you open the floodgates to allow God's rest to enter and make your life into something you have only dreamed of, a true garden of Eden.

However, even letting go of sin must be done by faith. Otherwise, if we try to get free from sin in our own strength, the carnal nature will rise up and we will fail. Yet if we release the sin into God's hands by faith, looking to Him to be strong through us, then sin loses its hold. The determining factor to this victory is whether we keep our eyes on God or on the sin we are trying to get rid of. Whatever we focus on is what we will move toward even if we do not mean to.

Let me explain it this way. I rode horses for many years. Any good rider will tell you that when you are going over a jump, your eyes should already be on the next jump. To look at the jump you are going over means you look down. And wherever your eyes go, your body follows. To not fall off your horse you have to always keep your focus on where you're heading. The same is true for overcoming sin. To overcome sin you cannot keep your eyes on the sin, but on the victory. A silly example of this would be someone trying to lose weight, saying, "I am not going to eat that chocolate cake". This tactic does not work. It will not be long before they are sitting down with a big fork. However, if this person begins to focus on healthy food, researching it, trying different types, learning to cook it, etc., they will move in that direction. This truth works the same for eradicating all kinds of sin from your life; from anger to pornography, to lying, etc.

The *third* way rest is hindered is lack of faith. To find rest you have to believe by faith that God truly wants rest for you. As you stay in His Word, you will begin to believe that more and more.

> "We see, then, that they [the children of Israel] were not able to enter the Promised Land, because they did not believe" (Heb. 3:19, GNB). "Now, God has offered us the promise that we may receive that rest He spoke about. Let us take care, then, that

> none of you will be found to have failed to receive that promised rest. For we have heard the Good News, just as they did. They heard the message, but it did them no good, because when they heard it, they did not accept it with faith. We who believe, then, do receive that rest which God promised…" (Heb. 4:1–3a, GNB).

These Scriptures are referring to Israel not entering into the rest God had for them. These powerful scriptures then challenge us to *not* make the same mistake! They exhort us to keep our eyes on the Lord and realize that we have to enter into rest by faith. This is a faith journey *not* a "works" journey. The fact that the children of Israel didn't enter rest actually upset God. Entering into rest is so simple, but it goes back to believing God is a good God. This "Rest" is exactly that. It is "resting" in God's goodness, love, and mercy. It is letting go of striving. When we are worried, anxious, and fearful, it frustrates the grace of God. God wants us at peace all the time. He wants us to look to Him and rest in Him continually. So, according to this, we know that when we cease from trying to make things happen on our own, we are in faith and at rest, then our Promised Land comes in sight.

Truth:

If we are not in rest, we are not in faith!

(There is a quick way you can gauge your faith). Faith is a rest, and rest is enjoyable. If you are resting in God's Word, the peace comes. You need to go to God and get quiet. Remember our first Scripture: "And He said, 'My presence shall go with you, and I will give you rest'" (Ex. 33:14). That Scripture is out of the book of Exodus. That was God's plan for the children of Israel in the desert and it is still His plan for us. When we cease from own labor we are in faith (Heb. 4). Even when you are working hard you can still be resting in the Lord. Let that thought sink in!

Peggy Joyce Ruth, my pastor's wife from my childhood, tells a story of how she and her husband were shoveling gravel. Her husband, Pastor Jack, was working as hard as he could, shoveling dirt from one side to the other. After hours of working he looked over at Peggy Joyce, who was not as physically strong as he was, and yet she had shoveled more dirt than he had and was not tired or sore; all because she was relaxed while she was working. She was actually more productive because she was at rest on the inside.[40]

If we can be at peace, we can be a rest, and if we can be at rest, we can be healed and have clarity of thought and mind. We must be in faith for God's life to flow through us. Rest is the proof of faith. If we remain in rest (peace), we will get our miracle. Do you need a miracle? Then you need to be at rest.

The good news is, what you have lost through unrest, you can recover through rest. You can regain everything you've lost—and infinitely more.

Warning:

My only warning is: "But as soon as they had rest, they did evil …" (Neh. 9:28). Believe it or not, I've known people who, as soon as they get rest (in the form of answered prayer and peace of mind), they slip back into sin and backslide. Make sure that as you begin to walk in rest that you guard your heart against complacency toward God. Some people only go to God when they are in need or crisis, and as soon as the pressure is off, they often forget God until the next need or crisis. However, real fellowship with God is birthed in those quiet, precious moments when you are loving on God just for who He is. Then, when you are in crisis you are close to God, and when you are not in crisis you are still close to God because you are in a living relationship with Him. This is where true rest comes on the scene. Relaxing in His loving arms brings rest on a level you never knew was possible! So next time you read your Bible and do your quiet time, be sure to take a deep breath, close your eyes, and relax in God's presence. Do not be intimidated by intimacy with the one and only Living God. Step into His ultimate "Rest Stop" and abide there.

Prayer

Heavenly Father,

I come to You in Jesus' Name and in the finished work of Calvary. You did all the work so I could rest in Your love and Your peace. Forgive me for not having done that fully.

Forgive me for the areas of fear and anxiety, where I haven't believed You would come through for me. I don't want to miss out on the "rest" You have for me because of unbelief. I don't want to miss Your Rest Stop even for a minute!

I love You and choose to let go of fear and worry. I choose to have an untroubled heart and to not only make my heart fertile soil for your promise to bear much fruit in my life, but to also make sure the door of my heart is *only* open to you!

Holy Spirit, quicken to me when I am slipping back into fear, anxiety or anger. I put my life in Your loving hands, once more.

I will keep my eyes on You, and live in expectancy of Your promises coming to pass.

In Jesus' Name,
Amen

Truth in Action:

1. What analogy about the heart spoke to you the most?

____

____

____

____

____

____

2. Where have you been missing it, in the above analogy, that stood out to you?

____

____

____

____

____

____

3. Recap the three hindrances to rest.

____

____

____

____

____

Nugget:

We retain information much longer if we will both receive it in and then repeat it back. Therefore, if we want to remember important facts on entering rest, we will receive the most benefit from writing down what we have just read. Some studies show that we remember approximately:

- *10% of what we read,*
- *20% of what we hear,*
- *30% of what we see,*
- *50% of what we both hear and see,*
- *70% of what we both say and write, and*
- *90% of what we do.*[41]

4. Put in your own words how one enters rest by faith. Write it down, along with practical steps to accomplish it. E.g. 1) Find a promise from God. 2) Stop worrying. 3) …… (Re-read that section if you need to.)

____

____

____

____

____

Steps to Loving Your Journey

"For he that will love life, and see good days. . ." (1 Peter 3:10a KJV).

Make these simple steps a daily part of your life and see the blessings abound!

- **Repent from the sin of dissatisfaction.**
- **Stop envying others and wishing you had someone else's life.**
- **Learn to love your life:** Do not curse your day by starting it out saying, "If my life was only different," or "I hate my life." Instead say, "God, You gave my today, and I choose to love it! Now, what can I do to make it special?"
- **Get rid of the "ifs":** ("If this or that changed, I would be happy.") No! What are you enjoying now? Those who enjoy what they have receive more!
- **Love the process:** Our lives are a constant journey. If we do not learn to love the process, we miss our entire lives!
- **Contentment for the journey:** "But Godliness with contentment is great gain" (1 Tim. 6:6). Remember that whatever you are going through is not the big picture; it is just today's picture! Enjoy life today!
- **Peace for the journey:**

  a) Settle Salvation

  b) Never be at odds with God

  c) Be at peace with yourself

  d) Be at peace with others
- **Grace for the journey**: "My grace is sufficient for you, for My power is perfected in weakness" (2 Cor. 12:9). Daily ask God for His grace to help you love your life, complete your journey, and go the extra mile.
- **Spend time with God:** This daily time with God will send you out with joy and strength for the day, a heart for your responsibilities, and a passion to glorify God in all you do.
- **Rest for the journey:** "And He said, 'My presence shall go with you and I will give you rest'" (Ex. 33:14). "Therefore let us be diligent to enter that rest …"(Heb. 4:11).
- **Learn not to dread:** Pray, "I am going to do the will of God today without thinking about tomorrow."[42] "Casting *all* your cares upon Him, for He cares for you" (1 Peter 5:7).

Chapter Thirteen

A Journey of Love

"I have loved you with an everlasting love;
Therefore I have drawn you with lovingkindness."
Jeremiah 31:3

The one thing that everyone in the world wants … is love. *Every boy* wants a father that is a hero whom he can model his life after and get approval from. *Every man* is looking for someone he can be a hero for, someone to lay down his life for, someone that brings out the hero in him. *Every woman* wants a man that will always keep her as the apple of his eye, always pursuing her, protecting her, longing to be with her, and providing for her. *Every little girl* longs for the protection of a strong, loving Daddy; one that will treat her like a little lady, who makes her feels pretty and sheltered from the cruel world; one who has a big lap she can always crawl into and whose hugs are readily available. *Love … what the world longs for but seldom finds.*

Love is certainly a journey. You do not have to live long to begin to realize that. It does not have to be a hard journey, however. It can be a wonderful journey. Love is the most important element that exists. In fact, everything good was created through love and everything good works by love. In this chapter I want you to be moved by the power of love; I want you to be healed by the power of love, and I want you to be determined to have the power of love working through every single aspect of your life. The true love of God moves mountains and makes peace with others and peace with yourself truly attainable.

If you have to ask someone what love really is, it would most likely be hard for him or her to explain. It can seem challenging to put into words, but if you use one word to describe love; it would be—God. God *is* love! God's love is deep; God's love is wide. Yet His amazing love has boundaries. This too is love. The natural consequences of reaping what you sow for example, is love allowing us to mature into compassionate loving people. God is merciful, full of compassion, and easy to entreat. God's so amazing that by His children He prefers the name of "Daddy" to the name of "King". His desire is for *all* of His creation to know Him as "Daddy." That's something to think about!

We see through Scripture that God loves intimacy with us and is quick to receive our repentance. Why? Because God hates separation as much as we do. Have you ever been in a relationship where there is a schism and you have knots in your stomach? Until everything is settled you have no peace in your life. It is the same with God; until we get it right with God we have no peace. And what is more amazing, I believe God longs for that peace with us the same way we do. That is why He went to such lengths to reconcile us to Himself. In fact, it is the greatest story ever told!

Love unimaginable; this is the love of God! Since God *is* this amazing *love*, the two names are interchangeable. You can say God is *love*, but you can also say *love* is God. In fact, you can take your favorite Scripture verses and exchange the word "God" for the word "love." Let's look,

> Ex: "But (He) Love was pierced through for our transgressions, (He) Love was crushed for our iniquities; The chastening for our well-being fell upon (Him) Love, And by (His) Love's scourging we are healed" (Isa. 53:5). Now that's a revelation!

To know the love of the almighty God is to be totally filled with God so it is to God and His Word we must go to learn what love is. The world cannot give us the answers we are looking for, as the Love of the Father is not found there. Matthew 24:12 says that a sign of the end times is that people's love will grow cold. Haven't we seen that in today's world? Yet God's love never grows cold!

Today's world finds it so hard to define love. In the modern vernacular its meaning alone can be so vague. In the English language people use love for all kinds of feelings that are unrelated to love. I could tell you I love roast lamb, or I love chocolate, or that I love that movie, or that painting. Or I could tell you I love my family, I love my children, I love my husband, I love my dog. I could look at someone and say, "Oh, isn't she funny? I just love her!" Or, a young lady who sees a very handsome young man she hasn't met yet, says, "Oh, I think I am in love!"

That's a lot of love. Or is it? Allow me to correct these sentences for you. The proper way would be to say: "Roast lamb is great; it is my favorite food," or "I am addicted to chocolate," which is the truth with most of us. You can definitely say that it was a well-done movie, a beautiful painting. You can certainly say that you love your children and you love your family, but you love your husband in a different way than you love anyone else. And the truth is for that young lady who sees that good-looking man and says, "Oh, I think I am in love!" she's actually saying, "Oh, I am lusting over him." We use the word "love" to cover so many different areas of our hearts when it's really not what we are saying at all. The Greeks never did that. For everything they felt they had a different word. In fact, they used four different words for our word "love." Differentiating these types of love is so important to God that He had the New Testament written in Greek.

It took writing the New Testament in Greek for many people to understand real love; yet most still do not even know it exists. I was talking to a young man the other day and he said that his father never once in his life told him he loved him. He said his mother has only said it once or twice, and that was only after they had a three-hour fight. I know many husbands who have never told their wives that they love them. I know mothers who have never told their children that they love them. Many people do not understand the God kind of love and what it is all about because they've never seen it demonstrated.

There was a joke (albeit not a very funny one) in which a couple got married. After years and years of the husband never telling his wife that he loved her, she complained one day. She said, "Why is it that you never tell me you love me?" He said, "I told you I loved you when I married you, and if that changes, I will let you know." That's not the way it works. Love is not something to conserve on; love grows as you give it away.

Different types of love:

To truly understand the God kind of love, we need to take a minute and look at the three other types of human love. The first being *phileo.* Phileo is affectionate love, friendship, or brotherly love. There's a city in the United States called Philadelphia, which means "the city of brotherly love." The Bible talks about this kind of love in Matthew 5:46–47,where Jesus says, "For if you love those who love you, what reward have you, do not even the tax gatherers do the same, if you greet your brothers only, what more have you? Do not the Gentiles do the same?" So phileo, though it may run deep, is loving the loveable. You have been through so much with these people in your life so you have a love, a bond, with them. But if they were to do something really ugly to you, you might just walk away. You might grieve over the loss of the relationship, but your love for them would change. Phileo is a soulish love. That's not bad; it is just what it is: soulish. It is an important part of life, but there is something more.

The second kind of love is *eros.* Eros is a physical love between a man and a woman. God made it beautiful, but it has boundaries. Not boundaries that we set, but boundaries that God has set; not to take away our fun, but to help us love our lives. God has set certain laws in the universe, i.e.: general relativity (gravity), Boyle's Law (pressure and volume are inversely proportional), Newton's Law of Motion, etc. You must know and understand the rules/boundaries so that you can benefit from these laws and not have them hurt you. They were given to bless, not to kill. God has also set certain spiritual laws governing this gift of eros. They can bless, but if the boundaries are not respected, they can harm and in some cases even kill.

Let me give you an example and then back it up with statistics. Kevin and I were talking to a woman who said, "My husband and I were physically involved before we were married. Now I struggle in that area." Is that normal? Well, my pastors from my youth, Peggy Joyce and Jack Ruth, who have also been marriage counselors for over thirty years, said that out of all the people they have helped, they noted that those who had relations before they were married all recognized that something died in that area of their lives after they got married. The good news is that when they repented and got on their knees and said, "God, I repent for having sex before marriage," God incredibly restored their marriage and truly revived that area!

The statistics on sexual relations exclusively in marriage are astounding! "Couples who wait until after marriage to have sex are 29–47 percent more likely to enjoy sex during marriage."[43] "Research is clear: Married people have the most sex, and they have the best sex," according to Dr. John P. Splinter.[44] Again, even if you have made mistakes in your past, remember that God's mercies are new every day. We are never locked into something we have done in the past; He always restores us if we ask Him to.

In addition, married couples who pray together just five minutes per day saw dramatic increases in their intimacy. Husband and wife team Squire Rushnell (well-known as an award-winning television executive at ABC) and Louise DuArt co-authored *Couples Who Pray.* In their book, they show the findings of their study: "The Forty Day Challenge." In this experiment, couples committed to pray together daily. The findings showed that couples saw an increase of "20 to 30 percent in romance, conversation, and overall happiness as a result of praying together." Among the couples who pray together frequently and not only on occasion, those tested showed that the fear of divorce drops to a staggering zero.[45] God created sex and created marriage. Let Him get involved in your marriage and in your life and He can make it so much better than you imagined!

For those of you who are single or have single children, a powerful analogy used to describe sex is "fire." If you build a fire in a fireplace, it produces warmth; it makes you feel cozy and safe; it is a comfort. If you build a fire in the middle of the living room, it is going to burn down your house and hurt more than just you. That's what physical love outside of marriage is; it will consume everything around you. God created sex to be great, but it is a covenant act and was designed for marriage. It is actually the last God-ordained blood covenant in the world. To best explain this as discretely as possible, let's take a peek at Jewish tradition.

> "When the wedding party arrived at the father's house the newlyweds went into the wedding chamber for a seven-day honeymoon and the groom's best friend stood outside waiting for the groom to tell him that the marriage had been consummated. The proof of this was the bed sheet bearing the bloodshed by the bride as a result of her first sexual intercourse (her hymen being broken). This is notable for two reasons. It speaks of purity before marriage, but it also shows a blood covenant (the most solemn and binding kind) such as God's covenant with his people."[46]

People, especially young people, tend to think that eros love is the strongest kind of love because it feels so strong. It is actually the weakest form of love, and even though it is an important part of a marriage, it is not the part of the marriage that keeps you together (helping you honor your commitment and covenant to each other) when you have differences of personality, differences of opinion, or when hard times take you through life. Eros is not the glue that holds you together, but we will talk about that glue in just a minute.

Number three is *storge.* Storge just means "fond of natural relations, cherishing what's kindred, especially parents to children."[47] This is a soulish love as well, but it is an important part of life. It is a very strong love, probably by far the strongest of the above three.

Number four is *agape.* Vine's Dictionary defines agape love as: a deliberate choice to love, not drawn out of the excellency of its object; in other words, not because the object is special or because it has any defining characteristics; a choice made without a signable cause. This is the type of love God has for us! There is no logical explanation for it except that it is part of His nature to love this way. Think of it like this: have you ever loved someone you are not even connected to? Have you loved someone that might not even like you, may even hate you, or perhaps made your life miserable? Perhaps someone who smells or looks vile? Have you loved them with a love so intense you would lay down your life for them? It is in truth unfathomable to the human mind.

The Strong's Concordance defines agape love as 'love, heart, affection, benevolence,' meaning you're giving it out to someone who cannot give it back. Agape is "a love feast."[48] This is the strongest love known to man because it is not human love, it is God's love.

People give their lives to the Lord because they feel the agape love of Christ. In comparison to agape love, even storge love for your children, husband, or family is weak. As you begin to receive this agape love from Christ, only then will you be able to walk in it. You cannot walk in it, however, until you first start receiving it.

God's love for you is so intense and so unwavering! The intensity of His love for you is best illustrated through the prophet Hosea in the Old Testament. At the time in history that Hosea lived, Israel was not serving the living God, but was serving dead idols. Therefore, they could not believe that God loved them as much as He did. (Have you been in that place? Are you there now?) God asked His prophet, Hosea, to marry a prostitute named Gomer as a living illustration of His love for His people. Hosea loved Gomer intensely, and even though Gomer would leave him continually and return to prostitution, he would bring her back with kind, loving words. He had Hosea be a living picture of how God is with us. No matter what we have done, He will always come back for us! Never be ashamed to return to God! There is nothing you could have done that would make Him not want to see you or not want to be with you. He sent His only Son on our behalf so when we fall all we have to do is ask Him to forgive us and we are amazingly forgiven and restored to right relationship with Him.

This reminds me of one of my favorite Scriptures "'So I have sworn that I will not be angry with you nor will I rebuke you. For the mountains may be removed and the hills may shake, But My lovingkindness will not be removed from you, And My covenant of peace will not be shaken,' Says the LORD who has compassion on you" (Isa. 54:9–10). Do you see that God is not mad at you? God loves you so much that He has withheld nothing from you; even His Son. All that is left is for us to take a deep breath, let go of the guilt and/or excuses, and tell God that we desire His love. He will not fail you. He loves you intensely. Meditate on Scriptures of His great love for you. Invite Him in, learn of this love, and then have the great joy of extending that love to someone else. Though God is powerful, He is also gentle. "You have also given me the shield of Your salvation, And Your right hand upholds me; And Your gentleness makes me great" (Ps. 18:35). As you spend time in His Word and in His presence, He will teach you how to love the unlovable. You cannot begin to love people with unconditional love until you have experienced it.

Agape love is the ability to love someone who is not lovable at all. Through the love of God, we can learn to bless those that curse us, we can bless their families, we can bless everything about them. I heard a man in the United States whose wife was murdered say on the news, "He [the murderer] took what meant the most to me, but I cannot let that hole be replaced with hate." That's agape!

It is incredibly freeing when you come to the point where you love a person and it has nothing to do with the person. Then you have the freedom to love all you want because God is filling you back up again. Through the love of God you can even love people you have just met.

In Matthew 5:44, Jesus goes so far as to say, "Agape-love your enemies, pray for those who persecute you in order for you to be sons and daughters of your Father, who is in Heaven, for he causes the sun to rise on the evil and the good, he brings rain on the righteous and the unrighteous." Why did he add that part? Because He wants us to know that He agape-loves, too. We love everyone when we walk in agape love, and so does God. That's why He lets the sun shine and the rain fall on the righteous *and* the unrighteous.

Truth:

Love is an action.

A well-known example of agape love occurred in the early 1950s when five men went to South America to bring Christ to a very ferocious tribe called the Auca Indians. After a time working with the Indians these men were brutally murdered by the tribe. One of their wives, Elisabeth Elliot, her daughter, and Rachel Saint returned to this tribe. The tribe allowed them to come in, live among them, and preach Jesus Christ to them. The tribe all gave their lives to the Lord because they could not understand what kind of love these women had for them after they had murdered their husbands.[49]

These women could have responded in several different ways. They could have forgiven the tribe yet stayed in the States, but they went the extra mile. They reached out to the very tribe that had killed their husbands. That act meant that their husbands' deaths were not in vain. That is agape love. It is not human, but divine.

How can you have love like this? How is it possible? By letting God love you. You may say, "What I really need is for my husband to tell me that he loves me just once, and then I would be free to love others openly," or, "What I've really been waiting for is for my mother to say that she loves me and is proud of me. If I had that, it would heal me and I could love others freely." It does not work that way. The people you need so desperately to love you cannot give love because they were never loved that way themselves. Damaged people have a hard time loving. They do not love themselves, so they cannot return love. They are so desperate for unconditional love, yet they often push it away, thinking that everyone else's love has an angle. You'll notice that the people who are the most damaged and the most love-starved will not let you hug them. They will not let you near them because they do not believe that you could love them. They think you have an ulterior motive. They are convinced of it. So they are actually pushing away the very thing that they need most in their lives. These same people say, "I can't love, I am too busy looking for someone to love me." If you ever find yourself saying these words, then it is because you need to experience the love of Christ. The love of a human will not heal you.

How Do You Walk in Agape Love?

Number one: If you've already given your heart to the Lord, you start by forgiving those who cannot love you. Jesus said that if you cannot forgive those who have hurt you, you're going to end up in the same prison of misery your whole life that they are in. The people who do not love you are not refusing to love you because they want to hurt you, regardless of what it looks like or even what they think. They are refusing to love you because they are so hurt and so miserable that they literally *cannot* love you. Stop looking for love from these people and accept that they may never be able to love you the way you need.

Which brings me to the all-important **number two**: Begin to look for love from the One who created love and the One who is love. Then your life will change. Many people do not realize that they need to look up, not out, for the love, security, and confidence they need. I did a study once on many of the remarkable women through history that accomplished so much, and I found it interesting that they all had one thing in common—a great relationship with their dads. I found it equally remarkable that most of our Bible heroes didn't have great dads, but they learned to look to God for the love they had missed. This is neither the book nor the time to go through all the examples, but suffice it to say that those who looked to God for love and looked to God to be their Father, changed history. Whether you are male or female, the answer is the same; only God can fill the void that people have left in your life. But fill it He will! Do not be intimidated to find a quiet moment and go to Him for love. The results will be life changing.

A member of our church learned this lesson in college. Here is Jennifer's story:

> My small circle of friends in college was very close and we spent all our time together. One day one of the members of the group, Tim, suddenly refused to speak to any of us or spend time with us anymore. He changed overnight. He would not return phone calls or even acknowledge the existence of his once close friends. We all became angry and rejected Tim because of his odd and indifferent behavior. At first, I was as hurt and embittered as everyone else. I had never had someone close to me reject me like this. His behavior was completely unjustified, unexpected, and ruthless. My initial reaction was just like everyone else: I was deeply hurt and very angry.

> However, I soon came to realize that Tim's behavior had nothing to do with me personally or our circle of friends. Tim was simply a person who was still working through deep emotional issues. He would reject others so that they would in turn reject him, and he could then have a real excuse for his anger and hatred. I began to send him birthday gifts, letters, and small surprises just as if nothing had ever happened. Even after I graduated and moved away, I continued to write him. He never once responded. After a year or two, Tim opened up to someone else, "You know, I just don't get it … I was so cruel, especially to Jennifer, and she still writes me. I just don't understand how she could be nice to me after how I treated her." Even though Tim never returned the compassion I showed, I gained an invaluable gift and learned a life-changing revelation. By refusing to reject Tim when he deserved it, I was freed from the bitterness that set in on those around me. Never again will I be trapped by someone else's weaknesses. Never again will I play the rejection game and be caught in its downward spiral. I learned the secret of loving someone who was not able to return it.

As you begin to agape love people, the people who cannot love you back may actually surprise you. You may see them begin to change because you are able to pray for them in a way that you were never able to before. They may not, but either way you win.

If your spouse cannot love you, God can. If you stop looking for love from hurtful people and start looking for love from God, then and only then will you open up your heart to receive God's beautiful and powerful love. If you are looking desperately toward the person who cannot love you, you cannot receive the love of God, because your heart is closed off. I challenge you to fall in love with the One who loved you first, and that's Jesus Christ. Do you really know how much God loves you? I am going to share a couple of Scriptures.

"I have loved you with an everlasting love; therefore I have drawn you with loving-kindness" (Jer. 31:3). When you read Scriptures like this, you need to put your name in them. "'I have loved _______ with an everlasting love; therefore I have drawn _______ with loving-kindness.' God loves me so much!"

"Who can separate us from the love of Christ?" Paul says, "For I am persuaded that neither death nor life nor angels nor principalities nor powers nor height nor depth nor any other creature should be able to separate us from the love of God, which is in Jesus Christ" (Rom. 8:35, 38–39). That's how much He loves you!

Many of you have labored tirelessly for your families or for you church and you do not feel like you've gotten the love or the gratitude that you deserve, and you're tired and maybe a little frustrated. That's because as the old song says, "You're looking for love in all the wrong places, looking for love in too many faces …"[50] You simply need to look in one place, in One Face. God says in Heb. 6:10 (NKJV), "For God is not unjust to forget your work and labor of love which you have shown toward His name, in that you have ministered to the saints, and do minister." You may say, "My family are not saints." They are to God. As you minister to them, He will not forget your labor of love. "When You said, 'Seek My face,' my heart said to You, 'Your face, O LORD, I shall seek'" (Psalm 27:8). Let's make that verse our heart's cry.

The Bible says we are able to love God. Why? Because He first loved us. Have you ever really acknowledged how much God really knows about you and still loves you? Most of us do not like to think about that. We like to pretend that those areas in our lives and our personalities are not there. We figure God only loves the nice part of us and that is why we only love the nice part of others. But if we would be willing to acknowledge that God loves all of us, even the ugly part of us, then we will find that we are able to love even the ugly parts of other people. Let's read what real love is.

> "Now one of the Pharisees was requesting him to dine with him (speaking of Jesus) and Jesus entered the Pharisees' house and reclined at the table; and behold there was a woman in the city who was a sinner and when she learned that Jesus was reclining at the table in the Pharisees' house, she brought an alabaster vile of perfume, and standing before him, she began to wet his feet with her tears and wiping them with the hair from her head and kissing his feet and anointing them with the perfume. Now when the Pharisees who had invited them saw this, he said to himself, 'now if this man was a prophet, he would know who and what sort of person this woman is who is touching him, that she is a sinner. And Jesus answered and said unto him, 'Simon, I have something to say to you,' and he replied, 'Say it teacher.' 'A certain money lender had two different debtors, one owed 500 denari and one owed 50. When they were unable to repay, he graciously forgave them both. Which of them, therefore, would love him more?' Simon answered and said, 'I suppose the one whom He forgave more,' and He said to him, 'You have judged correctly.' And turning toward the woman he said, 'Do you see this woman? I entered your house, but you gave me no water for my feet. But she has wet my feet with her tears and wipes them with her hair. You gave me no kiss, but she, since the time I came in, has not ceased to kiss my feet. You did not anoint my head with oil, but she anointed my head with perfume; for this reason I say to you her sins, which are many, have been forgiven, for he who has been forgiven little, loves little.' And He said to her, 'Your sins have been forgiven'" (Luke 7:36–48).

Agape love surpasses the embarrassment button and the selfish button. Lavish your love upon the Lord, and love Him with abandon. In your life, do you play the part of this lady, or do you play the role of Simon, being reserved with your love toward Christ? Where are you? Some people say, "It is just my personality to be reserved." Simon could have said that, but it didn't matter to Jesus, did it? All that mattered to Him was the lady who was vulnerable. Is the Lord Jesus just a moment in your day, or is He the purpose for your day?

Let's review how you walk in this kind of love:

- Receive God's love and dwell in it. I John 2:5 says, "Whoever keeps God's Word in Him, the love of God has truly been perfected; by this we know that we are in Him." So as you begin to not only read but meditate on His words, you will be filled with His love. David understood God's love, therefore the Psalms are a nice place to start.

- Stop looking for love in the wrong places by expecting it from those who can never give it.

- B*e a doer of God's Word and not a hearer only* (James 1:22). Be kind to your enemies. Feed the poor. Encourage the weak. Never return evil for evil.

- The love of the world will drain agape love faster than anything else I know. "Do not love the world nor the things in the world. If anyone loves the world, the love of the Father is not in him" (1 John 2:15). You know you have a hunger for the world:
    - o If you are more hungry for what's in it (fashion, money, etc.) than for God.
    - o If you are more interested in the approval of man than the approval of God.
    - o If "things" make you feel important instead of finding your importance in Christ.

  If you answered yes to these you may find yourself running low in the love department. Put God first and He will add these things unto you, but it will not matter to you because you are so filled with His love.

Be quick to give a word of kindness or encouragement. Praise changes people's lives. So on the days you think, "I have no love to give," take a step back, meditate on God, receive what He has for you, and all of a sudden, the love will rise up and flow out of your words. The Bible says, "God is love" (1 John 4:16). Therefore, love is as powerful as God Himself. Do you know how faith works? The Bible says that, "faith works by love" (Gal. 5:6). What about fear? Fear does not stand a chance against love; love is so powerful. In 1 John 4:18 it says that *perfect love casts out all fear.*

Someone in your life needs to hear you say, "I love you." Are you going to make them wait another day? Someone is waiting for you to reach out to them, and it may be the very person that you have prayed on your knees, "God, just let them say that they are proud of me." It may be an aging parent and you need to reach out to them. Are you going to make them wait? Will you continue the iniquity in the family of not loving? Or are you going to change that, receive the love from God, and not expect anything in return? The world cannot love like this, but God can. Will you do that? Will you show God's love today?

Prayer

Dear Lord,

I desire Your agape love in my life. I desire to receive it and to give it freely. Lord, more than anything I want a life of love. I want my life to count for eternity. I want to love those that cannot love me back. I want to feel Your compassion for the hurting. I want to be a whole vessel that You can pour Your love through.

Forgive me for the times I have been reserved in my love toward You. You are the first One I want to practice loving with reckless abandon! I love you Lord.

I once again release all those people (name them) that I have been looking for love and approval from that haven't given it, I release them into your loving arms and I release them from my expectations. I realize that they may never love me as I need and I am okay with that, because I am no longer going to look to them but to You!

In Your precious Name,
Amen.

Nugget:

Here are a couple of ways to check if you are walking in love:

- *If you are patient, kind, not jealous; if you do not brag and are not arrogant, if you do not act unbecomingly; if you do not seek your own, if you are not provoked, do not take into account a wrong suffered, do not rejoice in unrighteousness, but rejoice with the truth; if you bear all things, believe all things, hope all things and endure all things (1 Cor. 13:4).*
- *Love covers. Proverbs 10:12 says love covers and hate stirs up. There are going to be times in your life when you are going to have to love people no matter what.*
- *Love gives. "For God so loved the world that he gave his only begotten Son …" (John 3:16). Are you generous with others?*
- *Love forgives. How are you doing in this area?*
- *Love never clutches, it never holds on. When your children grow up, if you are clutching on to them, you are not agape loving them: you're storge loving them. Love lets people go. When people come in and out of our lives, love wants the best for those people more than it wants the comfort of having that person around. Love lets go, it never clutches.*

Truth in Action:

1. Have you let God have your heart 100 percent? If the answer is "no," bow your head in prayer, give Him all of your heart, and feel the love flood in. Relax in His arms.

2. a) What people in your life have you been waiting to receive love from?

____

____

____

____

____

____

____

____

____

b) Can you give them to God and love them instead, expecting nothing in return?

____

____

____

____

____

____

____

3. Pray 1 Corinthians 13:4–8 often. (I suggest changing it to first person so it really hits home. Here is how:)

Lord, I pray that I am patient, I am kind. I am not jealous; I do not brag and am not arrogant. I do not act unbecomingly; I do not seek my own, I am not provoked, I do not take into account a wrong suffered, I do not rejoice in unrighteousness, but rejoice with the truth; I bear all things, I believe all things, I hope all things, I endure all things. God's love through me never fails (1 Cor. 13:4–8a).

4. a) What sacrifices have you made others feel guilty over? No matter our sacrifice for others, if it is not with a heart of love it doesn't count. It is only a clanging gong to that person and to God! Our faces, our moods, our actions must reflect His love. First Corinthians 13:1–3 says, "If I speak with the tongues of men and of angels, but do not have love, I have become a noisy gong or a clanging cymbal. If I have the gift of prophecy, and know all mysteries and all knowledge; and if I have all faith, so as to remove mountains, but do not have love, I am nothing. And if I give all my possessions to feed the poor, and if I surrender my body to be burned, but do not have love, it profits me nothing."

____

____

____

____

   b) What changes can you make to love people more?

____

____

____

____

____

____

____

Steps to Loving Your Journey

- **Repent from the sin of dissatisfaction.**
- **Stop envying others and wishing you had someone else's life.**
- **Learn to love your life:** Do not curse your day by starting it out saying, "If my life was only different," or "I hate my life." Instead say, "God, You gave my today, and I choose to love it! Now, what can I do to make it special?"
- **Get rid of the "ifs":** ("If this or that changed, I would be happy.") No! What are you enjoying now? Those who enjoy what they have receive more!
- **Love the process:** Our lives are a constant journey. If we do not learn to love the process, we miss our entire lives!
- **Contentment for the journey:** "But Godliness with contentment is great gain" (1 Tim. 6:6). Remember that whatever you are going through is not the big picture; it is just today's picture! Enjoy life today!
- **Peace for the journey:**

  a) Settle Salvation
  b) Never be at odds with God
  c) Be at peace with yourself
  d) Be at peace with others
- **Grace for the journey**: "My grace is sufficient for you, for My power is perfected in weakness" (2 Cor. 12:9). Daily ask God for His grace to help you love your life, complete your journey, and go the extra mile.
- **Spend time with God:** This daily time with God will send you out with joy and strength for the day, a heart for your responsibilities, and a passion to glorify God in all you do.
- **Rest for the journey:** "And He said, 'My presence shall go with you and I will give you rest'" (Ex. 33:14). "Therefore let us be diligent to enter that rest ..."(Heb. 4:11).
- **Learn not to dread:** Pray, "I am going to do the will of God today without thinking about tomorrow."[51] "Casting *all* your cares upon Him, for He cares for you" (1 Peter 5:7).
- **A journey of love:** "Greater love has no one than this, that one lay down his life for his friends" (John 15:13). Love covers, heals, makes faith work, keeps you from having a critical spirit, teaches you to focus on good, and helps you to forgive.

Chapter Fourteen

Faith for the Journey

"Now faith is the substance of things hoped for, the evidence of things not seen."
Hebrews 11:1 (KJV)

I've been so excited to get to this chapter because in it I will share a revelation with you that was literally life-changing for me. God spoke to me so clearly as I wrote this. I can honestly say I've never understood this concept as clearly as I do now. When we realize what our faith was given for, it changes our perspective. Perspective makes all the difference in the world in our ability to enjoy life. If we believe something was created for a certain purpose and use it accordingly and it does not work, we are disappointed. But what a relief when we discover we were using it for the wrong purpose all along. And what a pure delight when we begin to use it for what it was created for and begin to see it work wonderfully, maybe for the first time in our lives. Please go with me on this journey to discover the true purpose of our "faith."

What do I mean by "Faith for the Journey"? I am not speaking of faith only in broad terms, such as "our common Christian faith." I am speaking of faith, like that of our heroes in the book of Hebrews. Faith that is an action verb! Faith that believes what God has spoken and acts on it. Many Christians do not even know that we've been given faith to act on.

So, what was your faith really created for? I am going to endeavor to show you. "And without faith it is impossible to please Him, for he who comes to God must believe that He is and that He is a rewarder of those who seek Him" (Heb. 11:6). Or the King James says "who diligently seek him." So God tells us we cannot please Him without faith. Then He graciously defines it. God makes it very simple and easy for us to understand the life of faith and to live it.

Faith defined #1*:* "He who comes to God must believe that God is ..." That is, you have to believe that you're not a cosmic accident; you're not a cosmic clash of electrons out in space somewhere, but that there is a God who created you. You have to believe that God is real, and Jesus is the Son of God.

Faith defined #2: "And that He is a rewarder of those who seek Him ..." In other words, you have to believe that He is a good God and that He is a rewarder. The second part of the definition is so precious to me. God could have left us with just the first part, but He wants us to understand His nature so we can receive the promises He has for us.

When I grasped this revelation, it changed my life. I was in Bible college in 1994 when I really *saw* this verse for the first time. I had no doubt of God's existence, or that Jesus was the Son of God, but I somehow thought the onus was only on my side to be faithful and to love God. I didn't realize how much He loved me or that He was a rewarder! This is an important revelation to grasp in order to understand this chapter. God is amazing and He is far more wonderful than we are, and He is far more faithful than we are. Begin to look to Him with expectancy and confident assurance that He will fulfill His promises. The Enemy is quick to steal your reward if you let him talk you out of it. What type of reward, do you say? Ahh, rewards come in as many different shapes and sizes as people do. A reward to one person is not a reward to another. Rewards may range from physical to emotional to material to relational and on and on. The most wonderful part is that the *real* amazing spiritual reward is eternal and will be received on the other side. Do not limit God. The neat part about God, though, is that He *is* a rewarder.

The principle of God being a rewarder is key when you begin to understand faith for the journey, because what I am about to say is in contrast to how the natural or carnal mind thinks. However, let's allow the Scripture to define faith for itself. Let's start with Heb. 11:7.

> "By faith Noah, Being warned by God about things not yet seen, in reverence prepared an ark for the salvation of his household, by which he condemned the world, and became an heir of the righteousness which is according to faith. (In other words, he believed God!) By faith Abraham, when he was called, obeyed by going out to a place which he was to receive for an inheritance; and he went out, not knowing where he was going. By faith he lived as an alien in the land of promise, as in a foreign land, dwelling in tents with Isaac and Jacob, fellow heirs of the same promise. For he was looking for the city which has foundations, whose architect and builder is God. (He was not settling for what the world offered him, he was looking for God's city.) By faith even Sarah herself received ability to conceive, even beyond the proper time of life, since she considered Him faithful who had promised … All these died in faith, without receiving the promises, but having seen them and having welcomed them from a distance, and having confessed that they were strangers and exiles on the earth" (Heb. 11:7–13, emphasis added).

I have noted that many Christians invest their faith (i.e.: their most fervent or believing prayers) in wanting to be liked and accepted by others. Our own insecurities, left unchecked, drive us to spend our prayers on the approval of men instead of the approval of God. James 4:4 says, "…know ye not that the friendship of the world is enmity with God?" Colossians 3:2 (KJV) tells us, "Set your affection on things above, not on things on the earth." These Christians seem to think their faith is mainly for being comfortable in this life. Often, these Christians do not want the persecution that comes along with being a believer and with having convictions. They haven't learned to be content in persecution like Paul did. Instead, they use their faith to be liked, to be accepted.

There are others that have thought faith was only for material things. Again, why would you only use your faith for material things except to be comfortable in this world. God wants to bless you with "things" because He loves you, but not for you to make this world your home or to make the "things" your god (the object of your affections). Abraham, who was very financially blessed, understood this (Gen. 13:2). Hebrews 13:10 says, Abraham was "looking for the city which has foundations, whose architect and builder is God." Abraham kept his eyes on God and lived for that Heavenly city called Heaven. He never let "things" trip him up or take his eyes off the "prize." Hebrews 11:13 goes so far as to say the saints of old "have confessed that they have been strangers and exiles in this world."

> "Therefore I say unto you, Take no thought for your life, what ye shall eat, or what ye shall drink; nor yet for your body, what ye shall put on. Is not the life more than meat, and the body than raiment? Behold the fowls of the air: for they sow not, neither do they reap, nor gather into barns; yet your Heavenly Father feedeth them. Are ye not much better than they? But seek ye first the Kingdom of God and His righteousness, and all these things shall be added to you" (Matt. 6:25–26, 33 KJV).

God does care about your material needs, but your job is to seek God first, not these things. God desires to deliver us from lack. He does not want you in debt. So praying Scriptures about provision over your life will make you wiser and free from lack … that is an important and good thing, but remember, it is a side goal. You want to be financially blessed *not* so you can "keep up with the Joneses," but so you are not hindered in doing God's will. The things themselves are not the goal. If you are struggling financially, then your focus is understandably on paying the bills, but if you were free from that debt, imagine what your life would look like. You could invest your prayers in lasting things, like the salvation of family, friends, or co-workers. When a missionary comes to your church you could actually give something substantial instead of just feeling sorry for all the needs out there. Wouldn't it be an amazing feeling to help provide for someone else in need or to be in a position to pay for the spreading of the Gospel? God has given amazing promises to us regarding meeting our financial needs. Just remember the reason is for His Kingdom, not ours.

Truth:

Faith was given for the journey.

The pattern is clear. Though you can use faith for many reasons, it was given to us for one purpose. It was given to us for the journey; the journey of establishing God's covenant in the earth!

"Now faith is the substance of things hoped for, the evidence of things not seen" (Heb. 11:1). Faith is the steady trust in God's character and goodness. This gives you the power to obey God regardless of adverse circumstances around you.

This next statement may shock you so I want you to remember you have to believe that God is a good God. Are you ready? Faith is not really for our happiness so much as it is for us completing our call. Faith is for getting the job done! Happiness is a choice, but faith is for the journey. As you begin to discover the life of faith and begin to use your faith for what it was meant for (to live for God), happiness will follow and you will really begin to love your life (Ps. 144:15)!

Truth:

Real happiness comes when you use your faith for what it was created for.

To make this point very real and tangible, we need to look at the lives of some true heroes of faith. As the saying goes, a picture is worth a thousand words, therefore a glimpse into these lives will do more to explain the Bible kind of faith, than all the dissertations in the world. With that in mind, let's look and see how these heroes, that God so highly praises, actually used their faith.

Noah

Noah did not use his faith to ask God or believe God for happiness, but to obey God. Can you imagine how people must have mocked and made fun of Noah for building this huge boat? (Talk about an eyesore in your backyard!) And imagine, he was waiting for rain? A flood? What was that? There had never been rain on the earth prior to this, only a mist (Gen. 2:6). They didn't even know what rain was. His family would have had great opportunity to be embarrassed as well. Noah could have used his faith to make them happy, but instead he used his faith to build an ark for the salvation of his household. It took Noah faith to complete the call of God on his life, to do what he was called to do. Building that ark didn't bring happiness to him in the worldly sense, not at first, anyway, but it brought great satisfaction and joy in knowing that he was building this for God. I do not know that Noah fully understood that he and his family would be the only ones that would really survive. What Noah did was obey God and use his faith to do so. In the process his family was protected. Deuteronomy 30:19 says "Choose life and blessing so that you and your children can live and be blessed." Your choices affect your family now and those after you. God's system will not work when we focus all our prayers and use all our faith just for our own happiness. God will bless you with many things because He is a good God, but I will say it again: faith is for the journey.

Abraham

Let's look closer at Abraham. Abraham used his faith to leave his relatives, and to go out not knowing where he was going (Heb. 11:8). Abraham left everything he knew to follow God. That's not comfortable. If you are going to use your faith for what it was meant for, your life may not always be comfortable.

Abraham was even willing to give Isaac back to God. "By faith Abraham, when he was tested, offered up Isaac, and he who had received the promises was offering up his only begotten son; It was he to whom it was said, 'In Isaac your descendants shall be called.' He considered that God is able to raise people even from the dead, from which he also received him back as a type" (Heb. 11:17–19). Why the last part of this verse? Because Abraham believed in his core that God was good and loving; that He would even raise Isaac from the dead if He needed to! Therefore, he was willing to give back to God what God gave him. (Some scholars believe that the vision Abraham saw of a son being raised from the dead was not actually his own, but a future picture of God's Son, the Lord Jesus, two thousand years later![52])

God is a God of order. He does not violate even His own laws. Just as God requires us to sow a seed before we reap a harvest, He works off the same spiritual laws. God needed a man who was willing to sacrifice his only son begotten by Sarah, whom he loved very much (Gen. 20:2) so that God could sacrifice His only son legally. Once God saw Abraham's heart, He didn't require the deed. God simply needed a door. On that amazing day God provided Abraham a ram in the thicket. Abraham then called God, for the first time in Scripture, Jehovah Jireh, "The Lord will provide!" (Gen. 22:14).

How many people do you think Abraham blessed by being willing to sacrifice his son Isaac? Untold numbers! Through Abraham's faith and act of obedience, God was able to send His only begotten Son to earth. The

Bible calls Abraham the "father of our faith", but that faith was not for him, it was for us. Your faith for today is for the people that will follow you tomorrow. We must come to the understanding that our faith was not created *just* for us, but also for God and for others. Abraham could not have trusted God so completely had he not believed with all of his being that God was truly good and truly righteous.

Mary

Was life comfortable for Mary, the mother of Jesus? No. Think of it! She was accused of being pregnant out of wedlock, birthed her child in a barn after traveling many miles, very pregnant, had to flee to Egypt for years and had to watch her son die on a cross. But imagine the joy of raising the Son of God! Wow! The joy of seeing His miracles. People admire her, but they do not want to live by faith like she did. They are missing the point. She did what she did by faith. When you're full of faith, there's a grace for what you're doing. Did she impact the next generation? I would say so! She not only impacted the next generation but every one thereafter.

Elisha

Can we get real for a minute and look at a few Scriptures just as they are written, without seeing them religiously? Sometimes we forget that the people in the Bible were just that: people. They had flaws and problems just like you and me. That's what makes the Bible so wonderful and so applicable to us. God would not have given us His Word if it weren't possible for us to live it. God does not put limitations on our success. Religion does. So let's take a glimpse at the life of Elisha and see how it applies to us.

Elisha washed the hands of the prophet Elijah. Elijah, however, did not come across in Scripture as overly grateful. Don't get me wrong; Elijah was one of the greatest prophets that ever lived and was used mightily, but we must remember that even people used by God are still people.

Everyone has their own rough edges … even those in the Bible. In the entire biblical account of their relationship, there is not one recorded conversation between the two men other than the day Elisha started the ministry and the day Elijah was caught up to Heaven. In fact, those two recorded conversations were dry and somewhat abrupt (1 Kings 19:19–21, 2 Kings 2:1–17). Elisha served Elijah for nearly twenty years and even at the end Elijah appeared to begrudge giving his mantle to Elisha. Have you ever met an old farmer that was rough as a cob? He may have a heart of gold on the inside, but if you didn't know him well, you would swear that he didn't like you. That's probably how Elijah was.

I want you to take note that this did not affect God's ability to use Elijah. Elijah was one of the greats. We often think God cannot use people that "offend" us, but in reality it is us that cannot be used if we are "offendable." That is where faith comes in. Can you stay the course regardless of people?

Truth:

God cannot use us if we are offendable.

If you use your faith for what it was meant for, you will find it far easier to not be offended. Remember, "faith" is for the journey. Here is a great place to see the importance of being "unoffendable" and blooming where God plants you. And trust me, it takes faith to do that. We must realize that people in the ministry are not perfect, yet they can still be very powerful in their gifting. This realization will set us free. I am not talking about sin issues, but rather how gracious they are (or are not) in their communication or personality styles. Most people get offended with ministers not because the minister has gotten into sin, but because the minister hurt their feelings. We should not go to a church or leave a church because of the personality of the pastor or leaders. We should go because that is where God has called us to serve and receive. It takes faith to be "planted" in a local church. It takes faith to be around people that are not your "size or fit" and enjoy them. I've learned this through the years, after having grown-up in church and now having pastured two churches. Imagine the blessing Elisha would have missed (being a prophet with the double anointing) had he been easily offended.

And not only was Elisha blessed with a powerful ministry and a *double* anointing, he was also blessed naturally, even more than gruff Elijah. Remember that Elijah was sent to a poor widow, Elisha to a wealthy woman. Do not forget, though, that Elisha left a lot behind and God was obviously blessing him back for it.

Don't ever become critical of someone else's blessing. You just do not know what they may have given up to follow God. Elisha came from a lot of money (a big family farm with twenty-four oxen, twelve plows, and at least eleven workers, 1 Kings 19). He left all of that to use his faith to fulfill the reason he was born. This life is not going to last forever. It may feel like it, but in reality it is quick. Eternity does last forever, and this side is just a practice run. We need to have the wisdom Elisha had and use our faith for the journey. He could have enjoyed his big family farm, but wow, what an amazing life he would have missed! Scripture tells us that, "For whoever wishes to save his life will lose it; but whoever loses his life for My sake will find it" (Matt. 16:25). The secret to "finding" your life and "finding" yourself is in giving it to the Lord. Only in giving it away will you find it. (This doesn't mean you will be called to missions in Timbuktu. It does mean that when you are not so focused on self, God can actually move you into His plan for your life, which might actually be right where you are.)

Esther

Even Esther used her faith, not to become queen, but to intercede on behalf of her people. The book of Esther tells the story of a woman "who, for the sake of her people, was willing to say, 'If I perish, I perish.'" Because of her selfless act of courage, the Jewish feast of Purim (which has endured over two thousand four hundred years) was named in her honor.[53] Having looked at Esther in chapter one of this book and told the story of Haman in chapter twelve, let's now look at Esther's story in a bit more detail.

Esther was a young Jewish girl who lived around 473 BC. At this time, many Jews were still living in exile in Persia. The current king, Ahasuerus, had recently banished his wife and was looking for a new queen. Esther was one of the young virgins chosen to go before the king. From all of the young women gathered, she was selected. However, this was hardly the thrilling life most of us imagine for royalty. Even in the land of her captivity she had more freedoms than she did in the palace.

While queen, an edict went out from the palace to destroy her people on a specified day. In those days, once the king made a decree, there was no revoking it. Esther was faced with a choice few have to make. She decided to entreat the king to save her people. Even coming into his presence without being summoned was a crime punishable by death. Yet Esther risked it not once, but twice! When the time came that her nation was to be destroyed she used her faith. She went without food or water for three days prior. How many days can you live without water? Three. She went the full three days without water, fasting on behalf of her people. If she had been killed by the king, she would not have saved her people. God gave Esther great favor with the king and he listened to her request, thus saving her people and destroying the enemies of her people. Esther used her faith to stand in the gap for a nation of God's people, and that's what her faith was for. That was what made a difference. That was what changed history. This correct use of faith, certainly didn't make her giddy, or happy in the short run, but it absolutely did in the long run!

Esther didn't go out of her way to find God's plan for her life; because she clearly put God first, it came to her. Would you have been willing to go without food *or water* for three days and lay your life on the line for your God? Many have! Many will!

Moses

"By faith Moses, when he had grown up, refused to be called the son of Pharaoh's daughter, choosing rather to endure ill-treatment with the people of God than to enjoy the passing pleasures of sin, considering the reproach of Christ greater riches than the treasures of Egypt; for he was looking to the reward" (Heb. 11:24–26). Moses believed in a reward that was greater than living in Pharaoh's house. There is a reward that is greater than a new car. There is a reward that is greater than making everyone and everything perfect so that you can be happy. There is a reward greater than satisfying your desires. There is a reward worth being uncomfortable for. The Bible does not say the reproach of Christ is a maybe. "Indeed, *all* who desire to live godly in Christ Jesus will be persecuted" (2 Tim. 3:12).

If you are going to live for Jesus, you will suffer reproach in this lifetime so don't be upset about it. Just go ahead and learn to be content in it, and learn to serve God. Don't be like "The one on whom seed was sown on the rocky places, this is the man who hears the word and immediately receives it with joy; Yet he has no firm root in himself, but is only temporary, and when affliction or persecution arises because of the word, immediately he falls away" (Matt. 13:20–21).

Remember that Moses considered the reproach of Christ greater riches than what he could receive in this lifetime, greater riches than the untold riches of Egypt, for he was looking to the reward. Wait! Did you see that? That means it is not wrong to do it for the reward. He just had discernment for what the real reward was. Oh, to please Him!

What we do in this life really does make a difference in eternity. If we can learn these lessons now, they will make a difference for us when we go on to be with the Lord. When we step into eternity we will find that God is so much more faithful than we ever imagined. The principle "He who is faithful in a very little thing will be made faithful also in much"

(Luke 16:10) is not just for this side of Heaven, but for the other side too. There are many people who have been faithful with their "little" yet will not receive their "much" until Heaven. But when they receive it, their "much", will be MUCH!

I believe that eternity is really going to be amazing! Remember, we will only get one chance at this life. I do not want to get to Heaven and regret that I didn't use my faith for what it was meant for. You can have great faith that can even move mountains, Paul said, but if not used properly to express the love of God, it is of *no* value.

Our faith is for getting the job done, but many of you reading this book may not even know why you were born. You may have no idea of the journey set before you. Yet in order to love your life today, you need to begin to say, "God, use me where I am." If there is a work night at your church, sign up! If there is a neighbor or stranger in need, help them! There are needs all around.

The Jews have something called a *Mitzvah.* The practicing Jew is looking throughout his day for an opportunity to do a good deed for someone, thus fulfilling the commandment "Mitzvah." He is not supposed to let his day close without doing something good for someone.[54] Be faithful with the small things so that you can begin to step into your destiny.

"Then the LORD said to Noah, 'Enter the ark, you and *all your household*, for you alone I have seen to be righteous before Me in this time'" (Gen. 7:1). We also see Joshua says "Choose for yourselves today whom you will serve … but as for me *and my house*, we will serve the LORD" (Jos. 24:15). Again in Deuteronomy, we see "I call Heaven and earth to witness against you today, that I have set before you life and death, the blessing and the curse. So choose life in order that you may live, *you and your descendants*" (Deut. 30:19). Notice it says that you and your descendants may live. The choices we make really do make a difference for the next generation. Though receiving Christ is an individual decision, the decisions we make and act on, impact the next generation profoundly for Christ based on these Scriptures. By loving people and serving God I can influence for good, for God, and for blessing not only my children and grandchildren, but for generations and generations and generations to come after me. I can prepare an "ark" for the salvation of my household if I do not live my life for myself but live it for Christ. Every good choice I make is a "plank" for their salvation. And that's exciting.

The Legacy of Jonathan Edwards

Jonathan Edwards, a famous early American revivalist, theologian, preacher, and missionary provides another great example of faith. Considered the "spiritual father of the first Great Awakening," Edwards lived from 1703–1758. His incredible zeal for God saw revival fires sweep New England for twenty years and some sixty thousand people came to Christ as a result.[55] He was a great man of God! Many, many lives were impacted and changed because of him. Most importantly, Jonathan Edwards' own family was impacted not just in his lifetime but for generations to follow all because he chose to serve God with a whole heart. From him came a remarkable line of descendants: "300 were preachers, 295 were college graduates, 100 were missionaries, 100 were lawyers, 80 held public office including 1 Vice President of the United States (Aaron Burr), 13 U.S. senators, 1 state governor, 3 big city mayors and 1 U.S. comptroller, 75 military officers, 65 college professors including 13 college presidents, 56 physicians including 1 Dean of Medical School."[56] They are still counting the *remarkable* people who followed Jonathan Edwards in his lineage, and hopefully they will be in ours, too.

A Different Legacy

In a stark contrast to Jonathan Edwards, consider the lineage of Max Jukes. Jukes was an "atheist who lived in New York during the 19 century. Of Jukes' 560 known descendants: 7 were murderers, 60 became thieves,

67 reported having syphilis, 100 were alcoholics, 50% of the women in his family line became prostitutes, and 300 died prematurely."[57]

Amazing! What a difference we make to the next generation! Max Jukes' descendants were radically impacted because of the choices he made to *exclude* God from his life and home. Jonathan Edwards' descendants were radically impacted because of the choices he made to *include* God in his life and home. What legacy will you leave?

Our Children

Truth:

It takes faith to release your children to become who they were born to be!

If you have children and you raise them to serve God, then you have to raise them to leave and to do what they are called to do, not what you want them to do. That takes faith.

For example, I live in Ireland and my parents hardly ever get to see their grandbabies. Yet because my parents are godly, they have "released" us by faith, which has removed all tension on this side of Heaven and has a reward on the other side. I honor my parents for that, and appreciate them more than words can say. Through the centuries however, many parents have had to do the same under far worse conditions.

Read the account of when the great missionary, Hudson Taylor, set sail for China:

> "My beloved, now sainted, mother had come to see me off from Liverpool. Never shall I forget that day, nor how she went with me into the little cabin that was to be my home for nearly six long months. With a mother's loving hand she smoothed the little bed. She sat by my side, and joined me in the last hymn that we should

> sing together before the long parting. We knelt down, and she prayed—the last mother's prayer I was to hear before starting for China. Then notice was given that we must separate, and we had to say good-bye, never expecting to meet on earth again.
>
> For my sake she restrained her feelings as much as possible. We parted; and she went on shore, giving me her blessing; I stood alone on deck, and she followed the ship as we moved towards the dock gates. As we passed through the gates, and the separation really commenced, I shall never forget the cry of anguish wrung from that mother's heart. It went through me like a knife. I never knew so fully, until then, what 'God so loved the world' meant. And I am quite sure that my precious mother learned more of the love of God to the perishing in that hour than in all her life before."[58]

All the great missionaries and evangelists, many revivalists too, have the same story! But whether we release our children by faith or begrudgingly they are still going to have to choose to serve the Lord. You can make it easy for them, or you can make it hard for them. Once your child becomes a single adult, the Scripture is clear: their singleness is for the Lord (1 Cor. 7:32–34). It is not for you. It is not for your physical needs. It is not for your emotional needs. Our children's singleness is for the Lord and it is for the house of God. We need to let them go, but let's receive a reward and do it by faith.

Our Communities

It is so important that we reach our communities for Christ. You do not need a pulpit to do that. You can reach your community with the love of God! When someone you know is in trouble ask them, "Can I pray for you?". Though some may say "no", some will say "yes". If so, stop and pray. Often these same people will come back and ask for more prayer. Some may give their hearts to the Lord, some may not. But that's okay.

Our job is to reach our communities just by loving people, praying for them, and never returning evil for evil. You too have a call on your life. You have a responsibility. You have a mission.

It is not too late for you! If you use your faith for the journey, you can make a difference. It takes faith to wake up in the morning and say, "I love my life!" Imagine being your children on the days when you do not like your life. Imagine what that would make them feel like. "Am I a mistake?" "If you wish your life was different, do you wish I was different?" How must it make our spouses, our relatives feel when we complain about our lives?

What must God feel like when we are serving Him, doing the job He has given us to do, but saying, "God, I hate it. I wish I was doing something different." Imagine! But imagine if we say, "God, this is the job before me now so I am going to do it with all my heart. If you want me to go a different direction, then I trust you with that. Until then, I am going to do what's set before me today. I am going to live today in joy and in faith."

You see, I want to become part of that great cloud of witnesses one day as I am sure you do too. I want people to say, "Because you followed the Lord Jesus, I came to the Lord," "Because you served God, many people in my community were saved." Don't you want that? By each act of kindness, by touching a neighbor, by cooking meals for someone, by sharing your faith, by bringing the love of God to someone who needs it so badly, you can reach your community. You can change your children, you can change your grandchildren, and you can change countless things just by choosing to love your life and to walk in faith. Remember what your faith is given to you for, and don't be so worried about getting what you're due in this generation. We can make a difference. If I worry about myself in the here and now, I might never impact another soul. But if I use my faith to fulfill my call, I can affect untold numbers *not* because I have a pulpit, but because I obey.

"And indeed if they had been thinking of that country from which they went out, they would have had opportunity to return" (Heb. 11:15). If your desire is for this world and its comforts, you will eventually return to the things of the world. But if you say, "God it's not about this world, it is about the faith journey. It is about what you've called me to do today," then you will not turn back. Let's continue to verse sixteen: "But as it is, they desire a better country, that is, a Heavenly one. Therefore God is not ashamed to be called their God; for He has prepared a city for them."

This was not true just for saints of old. It is true for all of us. I don't want God to be ashamed of being my God. I want to be able to say confidently, "God, this world has nothing in me." I am going to use my faith for the journey. How about you?

We all have our unique call. Not all of our journeys are the same. You are graced for yours, I am graced for mine. Not everyone is called to be outrageously rich like Abraham. Not everyone is called to endure what the prophets endured, but we are called to an amazing walk of faith.

It was easy for Paul to be content with trials and adversity because his eye was set on the joy of hitting the mark of the high call of God in Christ. He never got confused about what his faith was for. When we get confused and think our faith is only for ourselves it steals our joy. This makes us self-centered, disappointed, and disillusioned with this life. But when we know our faith is for "the journey," for God, and for the next generation we begin to have joy unspeakable! This insulates us from giving up or becoming disillusioned. The Bible says "we are surrounded by a great cloud of witnesses" (Heb. 12:1). What is the witness they left behind? It is the life of faith that they lived for Christ. That is the witness we too leave: doing what the Lord called us to do. It may not always be easy, but that's okay. If we do it by faith, not despising the challenges, looking to the reward, we will embrace the journey, run our race with joy, and love our lives.

Prayer

Dear Lord,

Wow! I didn't truly realize that "faith" was given to me to help me live my life for You. Lord, I am sorry for focusing my life on me! Lord, I've lived for my own happiness, my own ambition. I repent. I will live for You. I will spend time with You. I will get involved in my local church. I will endeavor to use "my faith" for what it was meant for.

Lord, Your Word says that faith comes by hearing. If I will be brave enough to embrace the Word of God and to remember that You are a Rewarder—so much greater than I can even understand—then I can embrace living for You!

In Jesus' Name,
Amen.

Truth in Action:

1. In what areas do you currently use your faith for more than anything else? (i.e. What do you spend most of your time praying over?)

____

____

____

____

____

____

____

2. Now that you have read this chapter, how do you need to change the focus of your faith-filled prayers?

3. If you are a parent, have you freed your children from your expectations and released them into God's plan for their lives? If you are still holding onto your own plans for them, write down how you can release them.

4. If you do not know what you were born for, take time to pray (and maybe even go on a fast) and seek God about it. He wants to show you! In the process of discovery, begin to be faithful in the small things. What area of "helps" can you get involved in at your church? How can you also begin to live your faith by helping in your neighborhood or community?

____

____

____

____

____

____

____

____

____

____

If you are unsure about how to believe God for answered prayer, there are recommended resources at the back of this book. Find more materials and build your faith! Remember, without faith it is impossible to please God. He is ready and waiting to reward.

Steps to Loving Your Journey

- **Repent from the sin of dissatisfaction.**
- **Stop envying others and wishing you had someone else's life.**
- **Learn to love your life:** Do not curse your day by starting it out saying, "If my life was only different," or "I hate my life." Instead say, "God, You gave my today, and I choose to love it! Now, what can I do to make it special?"
- **Get rid of the "ifs":** ("If this or that changed, I would be happy.") No! What are you enjoying now? Those who enjoy what they have receive more!
- **Love the process:** Our lives are a constant journey. If we do not learn to love the process, we miss our entire lives!
- **Contentment for the journey:** "But Godliness with contentment is great gain" (1 Tim. 6:6). Remember that whatever you are going through is not the big picture; it is just today's picture! Enjoy life today!
- **Peace for the journey:**

  a) Settle Salvation
  b) Never be at odds with God
  c) Be at peace with yourself
  d) Be at peace with others
- **Grace for the journey**: "My grace is sufficient for you, for My power is perfected in weakness" (2 Cor. 12:9). Daily ask God for His grace to help you love your life, complete your journey, and go the extra mile.
- **Spend time with God:** This daily time with God will send you out with joy and strength for the day, a heart for your responsibilities, and a passion to glorify God in all you do.
- **Rest for the journey:** "And He said, 'My presence shall go with you and I will give you rest'" (Ex. 33:14). "Therefore let us be diligent to enter that rest ..."(Heb. 4:11).
- **Learn not to dread:** Pray, "I am going to do the will of God today without thinking about tomorrow."[59] "Casting *all* your cares upon Him, for He cares for you" (1 Peter 5:7).
- **A journey of love:** "Greater love has no one than this, that one lay down his life for his friends" (John 15:13). Love covers, heals, makes faith work, keeps you from having a critical spirit, teaches you to focus on good, and helps you to forgive.

- **Faith for the journey:** Faith is for getting the job done! It is for reaching the next generation for Jesus. Loving your life starts with making sure you are on the right journey (God's journey for your life, not the world's journey for you).

Chapter Fifteen

Don't Control the Journey

"Commit your way to the Lord,
Trust also in Him, and He will do it."
Psalm 37:5

The Bible is a tale of two gardens. In the first garden the first Adam decided not to obey the Almighty. He decided to chart his own course and make his own way. Sounds great, doesn't it? So pioneering, so daring. The problem with that is that we were created for the Creator. Just as the sun, the moon, the earth, and every heavenly body are set in a path, nothing was made to be random. Actually, when you find something out of orbit, you find something dangerous that's on a collision course. We, like they, were designed to travel a certain path. When we deviate from that path, we're headed for danger. Adam did just that. The second garden, however, gives us another picture. The Last Adam, Jesus Christ, kneels at an altar at midnight and prays three times, "Father, if it is possible, let this cup pass from Me; yet not as I will, but as You will." Jesus did not want to go down that road. He was praying for an out, if it was possible. But He submitted Himself to Heaven's will and not His own and drank the cup He was given. He was committed to pleasing the Father, not Himself. In the Garden of Eden Adam said, "Not Thy will but my will be done." He brought the curse to all mankind. In the Garden of Gethsemane Jesus said, "Not My will but Thy will be done." He brought redemption to all mankind.

Which one do we follow? Which garden do we pray in? What course will we stay on?

The secret to staying on course, (the secret even to finding your course) is found in *not* controlling the journey. In this chapter we are going to learn the benefits and tremendous victories we can have if we do not control every minute detail of our lives, but begin to put our lives in God's capable hands. What does this look like? This does not mean that we allow everything *into* our lives that just comes down the pike. The Enemy would certainly accommodate our "open door" policy with some unwanted visitors. But rather, it means we submit our lives to God. God therefore has given us authority to throw all the serpents out of our garden that we've been called to till. Just like He gave that same authority to Adam and Eve, though they didn't use it. God has also given us authority to "speak to the mountains" in our lives (Matt. 21:21). We need to use the authority of God's Word to stop the Enemy from wreaking havoc in our lives! In order to do that, we must learn the difference between God and the Enemy. This is vital if we are truly *not* going to control the journey. It means you are releasing your life into the hands of Good and not into the hands of Evil. To do that let me establish four safe measuring sticks that we have already briefly started to look at. Then we are off to discovering what not controlling the journey looks like.

- **God is not the enemy.** "The thief comes only to steal and kill and destroy; I (Jesus) came that they may have life, and have it abundantly" (John 10:10).
- **Every good gift in your life comes from God.** "Every good thing given and every perfect gift is from above, coming down from the Father of lights, with whom there is no variation or shifting shadow" (Jas. 1:17).
- **God will never tempt you or test you with evil.** "Let no one say when he is tempted, 'I am being tempted by God'; for God cannot be tempted by evil, and He Himself does not tempt anyone. But each one is tempted when he is carried away and enticed by his own lust" (Jas. 1:13–14).

- **God will show you how to escape temptations.** "No temptation has overtaken you but such as is common to man; and God is faithful, who will not allow you to be tempted beyond what you are able, but with the temptation will provide the way of escape also, so that you will be able to endure it" (1 Cor. 10:13).

Based on these measuring sticks, I think it is safe to say that I am not trying to teach you to accept poverty (Ps. 23), misery (Deut. 28:47), lack of success (Josh. 1:8), or sickness (1 Pet. 2:24). These are contrary to what the Lord bought on Calvary. Let's look at sickness as an example. When people get sick, their first inclination is to go to the doctor so they can get relief from the symptoms. Something inside every person lets him or her know that it is not right for them to be sick, and this is true! God does not desire for sickness to be in any life. Never feel guilty about getting "the curse" (sickness, poverty, broken relationships, etc.) healed or out of your life.

You are not trapped to receive or keep any part of "the curse" in your life. It is your choice to say, "No!" and get the curse out. However, not every bad thing that happens is directly from the Enemy. Much of the time it is simply a result of living in a fallen world or living out the result of our own bad choices. Yet we have been given a higher authority to Whom we can appeal to overcome this fallen nature. God has gone to great lengths to free us from the curse. Even our own natural tendencies recognize when something is not how it "should" be. God is not the author of sickness, poverty, or pain. But more than that, He has provided freedom from the curse for each of us (Gal. 3:13–14).

As we mature in the Lord, we begin to discern the difference between "the curse" versus the discomfort or "stretch" of obedience to the call of Christ. "Not controlling the journey" is about learning to follow Christ. When we truly trust the Lord it can be uncomfortable at first, but the rewards are amazing.

It can seem hard and somewhat strange to trust the One and only true

Living God. This is especially true, since most of us learn from a young age that people will disappoint us and let us down. The good news is, God is not a person, and His Word promises He will truly *never* leave us, forsake us, let us down, or ever disappoint us. A good analogy for letting go of your life and putting it into God's hands, is like getting into a river. At first we stick our toes in, then we go a little deeper, and before we know it, we find when we do not fight the water the water actually supports us, carrying our weight, even making the burden lighter. The book of Ezekiel shows how this all works.

> "He (the Lord) brought me out by way of the north gate and led me around on the outside to the outer gate by way of the gate that faces east. And behold, water was *trickling* from the south side. When the man went out toward the east with a line in his hand, he measured a thousand cubits, and He led me through the water, water reaching the *ankles*. Again he measured a thousand and led me through the water, water reaching the *knees*. Again he measured a thousand and led me through the water, water reaching the *loins*. Again he measured a thousand; and it was a river that I could not ford, for the water had risen, enough water *to swim in*, a river that could not be forded" (Eze. 47:2–5).

If a river "cannot be forded," it means it has a strong current. I can swim across any river with no current, but I can *not* swim across a river with a current. This is a tremendous analogy for God's plan for our lives. God has a strong current. Many people think of God as passive; God is anything but passive. God is a powerful God. He is a mighty God, and He is an awesome God. When you get in His river, He knows where He's going. If you get in the Corrib River here in Galway, Ireland, and the water is high, it is taking you out to sea whether you like it or not. You are going to go where the current takes you. If you will allow yourself to get into the plan God has for your life, then He will begin to take you somewhere ... by His own power and not yours! What a relief!

Revelation 22:1 says, "Then he showed me a river of the water of life, clear as crystal, coming from the throne of God and of the Lamb." This river, even the same as the one Ezekiel was speaking of, only comes from one place: God's very throne, representing His sovereignty. Wading this river is the only way to find God's will. As you do this, abandon your life completely to the mercy of Heaven's current. Then, you will truly find the power of God.

God will not always tell you where He is going to take you. I find a quote from *The Chronicles of Narnia* very telling of God's nature. At the end of the book, when referring to Aslan, the fawn says to little Lucy, "He's not a tame Lion you know." Lucy replies, "No, but He is good!" [60] Then the lion disappears. As this Christian novel depicts, God is God, He is a spirit, and you cannot pin Him down. He thinks on a whole other level than we think on. We may not understand His ways yet, He is good!

So how does God operate? It says in Psalm 119:105, "Your Word is a lamp to my feet And a light to my path." If you ponder this verse you will notice that a lamp only gives enough light for the next step. And so it is with God. He will show you each step of the way, but normally no more than that. God does not give us the big picture. I believe He does this so we won't mess it up; so we will walk by faith and will not control the journey. If we knew where we were going, the human nature in us would say, "I think I will take a short cut or go a different route," but God knows where we need to be to fulfill our destinies. He also knows all the people we need to touch in our lives on the given path He has chosen for us. Let's not miss a single step of His amazing journey.

He also knows which path has disaster for you and which path has protection for you. It may look like He is taking you the longer route, but in reality He is keeping you safe. We see the Lord did this with the children of Israel. "When the king of Egypt let the people go, God did not take them by the road that goes up the coast to Philistia, although it was the shortest way. God thought, 'I do not want the people to change their minds and return to Egypt when they see that they are going to have to fight.' Instead, he led them in a roundabout way through the desert toward the Red Sea …" (Ex. 13:17–18 GNB). God knows which ways we can handle and which ways we cannot. If we would only stay on His path, then we would find the blessing.

He also does not want us to be a "back-seat driver." Men hate that! That's how I know God's a man! (Just teasing, He's not a man. He's God!) In truth, I believe He will not give us the directions so we will not be backseat drivers. He just wants us to come along and enjoy the ride. He wants us to enjoy it every step of the way without nagging Him saying, "Hey, shouldn't we turn here?" Don't control where God leads or how He does things! We need to get so good at following the Lord that we don't need all the details when He gives instructions.

A Bizarre Story

> "And He sent two of His disciples and said to them, "Go into the city, and a man will meet you carrying a pitcher of water; follow him; and wherever he enters, say to the owner of the house, 'The Teacher says, Where is My guest room in which I may eat the Passover with My disciples?' And he himself will show you a large upper room furnished and ready; prepare for us there.'" The disciples went out and came to the city, and found it just as He had told them; and they prepared the Passover" (Mar. 14:13–16).

This story always amazes me. I love this story because it is so unique. It is such a good example of letting God be in control and not questioning Him. The disciples in this account did a fantastic job of following Jesus. However, I believe the disciples didn't question the Lord in this situation, not because they totally understood how to get into the "river," but out of respect. If a person addressed Jesus in public, He would deal with it in public. The disciples learned to pull Jesus aside and ask, "What does this mean," because they didn't want Him saying in front of everyone, "Why does this generation not understand this?" The disciples got really good at following Jesus, and we need to, as well. Whatever it takes.

Look at verse 13 again: "And He sent two of His disciples into the city and He said to them, 'Go into the city and a man will meet you carrying a pitcher of water, follow Him, and wherever he enters say to the owner of the house, The master says, Where is my guest room in which I may eat my Passover with my disciples?'"

Is it just me, or does anyone else find this strange? These disciples had been with Jesus for three and a half years, and they had never met these men where they were going to celebrate the Passover. He said for them to follow the man carrying a pitcher. Men didn't carry pitchers back then; otherwise they would have found a hundred men carrying pitchers and thought, "Which man is the right one?" Instead, Jesus said to find the man with the pitcher. God always makes sure you find where you're supposed to be. He is not going to send you out to find a needle in a hay stack. This guy was obvious. When God tells you where to go, it is obvious. God so desires to bless us that He gives us many opportunities to walk by faith. God's ways are not man's ways.

The disciples walked into a huge city and found a man carrying a pitcher just like Jesus said, so they followed him. They may have thought that they would walk into a house of someone they knew, but they didn't. They had to follow him into a strange man's house and ask for the owner and say, "Hi, where's your guest room? My master needs it to have the Passover." That can be a little embarrassing. The owner of the house didn't seem to think it was strange, but this is the point at which we feel self-conscious. God will say, "I want you to share the Gospel with that person," and we turn red, or want to hide. But remember, if the Lord is the one directing you to talk to someone about Him, then perhaps He knows something you do not know. You can trust that He has already been at work in that person's life and that the person most likely is ready to know more. We may feel self-conscious or strange, but it is not strange for the person you're sharing with; they have been praying for that. It's just that we are uncomfortable going into the unknown. You can trust that His instructions will work, regardless of how they may appear to you at first.

In verses 15 and 16, it says, "He himself will show you a large upper room already furnished and ready. Prepare for us there. The disciples went out, came to the city and found it just as he had told them, and they prepared the Passover."

God did it. They didn't have to be embarrassed. They didn't have to think, "Am I going to find him? Will he be there?" Yes, of course they were going to find him, of course the owner was ready for them, and of course they didn't have to know anything about it. Jesus knew. That man knew; I don't know how he knew, but he knew. I don't know if they met secretly by night; I don't know if God spoke to the man, but it does not matter, and we still will never know, because it is none of our business. When God guides and directs us, it is none of our business to know why; it is our business to follow, trusting a good God!

The more we ask questions, the more often we mess up. It would have been so hard for a woman to take those instructions. I think it was hard for them too, but they were smart enough not to say anything. We often want to ask, "What about this," or "What about that?" But part of finding rest is to set down all the "buts." Then get all the "buts" out of your life! Say, "God, I will do this! No more 'buts' and no more 'how is this going to work?'" No anxiety, no fear! If God tells you to do something, don't you think He loves you and He has a plan that's far better than your plan? Let's show God a little respect by trusting Him, by letting Him be the driver, by enjoying what He has for us and trusting that we'll have what we need when we need it.

Many of our control issues stem from a simple fear of the unknown. Fearing what may happen if we do not force things to go a certain way, fearing what others may say or do, without our say-so, fearing what lies ahead, etc. But with God, the unknown is not fearsome.

Truth:

You will have courage and faith when you need it, but often not until then.

Let's take a life lesson from a true hero and an amazing woman, Harriet Tubman. As a young girl, she would pray, "God, how can I have courage when it is time to have courage? I feel such fear all the time." Harriet felt the call and destiny of God on her life. She knew in her heart that slavery was wrong. She firmly believed that God was going to use her to do something about it, but she was afraid. God's answer to her was that she would have courage when she needed it, but she would not have it before she needed it.[61]

The same is true for faith. You will have faith when you need it, but you may not have it beforehand. Yes, you need to be working and growing your faith. "Faith comes by hearing, and hearing by the Word of God" (Rom. 10:17). You can grow your faith in God by spending time in His Word, but in some situations you will not have all the faith in God you need until you step out in obedience. It is in obeying God that we actually get to practice what we have learned. Sometimes that first step can take your breath away, but once you make it, you find accompanying that step is all the faith and courage you need. This was certainly the case for Harriet and it will be for you too.

I have certainly seen that to be the case in my own life. For example, every time we put on our Halloween outreach event, Kids' Fun Fest, the building is packed with people. When the time comes to step onto that stage to minister the Gospel I never feel courageous until I hit the stage. I have to choose to shut fear, anxiety, and everything else out. When I hit the stage, the faith is there when I need it, but it is never there ahead of time. My part is to obey, to show trust and respect for God, and everything else is provided. God says, "Do not worry about how or what you are to say; for it will be given you in that hour what you are to say" (Matt. 10:19). This has been a true faith journey for me, since I have never liked public speaking.

Being able to do this and so much more, starts with *not* controlling the journey, but following God's path, His destiny for you. Yet there is one more journey you cannot control – that of others! Often spouses want to control the other spouse; what they do, and how they do it. Let's not do that. This is a big area for so many, particularly for parents. As their children grow, parents often want to control what they become, or how they become who they are. Often it is simply because it has become a habit. Whenever children are small we have to control so many aspects of their lives. The hardest part of the parenting process is learning to let go bit by bit, not all at once when they turn eighteen. We should be controlling less when they are ten than when they were two, and less again when they are fifteen instead of more and more. It is part of us growing in faith. Sure, we need to set boundaries with our children. They have to clean up, respect others' property, be home on time, etc. And by all means, we need to teach them God's Word and introduce them to the Lord as their best friend. We need to give them that moral and eternal mooring they would be lost without. Then we need to pray and leave them to God. God may take them in a way we didn't expect. Anything we pray about, we birth for God, not for ourselves; whether children, ministry, job, spouse. God needs to be in control of the direction, not us. We need to trust God enough to be able to let go of our loved ones and our jobs and let God take them where He wants to go.

Stepping into the amazing plan of God, that He has for us and our loved ones, takes faith. It takes faith to let God be in control everyday and every hour of everyday. However, letting go is often as simple as taking a deep breath, letting it out and putting your life and your situations back in God's hands. Let Him take you where He wants you to go. I dare you to take your feet off the ground and get into God's current.

Prayer

Dearest Lord,

First of all, I want to acknowledge all the times I have tried to control my journey and others' journeys. I am so sorry. Forgive me for trying to be You in my life and other people's lives. You do a much better job than I do!

Lord, I let go of the fear of not controlling circumstances, and now I hand you my circumstances, my life, and my loved ones. I am going to trust You, look to You, and lean not unto my own understanding (Prov. 3:5). I am excited about letting You control my journey. I put it into Your hands and I jump into Your river by keeping my eyes on You and not worrying about the outcome. It is my desire to become great at following Your Word and those subtle nudges from the Spirit!

In Jesus' Name,
Amen.

Truth in Action:

1. Start each day handing your journey over to God.

2. a) In what areas in your life are you the driver instead of God?

   ____

   ____

   ____

   ____

b) Can you let these areas go? How?

____

____

____

____

3. a) Are there directions from God you know you should be taking and haven't? What are they? What has stopped you?

____

____

____

____

____

b) What can you do today to build trust and faith in God for your journey?

____

____

____

____

____

c) Can you live without all of the details of your future upfront and follow God whole-heartedly?

____

____

____

4. What can you do to stop from trying to control other people or situations?

____

____

____

____

____

Steps to Loving Your Journey

- **Repent from the sin of dissatisfaction.**
- **Stop envying others and wishing you had someone else's life.**
- **Learn to love your life:** Do not curse your day by starting it out saying, "If my life was only different," or "I hate my life." Instead say, "God, You gave my today, and I choose to love it! Now, what can I do to make it special?"
- **Get rid of the "ifs":** ("If this or that changed, I would be happy.") No! What are you enjoying now? Those who enjoy what they have receive more!
- **Love the process:** Our lives are a constant journey. If we do not learn to love the process, we miss our entire lives!
- **Contentment for the journey:** "But Godliness with contentment is great gain" (1 Tim. 6:6). Remember that whatever you are going through is not the big picture; it is just today's picture! Enjoy life today!
- **Peace for the journey:**

  a) Settle Salvation   b) Never be at odds with God

  c) Be at peace with yourself   d) Be at peace with others
- **Grace for the journey**: "My grace is sufficient for you, for My power is perfected in weakness" (2 Cor. 12:9). Daily ask God for His grace to help you love your life, complete your journey, and go the extra mile.
- **Spend time with God:** This daily time with God will send you out with joy and strength for the day, a heart for your responsibilities, and a passion to glorify God in all you do.
- **Rest for the journey:** "And He said, 'My presence shall go with you and I will give you rest'" (Ex. 33:14). "Therefore let us be diligent to enter that rest …"(Heb. 4:11).
- **Learn not to dread:** Pray, "I am going to do the will of God today without thinking about tomorrow."[62] "Casting *all* your cares upon Him, for He cares for you" (1 Peter 5:7).
- **A journey of love:** "Greater love has no one than this, that one lay down his life for his friends" (John 15:13). Love covers, heals, makes faith work, keeps you from having a critical spirit, teaches you to focus on good, and helps you to forgive.

- **Faith for the journey:** Faith is for getting the job done! It is for reaching the next generation for Jesus. Loving your life starts with making sure you are on the right journey (God's journey for your life, not the world's journey for you).
- **Do not control the journey:** Pray: "Father, forgive me for trying to control my journey and other's journeys. I give my life anew into Your hands and I let go! I place my loved ones into Your loving hands."

Chapter Sixteen

A "Word" for the Journey

"In the beginning was the Word, and the Word was with God, and the Word was God."
John 1:1

Words are more powerful than we realize. They are the very vehicle that God Himself uses to bring life and blessing. Words are life-changing for the good or the bad. As children we all heard the adage, "Sticks and stones may break my bones, but words will never hurt me." And nothing could be further from the truth. Words can build up or tear down. If we are not careful, they can destroy the very ones we love, but if we are careful, our words can set our loved ones and us on a pathway of life. If you will recall, the hallmark Scripture of this book is: "For he that will love life, and see good days, let him refrain his tongue from evil, and his lips that they speak no guile" (1 Peter 3:10 KJV). Most people do not have a revelation of the power of their words or how to use them, which means many people do not "love their lives and see good days." The Bible says, "My people perish for lack of knowledge" (Hosea 4:6). Well, we do not want to perish, so we must learn how to use words properly. The right words at the right time cannot only put us on the right road, but also, as the Scripture says, cause us "to love our lives and see good days." And we all want that.

As I was praying the Lord began to impress upon me an urgency and a necessity to write on this all-important topic of "words". Most of the chapters in this book in truth cover the second part of our hallmark Scripture 1 Peter 3:11, "Let him eschew evil, and do good; let him seek peace, and ensue it." I hope you now have a picture of what this looks like in practicality. I have gone over the basics, established truths, and hopefully provided the tools needed for fulfilling the second half of this Scripture. Now that that is done, it is time for us to move on to the *skill* of using "words" as tools of healing and stepping stones to our destiny. God says that His word "is like a hammer" (Isa. 23:29). I've learned, however, that people use their hammers mostly for *de*struction instead of *con*struction. We must learn to build, not destroy. We all want to love our lives, so if words are an important part of that puzzle, then by all means, let's learn on. The best way to start this journey is to firmly establish the power of words.

Truth:

Every issue, problem, and fight in our lives is primarily due to *words.*

Things spoken over us, about us, or to us can be great causes of evil or pain. Words are so powerful that even wars are started over words, words that were misspoken and misinterpreted. Even Adam and Eve relinquished their beautiful garden of Eden because of words. They got in trouble from listening to wrong, beguiling words spoken by a serpent. (My husband always says you should not be speaking to serpents in the first place. They have a forked tongue. Anyone with two things coming out of the same mouth has a venomous effect!)

Most of the time when we make a mess relationally, it is because we got angry, we were offended, or even lazy and selfish, and answered with ugly words. Has someone ever asked you to do something and you just spouted out an answer gruffly? Then you thought later that your answer probably was not very gracious. When you think about it you may realize your only motivation was that you were lazy and simply did not want to do it. You did not want to be bothered, and so you threw them off with "words." Every time we respond incorrectly, doesn't it make everything worse? It makes everything a real mess! Then what is the result? We do not love our lives and we do not see good days. And it is all because of how we responded.

Words are so essential! Yet most of us are very careless with our words. Most people can be very impulsive, often speaking and *then* thinking. Yet how can well-meaning Christians be so poor at communication? How is it possible that there is such poor communication worldwide? We would expect this outside the body of Christ, but I have to say I hardly see any difference within the body of Christ. Christians may leave out the profanity, but the heart of what they are saying is the same. It is just slightly cleaned up.

That's why we must get control over what is coming out of our mouths in order to bring our lives under control. Can you see why, "For he that will love life, and see good days, let him refrain his tongue from evil, and his lips that they speak no guile" (1 Peter 3:10 KJV) is so important? It is not possible to love your life without making the necessary adjustments with the words that we speak. In order to make those adjustments, we must understand four fundamental spiritual laws.

Spiritual Law #1

We are made in God's image.

Then God said, "Let Us make man in Our image, according to Our likeness; and let them rule over the fish of the sea and over the birds of the sky and over the cattle and over all the earth, and over every creeping thing that creeps on the earth" (Gen. 1:26). The fact that we are made in God's image is foundational to our Christian belief. Scripture is clear.

Spiritual Law #2

God designed us to use words to build our lives.

Our God is a speaking God. Therefore, since we are made in His image, to emulate Him we need to start speaking. This concept of building our lives with our words, can seem so abstract to us; as abstract as God saying, "Let there be light and there was light." (Gen 1:3). Many have such a hard time understanding this spiritual law. I will tell you why. If I want a chair, I have to make it with wood or with steel. So the natural mind does not perceive that really I made that chair with my words. But in reality, before I started planning or building it, I began to say, "I need a chair. I am going to make some chairs." Picking up the wood and building was merely a result of my words or maybe my employers' words. Because it came about so naturally, we often do not realize it was a result of words. We can mistakenly think that it was merely a result of wood or a result of steel. And really, where did the wood and steel come from originally? Genesis chapter one, of course … Words!

Please note that nothing has come into being in your life without a word. Nothing! It works the same for the believer as the unbeliever. Spiritual laws are just like natural laws in that they do not discriminate. They work equally on everyone. It does not matter if you are rich, poor, young, old, black, white, Christian or non-Christian. Spiritual laws, such as the power of words, will work for you instead of against you if you will learn how to cooperate with them.

Although John D. Rockefeller was born into poverty, early on he began to say, "Someday I will be the richest man in the world."[63] Today he is still known for his wealth. When General MacArthur was driven out of the Philippines, the last thing he said was, "I shall return!" And he did! Words are powerful and creative.

Even our salvation comes as a result of words; by hearing words, believing words, and confessing words. "That if you confess with your mouth Jesus as Lord, and believe in your heart that God raised Him from the dead, you will be saved; for with the heart a person believes, resulting in righteousness, and with the mouth he confesses, resulting in salvation" (Rom. 10:9–10). The wonderful glory of our salvation is through words, simple words. It is not through our actions, no matter how elaborate or saintly. Why? So that we cannot boast. It is only through Jesus' actions and sacrifice, not ours, that redemption came. Therefore, God created our salvation to be a result of words spoken in simple belief and faith. The importance of words in Scripture is unmistakable.

Truth:

Without a revelation, we cannot change.

So we need to begin to look at words in a new light, in a way that gives such revelation that every one of us will genuinely change our words. Without a "revelation"/a "light bulb" moment, we cannot change. Wanting to change is not good enough. Have you ever wanted to change in an area and couldn't? And then you got a "revelation" and the change became easy. For example, maybe someone wanted to go on a diet, but he or she just "couldn't" lose the weight or change his or her eating habits. All of a sudden they got a "revelation" from their doctor that they have a diet-related disease and they are going to die in a very short amount of time if they do not change. Then it is not so hard to go on that diet and stick to it. This happens all of the time. People are given a life or death sentence, and you know what? They change! They get a revelation! The light bulb goes on! They had been hearing correct information over and over, but now they believe it really does pertain to them. It is the same way in every area of our lives. When all of a sudden we get a revelation, our desire to change becomes so intense that we do not even realize it is a desire. It seems like life or death.

Spiritual Law #3

Life and death are in the power of the tongue.

Well, our words are life or death. We need to get that revelation. "Death and life are in the power of the tongue, and those who love it will eat its fruit" (Prov. 18:21). That is Heaven's information from God's Word. This is a spiritual law. Just like natural laws, spiritual laws are a constant. There is nothing we can do to change these laws just as we cannot change the law of gravity. But we can learn to work with them, thus having them work effectively and properly for us. The Bible speaks so strongly on this subject that there are over a thousand Scriptures just on the power of words. Words are important! Let's see how important.

"In the beginning was the Word, and the Word was with God, and the Word was God" (John 1:1). What a powerful revelation John starts his Gospel with! In the beginning was the Word … just like in Genesis 1! The Word was with God, and the Word *was* God. When the Father wanted to save mankind, *He sent His Word* (John 3:16). "And the Word became flesh, and dwelt among us, and we saw His glory, glory as of the only begotten from the Father, full of grace and truth." (John 1:14). Incredible! Jesus is the Word of God! This is an amazing and fundamental revelation. We may not fully understand how this works until eternity. However, we *can* understand that for God to manifest in the earth He only does so through is Word. Hopefully this will shed some light on the importance God puts on words.

God's Word is His saving power, His helping power, His healing power. Psalms 107:20 says, "He sent His word and healed them, and delivered them from all their destructions." You see, our God is a speaking God, and when our God speaks, He is releasing His power.

In Genesis 1:2 we see God's Spirit was moving, but there was still chaos, darkness, and emptiness (Gen 1:2). It was not until He started speaking that "things" began to change. Likewise, many Christians sense God's Spirit present, even moving, but do not see much changing yet. Why? Simple: God's power is not released *only* when His Spirit is moving, but when His Word is spoken! Then the Spirit will work together with the Word (like in the baptism of Jesus) to bring the redemptive plan and power of God into the earth. As John said, "The Word became flesh (a manifest reality) …" (John 1:14).

In order for us to enjoy God's will for our lives and to become His agents in the world today, we must learn to speak His words and release His creative ability into our world. We were made to "imitate" Him, to be "like" Him (Spiritual Law #1). Though your words will have some power whether you are Heaven-led or hell-bent, it does not compare to the power of speaking God's Word. We believers *must* be intent on standing for God, listening to His voice, and speaking His Word into our lives. That is where the power of God is released. This in no way suggests that we are God as the New Age belief teaches. That is foolishness! We did not create the world and we all know it. We don't even do a very good job maintaining it. This is not about building our own kingdoms. This is about building God's Kingdom. Our "words" of prayer should be, "Thy Kingdom come and Thy will be done on earth as it is in Heaven!" I am determined to do just that.

Here is a testimony about the power of words from a member of our church. Iwona Machaj and her husband, Lukasz, are a Polish couple that came to Ireland several years ago. Here is Iwona's story in her own words.

Iwona Machaj's Story

> The recession time started in Ireland and affected everyone. My husband, Lukasz, and I knew there was a recession, but we hadn't realized how bad it really was until it hit us. The company I worked for manufactured products for another international company. I was told that the assembly line we were working on had to be moved to China, because it was not economically viable to manufacture products in Ireland any longer.
>
> Our company had two buildings, and one building had already been closed down. I was told that our building would also close down soon. The Vice President announced that we were closing and voluntary *redundancies were given to those who wanted

them. The rest of us were waiting for the company's closing date to come.

I remember walking through the dark, deserted building every day on the way to my office. It used to be filled with workers and machines, but now the only light was from the windows. Every day as I walked through I kept saying, "God, I just know, that I know, that I know, that as long as I am working here this company will not close down." I proclaimed, "I am a blessing to this business! God will not shut the business down as long as I am here! God, bless the company even double!" It looked hopeless. Many of the businesses in Galway were closing down.

I kept telling my co-workers. "No! We're not going to close. I am praying for a miracle!" Everyone knew I was praying and they kept thinking, "Oh, come on! Look at the recession. What are you talking about?"

I did not look for another job; I knew I had to believe God! I even told my manager I knew a miracle would happen if I kept standing on God's Word.

There were lots of negotiations, and the general manager was doing everything he could. He went to countless meetings to try and keep us open. One day the vice president called everyone together. Everyone expected him to say that the closing was now commenced. He said, "Listen, things have turned around. Not only that, but we now have double the business. We are also starting new production lines." My manager came running in to me and said, "I did not even listen to him. I was just thinking about Iwona and her miracle!"

Our business has now grown and expanded to new branches in Dublin and England.

Everyone who knew that I had been praying still comes to me asking for prayer because they believe that when I pray God hears my prayers.

I know without any doubt that if I had not been taught on the power of words and how to speak things in faith, I would not have a job today. I would have given up. I am so thankful for my church. Because of this, I knew what to do in a time of trial. I learned to speak the opposite of what the bad situation was, for you will have what you say. I learned to stand in faith.

*Note: "Redundancy" is the word used in Ireland for being laid off and given some form of severance package.

Best Camp in the West

Another fun example was with our children's summer camp here in Galway. For several years now I have been saying that we are the best camp in the west of Ireland. I really believed it! We recently received very good news confirming this. Ireland's nationwide primary school magazine had a reader's poll taken. We were awarded not only placement among the "Top camps in Ireland," but among the "Top 3 Best Camps in the West"! Although the honor is tremendous I was not surprised at all; I'd been telling everyone we were "the best in the West" for years. And truly believing it with all my heart. All those years when the camp was small, I was content. But I knew that God had more! And now we're seeing the fruition of those seeds. We must mix our words with a believing heart. Do you see the principle at work here?

Spiritual Law #4

You must mix your words with a believing heart.

Remember, Romans 10:9–10 says, "That if you confess with your mouth Jesus as Lord, and believe in your heart that God raised Him from the dead, you will be saved; for with the heart a person believes, resulting in righteousness, and with the mouth he confesses, resulting in salvation." *Believing is a vital part of speaking.* However, if you are having a hard time believing God's wonderful promises are for you, then don't worry. "Speaking" God's Word is still your answer. "So then faith comes by hearing, and hearing by the word of God" (Rom. 10:17 NKJV). If you will keep speaking God's Word, your believing will eventually kick in, and when it does, things will start changing. God's Word mixed with a believing heart makes an unbeatable combination.

My husband tells about how he learned the difference between just speaking, versus speaking with a believing heart. He was in a parking lot with our two older girls. They were still small at the time. He had taken Hannah, who was about three years old, out of the car and was getting Abbey out of her car seat; she was still a baby. Kevin hardly had Abbey out when he noticed a car pulling out of a nearby spot. He checked Hannah to make sure she was safely at his side, but at that moment she turned to walk away. Kevin said, "Hannah, there's a car there, honey." At three, those words didn't even register. Then Kevin, seeing her continue toward the open lot, said loudly and firmly, "Hannah, stop!" Immediately, she turned back and never went near the danger. At that moment he felt God speaking to him, saying, "You must learn to put that much weight into your words if you want better results." You need to believe what you say and say it with authority for it to move a mountain.

The next truth will give great insight into understanding the principle of words and using them correctly.

Truth:

Words are a very spiritual way to communicate!

Many people do not realize just how spiritual words really are, but there is no more spiritual way to communicate than through words.

There is a motivating spirit behind every conversation we ever have. The conversation that I am having with you right now is motivated by a spirit of love. What spirit motivates this chapter? The Holy Spirit. There are no neutral conversations. Words are spiritual. Your motivations behind every sentence you say will either make you love your life and see good days, or it will make you hate your life and see bad days. It will create crisis and confusion all around you, or it will create peace. The following is a story to illustrate this point.

Top Secret

A friend of the family was one of the scientists involved in developing the GPS system in the 1980s for NASA. He was recently sharing with us the power of words by illustrating how words, which are sound waves, will travel through space forever with an undiminished signal strength. Our friend explained that the government has listening devices that can pick up a conversation in a room up to twelve hours *after* it is finished. How is that possible? Well, the words that have been spoken are sound waves that can be recorded even after they have been spoken until the resistance in the atmosphere reduces the signal beyond our capacity to register it. That's why you can walk into a room and can tell if there has been strife, love, etc. *Your words linger even after you leave.* The last thing you say before you go to bed lingers. It is important to you and your family how you end your day or how you start your day.

Just as natural words linger for hours, God's words linger for eternity. "Heaven and earth will pass away, but My words will not pass away" (Matt. 24:35). When we speak His words it also lasts forever. Our words of grace go down to our children's children. When you are long gone if you speak God's Word, it still speaks up to a thousand generations (Exo. 34:7). It keeps speaking and speaking.

One important way to love God is to love others. This helps keep the motivating spirit behind our words clean. That is why Ephesians 4:29, which says, "Let no unwholesome word proceed from your mouth, but only such a word as is good for edification according to the need of the moment, so that it will give grace to those who hear," is followed by verse 30, "Do not grieve the Holy Spirit of God, by whom you were sealed for the day of redemption." When we are motivated by any spirit other than the Holy Spirit, we grieve the Holy Spirit in us. You are sealed by the Holy Spirit if Jesus is your Lord and Savior. He is with you whether you are doing the right thing or the wrong thing; He is not going to leave you. We are in the New Testament now and the Holy Spirit is here to stay, but when we make wrong choices, we grieve Him. We force Him to be around the "yuck" in our lives. Let's not do that. The Word and the Spirit work together. So let's make sure that the motivation behind our words is pure.

Principles

Since God has created words to have such impact, let us review the basic principles so we can use them effectively.

> "For if you cry for discernment, Lift your voice for understanding; If you seek her as silver and search for her as for hidden treasures; Then you will discern the fear of the LORD And discover the knowledge of God. For the LORD gives wisdom; From His mouth come knowledge and understanding" (Prov. 2:3–6).

To understand *words* you are going to have to search God's *Word* with all your heart. If you do this, God will flood your heart with wisdom. With that in mind, let's discover the clear-cut principles about words established in the Word of God. Let us be diligent to not only discover them, but also put them into practice and find the amazing lives God has for us!

Principle 1: Our words are a seed.

- "The sower sows the word" (Mark 4:14). All words are seeds and will be sown for good or for evil. This principle explains what we are currently seeing in our lives.

Principle 2: Our words have the power of life or death.

- "Death and life are in the power of the tongue, and they who indulge in it shall eat the fruit of it [for death or life]" (Prov. 18:21 AMP). Death or life are in your mouth everyday all day long, it is your choice which one you have.
- "Thou art snared with the words of thy mouth, thou art taken with the words of thy mouth" (Prov. 6:2).
- "Concerning the works of men, by the word of thy lips I have kept me from the paths of the destroyer" (Ps. 17:4 KJV). Our words keep us on God's hidden invisible path of safety *or* they put us on the destroyer's path. "He who guards his mouth and his tongue, Guards his soul from troubles" (Prov. 21:23).

Principle 3: We will be judged for every word we speak.

- "For by your words you will be justified, and by your words you will be condemned" (Matt. 12:37). "But I tell you that every careless word that people speak, they shall give an accounting for it in the day of judgment" (Matt. 12:36). People say, "You cannot take anything with you when you die but the souls you lead to the Lord." However, that's not true. When you die you will take every word with you that you have ever spoken. Your words precede you into eternity, and it is serious. It is important that we realize this.
- "Take words with you and return to the LORD. Say to Him, 'Take away all iniquity And receive us graciously, That we may present the fruit of our lips'" (Hosea 14:2). Words are what we present to God, words of thanksgiving, words of praise. We often think we're presenting our deeds, but in actual fact we're presenting our words because they precede our deeds.

Principle 4: Look to God for the right answer.

- "There is a way which seems right to a man, But its end is the way of death" (Prov. 16:25). If we make decisions based on what we see or based on our natural reactions, our plans will lead to failure. Have you ever had someone mistreat you and it just seemed "right" to have it out with them? It seemed the only thing that would clear everything up, but in actual fact it created failure (relational death). There's a way that looks right, but may not be. We need to ask God for His plan.

- "The plans of the heart belong to man, but the answer of the tongue is from the LORD" (Prov. 16:1). Let's let that be the case for all of our lives.

Principle 5: Too many words cause problems!

- "When there are many words, transgression is unavoidable, But he who restrains his lips is wise" (Prov. 10:19). People tease about how much women speak. Have you ever heard that women supposedly use twice as many words as men? I don't know if that's true or not, but if it is true that means women have twice as many opportunities to transgress! Because "where there are many words, transgression is unavoidable." So let's all learn (male or female) not to say so many words. Rambling will only get us into trouble.

Principle 6: Words of the mouth show the intent of the heart.

- "The good man out of the good treasure of his heart brings forth what is good; and the evil man out of the evil treasure brings forth what is evil; for his mouth speaks from that which fills his heart" (Luke 6:45). If evil comes out of your mouth, what is in your heart? I hear people often say, "But that's not what I meant". They are only fooling themselves. That's exactly what they meant. They said what came out of their heart. We need to begin to change our hearts so we can change what comes out of our mouths.
- "It is not what enters into the mouth that defiles the man, but what proceeds out of the mouth, this defiles the man" (Matt. 15:11). Your words can defile you. Do not be deceived and think you're wonderful but leave carnage everywhere you go. If everyone

was just slain all around you because of your words, then you have a problem!

Principle 7: There are no "little white lies."

- "Lying lips are an abomination to the LORD, But those who deal faithfully are His delight" (Prov. 12:22). God hates a liar. You are never going to love your life and see good days if you lie. Some people do not lie for any particular reason; they just lie. Everything they say is not exactly the way it happened. If that's you, it is important that you speak the truth to love your life.
- "Righteous lips are the delight of kings, And he who speaks right is loved" (Prov. 16:13). God loves it when we speak righteously. It may not make you the most popular person at the moment, but you'll soon go to the top.

Learning the importance and power of words is very key to growing spiritually, pleasing God, and fulfilling your calling. Learning how to use words properly is a skill set each of us must develop. For that to happen, we need to build a revelation in our life of the real impact that our words have on our environment and future, as well as the responsibility we have concerning words. We will give an account for every one we have ever used! To help your personal understanding of this, I suggest you do a very fun and enlightening Bible study. Along with your regular devotions, add a study through the book of Proverbs. If you read just one chapter per day, you will complete the entire book in one month. Highlight or mark every verse that refers to words or speaking. You will be absolutely amazed, perhaps even shocked, to see the sheer amount of times God attempts to correct or instruct us on what comes out of our mouths.

If you have always wanted to know how to speed your journey along for a more successful, enriching, and truly rewarding life, then this next chapter is for you. Now that you have learned the basics, it is time to move into phase two and be propelled into a wonderful future.

Prayer

Dear Heavenly Father,

"Teach me, and I will be silent; And show me how I have erred. Set a guard, O LORD, over my mouth; Keep watch over the door of my lips. Deliver my soul, O LORD, from lying lips, From a deceitful tongue. Let the words of my mouth and the meditation of my heart Be acceptable in Your sight, O LORD, my Rock and my Redeemer. Lord, I pray that You give me the tongue of disciples, That I may know how to sustain the weary one with a word. That You awaken me morning by morning, that You awaken My ear to listen as a disciple." (Job 6:24; Ps. 141:3; Ps. 120:2; Ps. 19:14; Isa. 50:4).

In Jesus Holy Name,
Amen.

Truth in Action:

1. What areas in your life look impossible that you need to begin to speak God's Word over?

____

____

____

____

____

____

____

____

2. What Scriptures can you begin to speak today over those areas in your life?

____

____

____

____

____

____

____

____

3. Can you commit to speak what God says about those areas and not what you're currently seeing? First Corinthians 4:18 reminds us, "While we look not at the things which are seen, but at the things which are not seen; for the things which are seen are temporal, but the things which are not seen are eternal."

____

____

____

____

____

____

Steps to Loving Your Journey

- **Repent from the sin of dissatisfaction.**
- **Stop envying others and wishing you had someone else's life.**
- **Learn to love your life:** Do not curse your day by starting it out saying, "If my life was only different," or "I hate my life." Instead say, "God, You gave my today, and I choose to love it! Now, what can I do to make it special?"
- **Get rid of the "ifs":** ("If this or that changed, I would be happy.") No! What are you enjoying now? Those who enjoy what they have receive more!
- **Love the process:** Our lives are a constant journey. If we do not learn to love the process, we miss our entire lives!
- **Contentment for the journey:** "But Godliness with contentment is great gain" (1 Tim. 6:6). Remember that whatever you are going through is not the big picture; it is just today's picture! Enjoy life today!
- **Peace for the journey:**

  a) Settle Salvation — b) Never be at odds with God

  c) Be at peace with yourself — d) Be at peace with others
- **Grace for the journey**: "My grace is sufficient for you, for My power is perfected in weakness" (2 Cor. 12:9). Daily ask God for His grace to help you love your life, complete your journey, and go the extra mile.
- **Spend time with God:** This daily time with God will send you out with joy and strength for the day, a heart for your responsibilities, and a passion to glorify God in all you do.
- **Rest for the journey:** "And He said, 'My presence shall go with you and I will give you rest'" (Ex. 33:14). "Therefore let us be diligent to enter that rest …"(Heb. 4:11).
- **Learn not to dread:** Pray, "I am going to do the will of God today without thinking about tomorrow."[64] "Casting *all* your cares upon Him, for He cares for you" (1 Peter 5:7).
- **A journey of love:** "Greater love has no one than this, that one lay down his life for his friends" (John 15:13). Love covers, heals, makes faith work, keeps you from having a critical spirit, teaches you to focus on good, and helps you to forgive.

- **Faith for the journey:** Faith is for getting the job done! It is for reaching the next generation for Jesus. Loving your life starts with making sure you are on the right journey (God's journey for your life, not the world's journey for you).
- **Do not control the journey:** Pray: "Father, forgive me for trying to control my journey and other's journeys. I give my life anew into Your hands and I let go! I place my loved ones into Your loving hands."
- **A word for the journey:** "For he that will love life, and see good days, let him refrain his tongue from evil, and his lips that they speak no guile ..." (1 Peter 3:10–11). There is nothing more powerful than the Word of God, especially in your mouth and in your heart!

Chapter Seventeen

A Word that Speeds Your Journey Along

"Let no unwholesome word proceed from your mouth, but only such a word as is good for edification according to the need of the moment, so that it will give grace to those who hear."
Ephesians 4:19

We have just learned in the previous chapter how important words are. We have established four spiritual laws and learned that the most important words in the universe are God's Words. So if we want to speed our journey along, we need to learn how to put these words into the right gear and hit the accelerator. I do not know about you, but there are some areas in my life that have stayed the same for too long. What will make these areas move along? Words! So let's buckle up and get moving!

As Jesus taught: words are seeds. For us to have fruitful lives, we must first have seeds. For those seeds to produce they must be planted. If seeds are words, then for words to be planted, they must be spoken. Otherwise they are simply just thoughts. But Jesus did not tell us to "think" to our mountain, He said we must speak to our mountain (Mark 11:23). If we are willing to learn God's method of landscaping, we will start talking to the mountains in our lives and they will obey us. As the Lord said, they will be cast into the sea and we will have whatsoever we say. Wow, that's a weapon we need to learn how to fire.

However, this weapon fires both directions. To speed our journey along, we must learn to fire it in the right direction. All our words are seeds, and all produce a harvest. Do we really want a full harvest on all our words? Wow! If only we had to pass a test before we could use "words" like we do to drive a car or to become a doctor. That's why James says "For in many things we offend all. If any man offend not in word, the same is a perfect man, and able also to bridle the whole body" (Jas. 3:2 KJV). The Bible has truly allotted tremendous weight on this subject that we have too long ignored. Let's take out our manual of God's word and begin applying it to our lives straight away.

Once your soul is saved, and your name is written in the Lamb's Book of Life, your life still needs changes. How do we accomplish this? By the Word of God! As Peter said, "As newborn babes, desire the sincere milk of the word, that ye may grow thereby" (1 Peter 2:2 KJV). As a baby grows, it begins to speak. This is where true maturity levels are shown as we begin to speak the Word of God. You could have been a Christian for a long time, having Heaven as your home but still living in hell on earth, needing God to heal any broken areas of your life. Salvation for your everyday life comes through Words. The effort needs to be in your speaking. All day long, continually speaking, speaking, speaking the Word of God and nothing negative. Do not wait until circumstances are favorable or until the economy changes. Start today.

If we can bridle our tongues, not only does God consider us perfect, complete, lacking nothing, but we can actually begin to go the direction of real success. Not at a walk, but at a gallop.

> "Now if we put the bits into the horses' mouths so that they will obey us, we direct their entire body as well. Look at the ships also, though they are so great and are driven by strong winds,

are still directed by a very small rudder wherever the inclination of the pilot desires. So also the tongue is a small part of the body, and yet it boasts of great things. See how great a forest is set aflame by such a small fire! And the tongue is a fire, the very world of iniquity; the tongue is set among our members as that which defiles the entire body, and sets on fire the course of our life … With it we bless our Lord and Father, and with it we curse men, who have been made in the likeness of God; from the same mouth come both blessing and cursing. My brethren, these things ought not to be this way. Does a fountain send out from the same opening both fresh and bitter water? Can a fig tree, my brethren, produce olives, or a vine produce figs? Nor can salt water produce fresh" (Jas. 3:3–6; 9–12).

Truth:

Our tongue is *the* agent that guides the direction of our lives.

James is showing us with wonderful, figurative language that our tongues are *the* agents that guide our lives, even though they are small! He likens our tongues to a rudder on a ship. Only the rudder can point the ship in the right direction. In fact, the rudder was created to withstand great pressure, holding fast its course against the strong currents. Though the other parts of the ship are important, if the rudder breaks, the ship is out of control. It is the rudder that directs our course and nothing else. Is your rudder broken? If it is, humble yourself, go to God, the "rudder builder," and let Him fix it. It is never too late. Fixing your rudder/tongue is vital if you want to get where you are going. We see from James' text that our lives are set on a bad course solely by us not bridling our words, or we can be brought to safe harbor by properly using them. Let's learn some tips that will take our lives from a stand still or slow pace in certain areas to the race track.

Tips for Speeding Our Journey Along:

1. Speak blessings instead of cursings, all the time.

James explains this concept even further by stating very clearly that it is not possible for good and evil to come out of the same mouth without the evil polluting the good. That is a sobering thought for all of us.

Let's face it, at some point we have all spoken evil or guile. Have you ever said one thing and done another? That's guile according to *Nave's Topical Bible.*[65] It is that simple. Have your words ever produced sorrow in anyone? That is speaking evil according to *Merriam-Webster's Dictionary.*[66] Have you ever spoken a word with the intent of causing injury? In the heat of the moment, absolutely. Everyone at some point has. Remember, the Enemy deceives us into thinking that our retaliatory words will protect us, but they are not the sword of the Spirit. In fact, they make it worse and make us more vulnerable to future pain. Only God's Word spoken in love can protect us.

We cannot, however, change in the natural way. We cannot do it by just sheer grit. God clearly teaches principles that will make it easier to begin to change the way we say things, even the way that we see things. Unless we change we are no example whatsoever to the lost souls out there. It is no good for us to make it to Heaven and leave so many behind just because we refused to bridle our tongues. However, if we can change and begin to return good for evil every time, then God can begin to use us to win this generation for Christ. "Let him refrain his tongue from evil, and his lips that they speak no guile …"

One of the essential ways to speed your journey along is by speaking blessings instead of cursings. The word "blessing" in the Bible means "benediction," which translates literally to: good speaking, even, praise. The Lord went so far as to say, "But I say unto you, Love your enemies, bless them that curse you, do good to them that hate you, and pray for them which despitefully use you, and persecute you" (Matt. 5:44 KJV). A tall order, but only in doing this are we able to make sure that blessing and cursing do not come out of the same mouth.

Blessings are much more powerful and exciting than you think. Jesus was speaking to the Eastern mind of the day and they understood far more than we do in the modern Western culture about the power of a blessing. What Jesus was asking them to do to their enemies was quite revolutionary at the time.

How is it that we can bless someone? A Rabbi explains: "When I give someone a blessing, I feel that the blessing does not come *from me,* but it comes *through me.*"[67] The most powerful way to bless someone, of course, is using Scripture. "The LORD bless you, and keep you; The LORD make His face shine on you, And be gracious to you; The LORD lift up His countenance on you, And give you peace'" (Num. 6:24–26).

The following is an amazing story by an author that is not even a Christian, but has discovered Scriptural principles and spiritual laws. The author tells a story that happened to a woman who started putting this into practice.

> An Irish woman went home on the subway where she struck up a conversation with a young man. They got on so well that they continued talking on a bench at the station where they both got off. He saw a friend and hailed him over. The friend sat on the other side of the lady. A moment later, she left to go home. After a few steps, she realized the second young man had stolen her wallet. Instead of screaming or making a scandal of some sort, she told herself, "Well, if this blessing Pierre talked about works, I simply need to bless him." She did that for a few seconds and then turned around; the young pickpocket was coming toward her with her purse in his hand.[68]

The concept of blessing our enemies is truly revolutionary and will set you free. In fact, earlier in the book of James, James says: "If anyone thinks himself to be religious, and yet does not bridle his tongue but deceives his own heart, this man's religion is worthless" (Jas. 1:26). By this definition, how many of us would be considered un-Christian in the body of Christ? Amazing! Our religion is worthless if we cannot bridle our tongues! So obviously there is an expectation from God that we can.

2. Respond to anger with words of life.

Another way to learn to speed your journey along is to change how you respond to anger and begin to use words of life. What did Jesus do when He got angry? How did He respond? "And when he had looked round about on them with anger, being grieved for the hardness of their hearts, he saith unto the man, Stretch forth thine hand. And he stretched it out: and his hand was restored whole as the other" (Mark 3:5 KJV). When Jesus got mad, He healed. What would the body of Christ look like if when we got mad, we healed people instead of hurting people? Imagine. This is a right-side up Kingdom! This is true religion.

James expects us to not only bridle our tongues, but to bridle our hearts. He also says, "But everyone must be quick to hear, slow to speak and slow to anger; for the anger of man does not achieve the righteousness of God" (Jas. 1:19–20). Ephesians 4:26 says, "Be angry, and yet do not sin; do not let the sun go down on your anger." Wow! That's also a tall order, but we can do it. Again, God wants to bless you. You only hurt yourself by staying angry, and you certainly will not love your life! "Let all bitterness and wrath and anger and clamor and slander be put away from you, along with all malice. Be kind to one another, tender-hearted, forgiving each other, just as God in Christ also has forgiven you" (Eph. 4:31–32). Let's look at a good example of this.

The Innkeeper

The Vilna Gaon, who was a Jewish sage from Eastern Europe before WWI, related a fantastic story that illustrates the point.

> A poor man came to him on a snowy night seeking shelter. After providing him a small bit to eat by the warm fire, the man asked for something to drink. Appearing put out, the innkeeper poured the man the best he had to offer, then murmured something to himself, pounded his fist on the counter, and threw it out. This he did several more times before pouring the last and handing it to the stranger with a pleasant smile. When the traveler asked about the waste, the innkeeper gave an enlightening explanation. He said that he had at first resented having to give him more than he already had given. But he refused to give him help with malice in his heart and so threw it out until he could truly give it to the man with a pure heart so that God could reward him accordingly.[69]

We must also learn to "give" every word with the right spirit that we may be rewarded accordingly. Even if we say something nice, but we are mad on the inside, there is no reward for the nice thing that we said. We must get the spirit right that is motivating what we are saying and *then* we get a reward (the reward of loving our life or not). If you have to walk in the other room and say the thing ten times to yourself until you can say it with a pure, happy heart, then do that! You need to do whatever it takes.

I recently received an e-mail that really hurt my feelings, though that was not the intent of the e-mail. I wanted to be happy for the person, so I needed to give a happy, wonderful response. I had to rewrite my e-mail several times before I could whole-heartedly say I was happy for that person. It took me a few minutes, but I didn't want it to go until I was genuinely happy for them. That way I could genuinely "communicate" love and blessing to them. The Bible says it is okay to be angry, but just do

Nugget:

There's no way to become "truly" clean other than the Word of God. "That He might sanctify her (the church), having cleansed her by the washing of water with the Word" (Eph. 5:26). God's Word cleanses us. Negative words dirty us. No matter what has happened in your life, God can still only cleanse you through His Words. Amazing! God operates the same way He created us to. We can heal others with our words, and He heals us with His mighty Words of grace; not only comforting us, but washing us forever clean.

not sin. Adjust. Work through it. Tell God about it. God wants to know. God understands! Then let it go. With a pure heart let your words be a gift to the hearer! The Bible says, "You minister grace unto the hearer" (Eph. 4:29). Does every word you speak minister grace?

Is It Possible?

You bet it is. "Jesus saw Nathanael coming to him, and saith of him, Behold an Israelite indeed, in whom is no guile" (John 1:47 KJV). If he can do it, we can do it! The Bible further on says, "Let no unwholesome word proceed from your mouth, but only such a word as is good for edification according to the need of the moment, so that it will give grace to those who hear" (Eph. 4:29). Every moment of our lives, every circumstance, every conversation needs grace. And if you can find grace to speak about every situation and in every situation, no matter what it is, then you will begin to love your life and see good days, once again moving you to yet a higher gear. Grace is so powerful that some mountains only move by speaking grace to them (Zech. 4:7). "What are you, O great mountain? Before Zerubbabel you will become a plain; and he will bring forth the top stone with shouts of 'Grace, grace to it!'"

3. Speak to the mountains in your life.

"For verily I say unto you, That whosoever shall say unto this mountain, Be thou removed, and be thou cast into the sea; and shall not doubt in his heart, but shall believe that those things which he saith shall come to pass; he shall have whatsoever he saith. Therefore I say unto you, What things soever ye desire, when ye pray, believe that ye receive them, and ye shall have them" (Mark 11:23–24 KJV).

Truth:

There is nothing more powerful than the Word of God, especially in your mouth and in your heart!

When we speak God's Word to our mountains, they will move. We must simply believe, as we speak, that the mountains will respond. The whole reason that words can move mountains is that words put that mountain there to begin with (Gen. 1). Some mountains respond faster than others, but they will all respond. I heard one minister say, "If you are willing to stand forever, you will not have to stand very long!"

Our stance of "faith" is not an idle or unprotected stance. It is a stance with the *sword of the Spirit*, which is the Word of God in your mouth. It is a stance with the *shield of faith* that extinguishes *every* flaming missile of the Evil one. It is a stance with the *helmet of salvation*, the *breastplate of Jesus' righteousness*, the *belt of truth* and *feet shod with the Gospel* (Eph. 6:10–18). Now that is a stance of victory. Whatever your mountain or situation is you can overcome it if you will clothe yourself with salvation, read the Word, and then courageously speak the Word, staying in faith which is how you keep your *shield of faith* up!

If something is in your life that should not be there, you must stop telling God about it or pleading with God to get rid of it. He already knows! He wants it out of your life as much as you do, but you have to work within His spiritual laws. Remember spiritual laws one and two: We are made in God's image and God designed us to use words to build our lives. God died on the cross and rose again to give life and authority back to us. Now, start using that authority by confidently speaking God's Word and Name. Start telling the mountain in Jesus' name to leave. It is no longer welcome! This works on mountains, things that are very big; and it works on offense and unforgiveness, things that are deeply rooted (Luke 17).

Let me say this, some of the biggest mountains we face are not "out there somewhere" but are right between our ears. I like to call it "friendly fire." It does not come from an enemy, it comes from ourselves. It is not very friendly though, and it is deadly just the same. "For the weapons of our warfare are not of the flesh, but divinely powerful for the destruction of fortresses. We are destroying speculations and every lofty thing raised up against the knowledge of God, and we are *taking every thought captive* to the obedience of Christ" (2 Cor. 10:4, 5). How do you take a thought captive? You pick up the sword of the Spirit and the shield of faith, and you face the thought down by speaking God's Word out loud to yourself and over yourself when those negative or discouraging thoughts come. The great news is, it's a simple formula and it works for everything.

And you don't even need more faith; you just need to use what you have and begin to say, "Offense, you have no place in the soil of my heart. Be removed in Jesus' name. I forgive that person right now. I will not allow that seed to take root." Then begin, as Jesus said, to bless that person. Begin, from the depths of your heart, to say good things over them. E.g.: "God forgive them, they know not what they do. Lord, bless their family, their job, their joy. Help them, Oh God!" etc. If a cancer is trying to attack you or a loved one, God has already answered your prayer and provided healing for you through the Cross. You now have the authority to say to it, as Jesus did to the fig tree (Mark 11:12–26), "Cancer, you will no longer be allowed to grow in the soil of my body. I tell you to dry up, be plucked up, and be removed from my life, in Jesus' name!"

My mother, who is involved in the healing ministry at her local Episcopal church, gave me a wonderful report just the other day. A gentleman who had been diagnosed with terminal cancer came up for prayer. As he was speaking about the situation, he kept saying "my cancer." My mother simply told him that even though the cancer was in his body it was not his cancer, and he did not have to receive it as his own. All of a sudden, it "clicked" with him. He began to tell everyone that he did not have to receive the cancer. When he returned to the doctor for his checkup three weeks later, the doctor could not find a trance of cancer anywhere in his body! Once he realized it was not Heaven-sent, he rejected it. He simply said, "No," and the cancer literally left his body.

We are overcoming circumstances, not denying them.

God made you to be an over-comer, but you cannot be an over-comer unless there are negative things to overcome. Overcoming the negative circumstances around you does not mean you are in denial. You are not denying the facts. Jesus said to speak to the mountain, not to say, "There is no mountain." If it is raining outside, there is no power in speaking, "There is no rain. It's not raining." The fact is: yes, it is raining! The power is not in denial. The power is in the Word of God.

You are not denying the diagnosis given to you, but you do not have to receive that as God's diagnosis for you. Remember, only good things come from the Father. ("Every good thing given and every perfect gift is from above, coming down from the Father of lights, with whom there is no variation or shifting shadow" [James 1:17]. "The thief comes only to steal and kill and destroy; I came that they may have life, and have it abundantly" [John 10:10]). You do not have to receive the diagnosis as your permanent reality. You instead begin to say, "By Jesus' stripes I was healed" (1 Peter 2:24). Whatever your circumstances are, they are real. However, God's Word is *more* real. "While we look *not* at the things which are seen, but at the things which are *not* seen; for the things which are seen are temporal, but the things which are not seen are eternal" (2 Cor. 4:18). God's Word is eternal and more real than your circumstances. Choose to put your confidence in His Word and not in your "temporary" circumstances. Look at your mountain, size it up, and speak God's Word to it without fear.

I remember my mother-in-law sharing her wonderful story with me. She said it was the first time she had ever seen an actual answer to prayer and a miracle from God. She discovered a weeping growth on the inside of her mouth. She had been going to church for a little while then, and decided not to be afraid of it. She bought a little book of healing Scriptures (many such exist) and prayed them every day with purpose and power over that growth. She woke up one morning and it was gone! She was seventy years old at the time and was delighted to have discovered the real power of faith-filled words.

It works the same for us as it does for others. When we speak God's Word to someone, it can "create" salvation in their lives if they only believe and receive it. We can speak God's Word to people with huge issues like alcoholism, drug-addiction, etc., and they can be totally delivered by God's Word. It heals, strengthens, and feeds a hungry soul. Whether we are speaking God's Word to a mountain (a stubborn problem) or we are speaking a word of healing, God's Word works if we will work it.

4. People are not your problem.

An additional way to speed your journey is to realize that the Bible says your fight is not against flesh and blood but powers and principalities (Eph. 6:12). Yet this is so hard for many to understand. Our fight is in the spirit realm, not in the natural realm. People are not our enemy, no matter how it looks. We have to trust the Word of God. It is at that point we go back to spiritual law three: "Death and life are in the power of the tongue: and they that love it shall eat the fruit thereof" (Prov. 18:21 KJV) and begin to speak life (God's Word) into the situation, bringing healing and not strife. Often we are still like Peter on the night Jesus was arrested. Peter ran to Jesus' defense and cut off the ear of the high priest's servant. Jesus must have thought, "Peter, you are not getting it. You're fighting in the wrong kingdom. If you live by the sword, you die by the sword" (Matt. 26:52). Instead, Jesus picked up the man's ear and healed him. God's Kingdom is so different to ours. If you will begin to pray for ways to heal the situation, ask God for wisdom, and speak words of life, you will begin to win battle after battle. It does not always happen immediately, but over time it will *always* work. You have to believe the Word of God and you have to get a revelation of how powerful, how strong, and how impacting the Word is in your mouth. "For the Word of God is living and active and sharper than any two-edged sword, and piercing as far as the division of soul and spirit, of both joints and marrow, and able to judge the thoughts and intentions of the heart" (Heb. 4:12).

Even at Armageddon, Jesus will not come with a sword in His hand, but with the sword in His mouth. When Jesus wins that victory at the end of the age it is with His Word. "He is clothed with a robe dipped in blood, and His name is called The Word of God. And the armies which are in Heaven, clothed in fine linen, white and clean, were following Him on white horses. From His *mouth* comes a sharp sword" (Rev. 19:13–15a, emphasis added).

5. Do not give up on the process.

The Process

"And let endurance have its perfect result, so that you may be perfect and complete, lacking in nothing" (Jas. 1:4). It takes a while to become perfect (or mature) in your speech. You may do it wrong a hundred times, but keep pressing to the goal, have endurance, and you will certainly get there. If we can truly grasp the biblical understanding that words are seeds, it becomes much easier to have patience to wait for a harvest. We all know the harvest process takes time. We also understand that when a farmer plants his seed, it is underground where it first begins to work. Then, as Jesus taught, comes the blade, followed by the ear, then the full corn in the ear (Mark 4:28). Words spoken into the realm of the spirit, go underground so to speak, in the invisible realm, like seeds in soil. That is where they begin their powerful budding process. Only after the process of time do they come to full bloom where everyone can see, above the ground. Remember, even if the farmer does not know what the seed is doing, he is confident that the process is working for him just fine. The soil does not discriminate. It simply works regardless of who planted it or what kind of seed it is. We must begin to have faith that speaking God's Word works just the same. In the process of time you will have a wonderful harvest.

6. Water the seeds you've sown with thanksgiving and praise to God.

The greatest way to nurture the seeds you are sowing is to water them by giving thanks and praise to God. Giving words of thanks and praise to God speeds the journey along so powerfully they have been given their own chapters. A simple paragraph or two would not suffice. So whatever you do, do not miss the power-packed revelation in the next chapters. It is a sure way to see your harvest come to fruition!

7. Do not allow yourself to grumble or complain.

Living the Process

Be warned: murmuring, complaining, and doubt, dig up your precious seed. Let's see how the process works. If you do not see the answers to your prayers straight away, do not be tempted to murmur and undo all the good you have done, digging up the good seeds you have sown, by speaking words of doubt and negativity. Instead of complaining, begin to say, for example, "Lord, thank You for that job. Your Word says You supply all my need and I need a job. So I look to you. My eyes are on You. I know You've heard my prayer so I refuse to pull up my precious seed!" That has the power to bring the job, not the murmuring or complaining or even begging. Some seeds (words) germinate longer than others depending on the conditions. Do not give up. And by all means do not dig up!

When the Hebrew children were coming out of Egypt, they didn't understand this process and paid a great price for it. When they got into a tight spot, they murmured because that was what was in their hearts. They complained instead of saying, "God, we trust that You can set a table here in the desert just as well as You can in the king's palace. I am confident You care for us. Our eyes are upon You." That expression of faith would have thrilled God. When we speak His Word, everything goes to work bringing deliverance and assistance toward us. *Man truly does not live by bread alone, but by every Word of God* (Matt. 4:4). Even the angels are triggered by the spoken Word of God. Psalm 103:20 says these mighty beings "hearken to the voice of His Word." Though you cannot see those seeds of faith, those words are indeed planted into the spirit world and activate the Kingdom of God. At this point Heaven is released to go to work for you! When you are in a tight spot do not let the pressure of it move you off of your faith in God's process. If you will not move, your problem will. No problem is such hard ground that the Word of God cannot break through. If even an acorn can break through cement, then no negative situation stands a chance against God's Word in your mouth.

Musts for a Speedy Journey

- **Always put God's Word in your mouth (and everywhere)!** (Jos. 1:8, Deut. 11:19–21 NKJV)
- **Put God's Word many places as a reminder to point your "rudder" the right direction.** (Ex. 13:9)
- **Keep (honor) your word.** (Deut. 23:23, Ps. 15:4)
- **Speak God's Word aggressively and consistently.** (Jer. 23:29)
- **Treasure God's Word and develop hunger.** (Job 23:12, Ps. 119:131, Ps. 42:1, Matt. 5:6)
- **Do not defend yourself.** (Isa. 53:7)
- **Do not avenge yourself either.** (Rom. 12:19)

Change the Influences Over Your Words

- **Leave the presence of a fool.** (Prov. 14:7)
- **Do not be boastful.** (1 Sa. 2:3)
- **Love correction.** (Prov. 3:11)

God's words are our greatest asset! If we can learn to be perfect in what we speak, we are the most valuable assets on the planet. I believe we can. Let's get "speaking."

Prayer

Dear Lord,

Forgive me for all of the harsh words I have spoken to those around me, especially to those I love the most. I genuinely did not realize that the power of life and death were in my tongue. I repent and pray that those words will not bear fruit in my life or theirs. I choose life and blessing for me and my family (Prov. 18:21; Deut. 30:19).

Holy Spirit, instruct my words. May my words minister grace to the hearers instead of sarcasm, bitterness, or anger. May my words bring health and healing. May my words keep me from the destroyer and speak truth, kindness, and love. Teach me how to use my words to bless and build others up. Remind me, Lord, to think before I speak. I will be more mindful of my words and endeavor to use them according to Your Word (Eph. 4:29).

In Jesus' Name,
Amen.

Truth in Action:

1. In what situations and with what people do you find that you need to change your tone of voice and the motivation behind your words?

 ____

 ____

 ____

 ____

2. Now that you understand the principle that "life and death" are in the power of the tongue, in the areas you have been negative in, what words of life can you commit to speak instead?

____

____

____

____

____

____

____

3. Are you quick to speak judgmental statements or criticize? As James explains, "this ought not be" (James 3:10). How can you begin to break this habit?

____

____

____

____

____

4. Can you begin to put God's Word in your mouth and in your surroundings? Where will you start?

____

____

____

____

____

Nugget:

Speaking and praying Scriptures has no power if you refuse to act on what the Scripture says. E.g. If you are praying that you "refrain your lips from evil", and someone asks you why you're late, do not tell them some big lie. Why? Because you prayed to keep evil away from your lips. By choosing deception you have just invited evil back onto your lips. Don't say, "I got caught in traffic", when there was no traffic at all. You can say, "I was just late. I am really sorry". God can help you in that situation. The Enemy is the father of lies (John 8:44) so only the truth can set you free. The Bible says through truth and mercy sin is purged. If you can tell the truth to people, you can find mercy. Over the years, I have heard the most outrageous excuses, like: "I couldn't be there because I was at a funeral", only to find out there was no funeral! Rather, if you obey the Scriptures you've prayed, about speaking the truth or walking in love, you will see God's blessing in those areas.

Steps to Loving Your Journey

- **Repent from the sin of dissatisfaction.**
- **Stop envying others and wishing you had someone else's life.**
- **Learn to love your life:** Do not curse your day by starting it out saying, "If my life was only different," or "I hate my life." Instead say, "God, You gave my today, and I choose to love it! Now, what can I do to make it special?"
- **Get rid of the "ifs":** ("If this or that changed, I would be happy.") No! What are you enjoying now? Those who enjoy what they have receive more!
- **Love the process:** Our lives are a constant journey. If we do not learn to love the process, we miss our entire lives!
- **Contentment for the journey:** "But Godliness with contentment is great gain" (1 Tim. 6:6). Remember that whatever you are going through is not the big picture; it is just today's picture! Enjoy life today!
- **Peace for the journey:**

  a) Settle Salvation b) Never be at odds with God

  c) Be at peace with yourself d) Be at peace with others
- **Grace for the journey**: "My grace is sufficient for you, for My power is perfected in weakness" (2 Cor. 12:9). Daily ask God for His grace to help you love your life, complete your journey, and go the extra mile.
- **Spend time with God:** This daily time with God will send you out with joy and strength for the day, a heart for your responsibilities, and a passion to glorify God in all you do.
- **Rest for the journey:** "And He said, 'My presence shall go with you and I will give you rest'" (Ex. 33:14). "Therefore let us be diligent to enter that rest …"(Heb. 4:11).
- **Learn not to dread:** Pray, "I am going to do the will of God today without thinking about tomorrow."[70] "Casting *all* your cares upon Him, for He cares for you" (1 Peter 5:7).
- **A journey of love:** "Greater love has no one than this, that one lay down his life for his friends" (John 15:13). Love covers, heals, makes faith work, keeps you from having a critical spirit, teaches you to focus on good, and helps you to forgive.

- **Faith for the journey:** Faith is for getting the job done! It is for reaching the next generation for Jesus. Loving your life starts with making sure you are on the right journey (God's journey for your life, not the world's journey for you).
- **Do not control the journey:** Pray: "Father, forgive me for trying to control my journey and other's journeys. I give my life anew into Your hands and I let go! I place my loved ones into Your loving hands."
- **A word for the journey:** "For he that will love life, and see good days, let him refrain his tongue from evil, and his lips that they speak no guile …" (1 Peter 3:10–11). There is nothing more powerful than the Word of God, especially in your mouth and in your heart!

Chapter Eighteen

Thanks for the Journey

"Therefore I will give thanks to You, O Lord, among the nations,
And I will sing praises to Your name."
2 Samuel 22:50

Never underestimate the power of a simple "thank you." With a quick glance at the life of a stubborn, run-away prophet, I will demonstrate a Biblical example of the power of thankfulness. A short read of the book of Jonah will reveal that this one attitude, yielded with faith and humility, can rescue someone from the deepest of all possible predicaments. Jonah, who was rebelling against the call of God, was thrown overboard to quell the storm and was swallowed by a big fish. After three days and nights Jonah "prayed from the fish's belly" (Jonah 2:1), or worse (Jonah 2:2), and God heard him! (One does not get any deeper in trouble than that.) He prayed, "But I will sacrifice to You with the voice of thanksgiving, that which I have vowed I will pay, salvation is from the LORD" (Jonah 2:9). Thanksgiving began to roll out of Jonah's mouth. Who could find something to thank God for there? Well, Jonah did! And God spoke to the fish and it vomited him out onto dry land. What a prayer! If we, in our dire circumstances, could employ such a tool, we would surely come out of our troubles, as well.

From this and many other stories and truths in God's Word we learn the importance of saying, "thanks for the journey"! Thanking God for *having* a journey, and thanking Him *in* the journey changes our lives. The following story illustrates this principle very well.

Corrie Ten Boom: Flea Story

In 1940, when Hitler took control of Holland, the Ten Boom family protected their Jewish neighbor. That began a two-year span in which they hid many Jews from the Nazis. Corrie Ten Boom (51 years old), her father, and older sister were eventually caught and put in notorious concentration camps where they were beaten and violated. However, Corrie's sister Betsie always tried to encourage Corrie to find something to be thankful for. After one of their transfers, the sisters were put in a barrack built to accommodate two hundred women, but instead there were seven hundred in it, not to mention millions of fleas. When Corrie heard their barracks assignment she groaned, but Betsie said, "Let's praise the Lord in all things." They immediately set up a Bible study in their new barracks. They had the Bible study every evening after doing hard labor dragging heavy pieces of metal from railroad cars to the factory building. After eleven exhausting hours, they had to march back to the concentration camp, seven days a week. Yet every night women gave their hearts to Jesus as the sisters taught. Each night more women joined the group.

One night Corrie said, "Betsie, isn't it interesting how we are able to have a Bible study here and share Jesus with so many women, and we've never had a guard come in here?" Then they realized that the very fleas that had been biting them were also keeping the guards from coming into their barracks. The fleas stopped the guards from coming in and violating the women and breaking up their Bible study. Betsie and Corrie began to say, "Lord, thank you for the fleas!"

Days before Betsie died, she woke up from a dream and said, "Corrie, I just saw the prettiest picture. I saw a concentration camp, but all the barracks were painted bright colors and had flowers all around them, and God turned it into a place of healing, not only for the victims, but for the guards." Corrie said, "What do you mean? These guards do not need any healing." Betsie said, "The guards need more healing than anyone." She understood that it destroys a human's soul to torture another person; twisting the abuser more than the abused. Shortly after this, Betsie went to be with the Lord. Not long after that, Corrie Ten Boom was released by "accident"; on a clerical error. Two weeks later, the guards killed every woman her age in her concentration camp. God spared her life so she determined not to waste it. Pursuing the vision and dreams God put in her heart, she was so dedicated to the Lord that she was even nicknamed "Tramp for the Lord." She died at the wonderful age of ninety-one.

Corrie learned through it all to be thankful and share a message of hope and healing to many. True to Betsie's dream, after the war was over Corrie turned that concentration camp into a place of healing, not only for the victims, but for the guards too. Many guards came to the saving knowledge of Jesus Christ in that place because Betsie understood thanksgiving. She understood how it all worked. [71]

Thank goodness for Betsie's precious heart of thankfulness. What a reminder of how God wants us to be. Most of us will never go through what Betsie or Corrie went through, yet thankfulness is just as essential to our lives as it was to theirs. Our trials seem so small in comparison, yet the principle is the same. In fact, if we cannot learn to be thankful in the everyday of life, it will be much harder to be thankful in the trials of life. One of the most powerful ways to overcome the ugly, selfish habit of dissatisfaction is to cultivate a lifestyle of thanksgiving.

Truth:

Cultivating a lifestyle of thanksgiving will increase your capacity to receive!

We need to cultivate a lifestyle of thanksgiving if we wish to increase our capacity to receive blessings from the hand of God. Our ability to be thankful is in direct proportion to our ability to receive. If we want to be able to receive more from God, we must learn to be more thankful. There are always things to be down about or even downright negative about, but when we give thanks in the midst of adversity, we magnify God and minimize problems. This opens the door to more blessings from God. Thanksgiving is imperative to enjoying life.

Thankfulness is so powerful. I was going through a circumstance recently that was so overwhelming I didn't think I could bear it. I was doing my morning Bible study and God spoke to me through His Word. (Please have a time every day when you open up God's Word.) I was praying and I said, "God, I don't know how I can handle this. I am so overwhelmed." In my reading that day was Psalm 50:14–15. God clearly pressed upon me to pray it and *do* what was in it! "Offer to God a sacrifice of thanksgiving And pay your vows to the Most High; Call upon Me in the day of trouble; I shall rescue you, and you will honor Me" (Ps. 50:14–15). The Lord showed me very clearly that the "rescue" in verse fifteen was attached to the "sacrifice of thanksgiving" in verse fourteen. Verse fourteen had to come first, since our trust in God activates Heaven.

When you are discouraged and things do not look like they are going to turn out the way you had hoped, it is in those moments that thanking God is a true sacrifice. Understand, however, you are not thanking God *for* the problem, you are thanking Him *in* the problem. You are thanking the Lord for everything He has ever done for you in the past. You are reminding yourself how great God is. This literally charges the spirit realm with faith. When we magnify God over the problem it opens the door for God to walk in and the miraculous to happen.

How do you order your way aright? You thank God in the problem. You say, "God, I thank you for the answer." You thank Him *in* the problem *for* the answer. On that day, I began to say: "God, I just want to thank you! I choose thankfulness. There is so much I can be thankful for, and right now I am thanking you for the answer to that problem." I began to thank Him all day long. Not only did it lift my spirits, giving me hope where I had none, but it also began to fill me with surety and I knew in my heart things were changing. And sure enough, over a period of time, everything worked out.

When we say thank you, we begin to see God's blessings and victories. Thanksgiving is one of the most powerful weapons that you can have. It is more powerful than any type of nuclear weapon or weapon of mass destruction. Thanksgiving brings something that doesn't already exist into the physical realm. It is not only bringing your answer into existence, but also utterly destroying the darkness surrounding you.

I believe that when God hears us thanking Him *even* before we receive our answer to prayer, the heavens open and God does whatever it takes to fast-track, federal express our answer right to us, because we're already thanking Him. The act of thanksgiving shows that we really believe God is good and is a "rewarder of those who diligently seek Him" (Heb. 11:6b). Scripture proves that He does not see this as audacious, but as having faith and trust in a loving, generous God.

The weapon of deliverance God gave me that day was thanksgiving. Everything began to change because I put God's Word into action. "He who offers a sacrifice of thanksgiving honors Me; And to him who orders his way aright I shall show the salvation of God" (Ps. 50:23).

"Whatever you do in word or deed, do all in the name of the Lord Jesus, giving thanks through Him to God the Father" (Col. 3:17). Let's learn to give thanks every day! All day! In everything! A lack of praise to God when we have success infers how great we are. Thankfulness to God shows how great He is. Pride is actually the culprit when we are not thankful for the victory! I cannot stress it enough, "For the mouth speaks out of that which fills the heart" (Matt. 12:34). Whatever is in your heart will come out of your mouth. Thanksgiving is vital to our future. So become a person that is vocally thankful to God. It guards against pride so God will allow us to continue being blessed. Ungrateful people cut off their futures!

Storms

Often when we go through a tight or rough spot we get our eyes off of the Lord and onto the storm. This makes things so much harder, and it makes our storm appear bigger and stronger than it is. Then we start to sink. Peter walking on the water is a visual we can really learn from. After Peter courageously stepped out onto the water to go to the Lord (Matt. 14:30) he all of a sudden started to look at the fierce storm and the intimidating waves, and he began to sink. The problems looked so big, so enormous that he lost his focus and began to doubt. What could Peter have done to prevent fear and distraction? If while Peter was on the water he had said, "Thank you, Lord for this opportunity! You are an awesome God. I will follow you anywhere. Thank you!" I can promise he would not have sunk. How can I say that? Because his eyes would have been on the Lord and not the circumstances.

Thankfulness keeps our eyes focused on the Lord. When we keep our eyes fixed on the Lord, we are assured that He is much bigger than any storm. In a moment of crisis, we *need* to begin to give thanks to Him. Start by thanking Him for *all* the past times you have called on Him and He has seen you through! King David was a master at this. Take some time and read through the psalms. Even in a time of trouble David would recount the wonderful things God had done for him. Then, full of faith he would proceed with his prayer request. Even on occasion, when David began to dwell on the problem first, he quickly corrected himself and began to give thanks and rehearse his victories, once again filling himself with faith and putting himself in a position to receive the miraculous. We must watch that our prayers do not become a format of complaining, but a format for receiving.

Missions

There are so many opportunities in life to fail to show gratitude. The natural tendency is to allow circumstances to dictate our response. This is true even when we are doing work for the Lord, whether it is in a volunteer capacity or a full time capacity. This can catch many people off guard. Kevin and I have noticed this in particular when church groups go on short-term mission trips, especially for the first time. The members of the group will often be stretched: being with a group 24/7, not having their own private space or their own schedule, having to be flexible, doing what the host church or host group needs, sharing the Lord with people, maybe for the first time and on top of it all being constantly on the go, which is physically demanding for many people. This is a legitimate stretch. Because of all of these new circumstances, there is often a strong temptation to be unthankful, even selfish and grumpy. It is important not to yield to this. Instead, that is the most important time to be thankful. Thankfulness helps us to love our lives. This is true not only for missions but also for any time we get involved in our local churches and communities. Especially if it is your first time to serve, expect the temptation to be unthankful and overcome it.

> *Nugget:*
>
> *If you have never been on a mission trip, please do not let this put you off. I cannot recommend it highly enough! It is a life-changing experience. You get to know God in a more intimate way and have many opportunities to lean on Him. There is nothing like leaving your home country and your comforts to clear away the distractions and begin to see the world through His eyes. Two-thirds of "God," as someone once said, is "Go".*

Head Thankfulness vs. Heart Thankfulness

In 1445 BC[72] in the Old Testament, when the children of Israel left Egypt and crossed over the Red Sea on dry land, they were so very thankful to God. Their enemy and enslaver, Pharaoh and his army, had been drowned. They no longer had to fear slavery and cruel treatment. They were so thankful! They sang to God in thankfulness, in dance and song. Yet a mere three days later, when they ran into hardship, they were negative and complaining. They began to grumble and complain against God and His leadership. Why? How could they lose their thankfulness so fast? Because their thankfulness was in their heads and not in their hearts. It was only a superficial emotion, so when trials came, they turned on the only hand that could save them.

We need to be careful of this ourselves. For Moses, thankfulness was a character trait; for Israel, it was an emotion and that was the difference! If thankfulness had been a character trait and not an emotion, Israel would have turned to God in time of trial like Moses did. That is one of the ways we can check to see if our thankfulness is in our heads or in our hearts. When it is a sacrifice of praise, when it is part of our character to thank God, thanksgiving, and not grumbling, flows out of our mouths- even when difficulties arise. Then we know we are on the road to success.

Beware: We can become *unthankful* …

- *When* (believe it or not) God's daily provision becomes ordinary. When His daily miracles in our lives can become almost "common" we need to be careful. At this point we begin to take things for granted, thinking, "Well, I deserve that." Then unthankfulness creeps in.
- *When* we begin complaining about our past. "What do you expect? I had a horrible upbringing. Life was hard for me!" People often use that as a crutch for not being thankful. If that's you, give your past to the Lord. Let go of your hurt, anger or even hatred. Remember, "Jesus Christ is the same yesterday and today and forever" (Heb. 13:8). He can heal yesterday so much that only "goodness and mercy" are following you. Allow God's healing power to make your heart and emotions new again. Let go of your unforgiveness toward any person or situation. Your holding onto it does not punish the other person. It only punishes you.

God has your permission to deal with it *if* you let go of it. If your past was difficult or harder than anyone else's, it still cannot be a reason to be unthankful. You need to determine that if there is only one thing in your past that you can be thankful for, that is the one and only thing you remember about your past. You need to decide to forget and forgive everything that God did not bring into your life in your past and rejoice over what He did bring into your life!

- *When* we look at what we do not have now. Maybe you need a new car and the car you have is barely making it; the temptation is to be unthankful and begin to complain about what you have and what you need more of. That is a real temptation, and once you know that, you can resist the temptation. Thankfulness will expedite your answer to prayer and keep your eyes on God, and will help you appreciate what you do have.
- *When* we have just plain ole' bad manners and self-absorption. A good example of this is found in the story of the ten lepers, given below.
- Lastly, *when* things do not work out the way we expect them to, we can become very unthankful and miss the miracle.

As you can see, the natural course of things does not lend itself to being thankful. It is up to us to choose thankfulness regardless of how things may appear, but if we will, we'll discover one of the most powerful secrets to loving our lives. Just look at the lives of a few people who did this the right way.

Where Are the Nine?

While He was on the way to Jerusalem, He was passing between Samaria and Galilee. As He entered a village, ten leprous men who stood at a distance met Him; and they raised their voices, saying, "Jesus, Master, have mercy on us!" When He saw them, He said to them, "Go and show yourselves to the priests." And as

> they were going, they were cleansed. Now one of them, when he saw that he had been healed, turned back, glorifying God with a loud voice, and he fell on his face at His feet, giving thanks to Him. And he was a Samaritan. Then Jesus answered and said, "Were there not ten cleansed? But the nine—where are they? Was no one found who returned to give glory to God, except this foreigner?" And He said to him, "Stand up and go; your faith has made you well" (Luke 17:11–19).

We see that as the lepers followed the Lord's instruction they were all healed. The word here for "healed" in the Greek is *Katharizo:* cleansed. The disease stopped where it was and was cleansed (no longer white, infected or oozing). Yet only one of the lepers came back to Jesus to say "Thank you." The other nine did not. However, when the one returned showing profound thankfulness, the Lord was surprised the others weren't with him.

And He said to him, "Stand up and go; your faith has made you well" (Luke 17:19). The Greek word here for "well" is *sozo.* Sozo: to save, heal, preserve, to be made whole. It is not the same word at all that was used above. It would not be a stretch here, given the Greek word, to believe that whatever body parts were "missing" due to leprosy were now not only clean but were now "whole." Restored! In addition, his emotions from such an ordeal would have also been made whole, and his life truly saved. Look at the power thankfulness has not just for realizing God's provision, but more importantly releasing His restoration. God wants us to realize the power in saying thank you. Thankfulness is key to healing and restoration. Do not let bad manners steal that from you! Be quick to say "thank you."

Nugget:

The word translated into English as "giving of thanks" is the Greek word eucharisteo. You can easily guess what word we derive from that—Eucharist. Unfortunately, for many Christians communion is simply just another part of a church service. In the Bible, though, it was a personal "thank you" to God for what He has done for us. This was not just any "thank you," though; it was a passionate one. When the one leper returned to Jesus to thank Him, the Bible says specifically that he came with a "loud voice"; In the Greek, mega[73] phone.[74] He could have cared less what anyone else thought. He was focused on thanking the One who had blessed him! How much more should we give thanks at all times, especially when we take communion? Remember that next time you take communion.

Miracle Story

Being thankful truly opens up the door to the miraculous and helps us see the miraculous in the ordinary. Here is a precious example of how this works: One of the daughters of the well-known Osteen family, Lisa, was born with cerebral palsy and brain damage. Lisa's family knew very little of God's healing power at that time in their walk with God, though her dad was a pastor. However, her parents began to see in Scripture that Jesus healed the sick everywhere He went, and they saw the Scripture that said, "Jesus is the same, yesterday, today and forever" (Heb. 13:8). So Lisa's parents prayed a simple, believing prayer, stayed in faith daily, giving thanks to God, and God totally healed Lisa.[75] She is now a perfectly healthy adult and a true testimony of the power in God's Word. Years later, after Lisa was married, she found that she was unable to have children. She and her husband prayed. They said, "God, we know we're supposed to have children. So we're going to rejoice and be thankful in however you want to bring them to us." God did a miracle for them, but not the way that you would think. Lisa and her husband were able to adopt twin girls through wonderful circumstances. If Lisa and her husband hadn't been able to let go of their plans, they would not have been able to accept God's plans to adopt these precious babies and add the fullness of life He had in mind for them in His way. We must be thankful in all situations. Even when things do not end the way we think they should, we must develop trust that God has a much bigger and better plan.[76]

We can get so stuck on God having to do things a certain way. Can we let go and trust God for the overall outcome? Can we thank God in the circumstances? There is always something wonderful to thank God for.

Harriet Tubman

Harriet Tubman being born into slavery, became the most famous conductor of the Underground Railroad. She was also known as the "Moses of her people." As a little girl, when a slave would escape from a plantation she would ask her mother where they went. Her mother would tell her that there was a rumor of a secret railroad that would take a slave to freedom, but no one believed it really existed, because no one had ever come back. At that point in her six-year-old heart Harriet thought, "If I can get free, I am coming back and I am taking people with me."

When Harriet was about sixteen years old, her plantation and a neighboring plantation came together for a corn shucking. Suddenly, during the festivities, a slave started to run away. One of the overseers from the other plantation looked at Harriet and yelled for her to stop the slave. Harriet was not about to do that so she froze. The overseer got so mad at her that he picked up a very heavy weight and threw it at Harriet and hit her in the head. He threw it so hard in his anger that it took out part of her skull and damaged her brain. She was unconscious for two months. When she finally woke up, the doctor explained that for the rest of her life she would have fits where she would fall asleep unexpectedly and she would not know when or where it would happen.

Harriet looked at her daddy and in tears said, "I thought God was going to use me like Moses, and now He can't." Her dad said, "No, honey, that's what Moses said to God, too. He said, 'You can't use me, I stutter.' Baby, whatever God wants to do, God can do." Another slave came to Harriet later and said, "You better thank the good Lord for that hole in your head! They were going to sell you further down south, but now no one would have you because of that!"

Years later, when Harriet finally escaped, it was at an incredibly dangerous time in history, when a law had been passed that escaped slaves could be caught in the North as well as in the South (which prior to that had not been the case). Harriet soon discovered that it took more courage to come back than it did to escape.

Harriet's concern was that God would not be able to use her, but use her mightily He did! Even though she still had fits of falling asleep throughout the years she was conducting the Underground Railroad, she conducted it by faith and led many people to freedom. Through her own testimony, she declared that it was never through her own strength that she did what she did; it was through God's strength. She understood the danger for everyone involved. She understood that if she fell asleep during the escape, everyone would die for she was the only one who knew the connections. Yet she still allowed God to use her.

God wants to use you too, but what can you be thankful for? In what area have you said, "God, you cannot use me because …" God *can* use you. God used Harriet. Her biography says she led 300 people to freedom (including her parents), and she didn't lose one of them! Her parents had much the same story as Corrie and her sister Betsy. When anyone would get angry about their treatment and situation, Harriet's father would say, "No, don't! Those people who have hurt you, been unjust, have done things that were wrong … they are God's children, too, and we're going to pray for them."[77] That is a miracle! That kind of thinking is not possible outside of God. We need to choose to be thankful in everything we do, in all circumstances. Look at the kind of person Harriet's parents produced because of their heart of love and thankfulness. They literally birthed their own deliverer.

"Be careful for nothing; but in everything by prayer and supplication with thanksgiving let your requests be made known unto God" (Phi 4:6 KJV). Our future success and the success of our children may well depend on it!

Prayer

Dear Lord,

There is so much to be thankful for! Once again I whole-heartedly repent for being unthankful in general. I want to develop a daily attitude of thankfulness in everything and in every situation so that I do not miss out on the blessings and the miracles! I love You so much, and I want to start this journey of thankfulness by saying thank You for my life! Thank You for my family! Thank You for my job! Thank You for my church! Thank You that You are so good! You are wonderful.

In Jesus' Name,
Amen.

Truth in Action:

1. When you receive an answer to prayer, do you forget to say thank You?

   ____

   ____

2. Where are the areas in your life in which you can be more thankful?

____

____

____

____

____

3. Even when things do not work out like you had thought, what can you do to be thankful?

____

____

____

____

4. Can you identify the obstacles that cause you not to be thankful?

____

____

____

____

Steps to Loving Your Journey

- **Repent from the sin of dissatisfaction.**
- **Stop envying others and wishing you had someone else's life.**
- **Learn to love your life:** Do not curse your day by starting it out saying, "If my life was only different," or "I hate my life." Instead say, "God, You gave my today, and I choose to love it! Now, what can I do to make it special?"
- **Get rid of the "ifs":** ("If this or that changed, I would be happy.") No! What are you enjoying now? Those who enjoy what they have receive more!
- **Love the process:** Our lives are a constant journey. If we do not learn to love the process, we miss our entire lives!
- **Contentment for the journey:** "But Godliness with contentment is great gain" (1 Tim. 6:6). Remember that whatever you are going through is not the big picture; it is just today's picture! Enjoy life today!
- **Peace for the journey:**

  a) Settle Salvation b) Never be at odds with God

  c) Be at peace with yourself d) Be at peace with others
- **Grace for the journey**: "My grace is sufficient for you, for My power is perfected in weakness" (2 Cor. 12:9). Daily ask God for His grace to help you love your life, complete your journey, and go the extra mile.
- **Spend time with God:** This daily time with God will send you out with joy and strength for the day, a heart for your responsibilities, and a passion to glorify God in all you do.
- **Rest for the journey:** "And He said, 'My presence shall go with you and I will give you rest'" (Ex. 33:14). "Therefore let us be diligent to enter that rest ..."(Heb. 4:11).
- **Learn not to dread:** Pray, "I am going to do the will of God today without thinking about tomorrow."[78] "Casting *all* your cares upon Him, for He cares for you" (1 Peter 5:7).
- **A journey of love:** "Greater love has no one than this, that one lay down his life for his friends" (John 15:13). Love covers, heals, makes faith work, keeps you from having a critical spirit, teaches you to focus on good, and helps you to forgive.

- **Faith for the journey:** Faith is for getting the job done! It is for reaching the next generation for Jesus. Loving your life starts with making sure you are on the right journey (God's journey for your life, not the world's journey for you).
- **Do not control the journey:** Pray: "Father, forgive me for trying to control my journey and other's journeys. I give my life anew into Your hands and I let go! I place my loved ones into Your loving hands."
- **A word for the journey:** "For he that will love life, and see good days, let him refrain his tongue from evil, and his lips that they speak no guile …" (1 Peter 3:10–11). There is nothing more powerful than the Word of God, especially in your mouth and in your heart!
- **Thanks for the journey:** Cultivating a lifestyle of thanksgiving will increase your capacity to receive! "He who offers a sacrifice of thanksgiving honors Me" (Ps. 50:23).

Chapter Nineteen

Joy for the Journey

"Do not be grieved, for the joy of the Lord is your strength."
Nehemiah 8:10b

I hope that you have learned so much through these chapters, but we are still missing the final ingredient—JOY! It is the icing on the cake, the crème de la crème. I cannot begin to express how wonderfully important this often missing element is! Joy is possibly the least understood and the least used of all of the ways to love your life, yet it is the element that gives us strength and gives us zest for life. And it is probably also the easiest of all the ways to love your life!

Joy: everyone wants it. People spend a lot of money trying to create it in their lives. However, real joy cannot be bought and real joy is not dictated to by circumstances! So what can we do when we have less than perfect moments? What do we do with sad moments or trials? The Bible says to count it all joy! If you have not marked this in your Bible, you certainly will want to. "My brethren, count it all joy when ye fall into divers temptations; Knowing this, that the trying of your faith worketh patience. But let patience have her perfect work, that ye may be perfect and entire, wanting nothing" (Jas. 1:2–4 KJV). "Perfect and entire, wanting nothing"! Wow! I want that. I don't know about you, but I have missed that more times than I've gotten it right. And you? How have you done counting every test, every trial and every temptation as joy? Okay, so I am not the only one. If we want to love our life, we're going to have to radically change in every area, we're going to have to count it all joy.

With joy we come full circle. Do you remember the first question we asked? "If your life never changed could you be happy?" Well, we have come a long way since that question. Hopefully you have learned what things you cannot change, what things you can change about you, what areas you need to speak the Word in and what areas you need to stop fantasizing about. If you will recall, we said: be on the alert against fantasy! Why? Because it robs us of all the joy in our lives. No circumstance, event, holiday, person, or lifestyle can match up to what you have built it up to be in your mind. If we can choose to not fantasize in certain areas, we can begin to see joy break loose.

Truth:

Joy is paramount in our Christian walk!

Yet depending on your personality, joy seems to come easier for some than it does for others. However, God knew this, so He wanted to make sure that we had no out. He made joy part of the fruit of the Spirit! Which means every believer is required to walk in it regardless of his or her personality! Upon reflection, I thought I better really learn what biblical joy is and be able to impart it in an effective way. To do this, I began to study hard on everything I could find having to do with joy, listening to teaching tapes, reading books, and of course, poring over my Bible. As I began to study, I thought I should take a personal inventory, and I recommend that you do the same. It is important to know the areas of our strengths and weaknesses.

As I began to look at my life I realized: I am good at loving God, setting goals, being focused, and even stepping out in faith to do things that look impossible. However, I am not that great at joy! Oh, I am happy and I laugh, but that is different from *joy*. Joy is not happiness; joy is not a funny joke or a quick sense of humor. In fact, some of the people who have the best sense of humor have no joy in their lives. They are just naturally quick-witted, but that does not mean they are joyful. In fact, some of the world's greatest comedians are constantly depressed.

What Is Joy?

When everything in your day goes wrong, that could possibly go wrong, do you smile, throw your head back, laugh, and count it all joy? No stressing out? No getting grumpy? No feeling fearful? That is what having real Bible joy is like. How do you rate?

Several years ago, Kevin and I went to see "Fiddler On The Roof" at a local theatre. One of my favorite lines is in the first couple of minutes of the production. (I couldn't keep from laughing when I heard it). The mother is kneading bread, she's sweating and laboring, and her little girl comes scampering happily into the room and says something like this, "Mama, I finished my chores. Can I go play?" and the mother, who was working very hard, says flatly, "You have feet, don't ya? Well use 'em!" The girl takes that as a yes, gets excited, and runs out. Then her little sister comes in and says, "Can I go too, Mama?" The mother does not answer, so the little girl runs out happily to go play.

The girls absolutely know that Mama loves them, would do anything for them, and that she would lay down her life for them, but they also know that Mama is tired, Mama is grumpy, Mama is stressed, and Mama is overworked! How does that happen so often when we grow up?

Your average grumpy adult started out as a happy little child. In fact, I have never seen a little child who is *continually* grumpy. This was true even when Kevin and I lived in Nicaragua, which is the second poorest country in the Western hemisphere. Many of the children there were literally raised on the streets or in little houses made from scraps of aluminum. Even without enough food and shelter, these children managed to play, laugh and sing. Life has a way of stealing their joy, but it is not because they didn't start with it. Little children are born happy and full of hope. Much of the time, they go around with their toys and sing. The mother's response in "Fiddler On The Roof" didn't even discourage the girls. They were still happy because they were little, but if they follow the natural course of life, they are going to become grumpy mamas one day, too. They are going to end up just the same as their mother.

Every generation thinks they are going to make it into being happy, joyful, carefree adults without any effort. However, it takes a lot of effort. Joy does not happen just because you want it to! It is a fight of faith! We have fought so many other battles that many times we haven't realized that the first battle should have been for joy; joy despite circumstances! That is worth fighting for.

If you leave a car without maintaining it, it naturally corrodes. If you leave it in a field, it will begin to rust. Not having joy is like rust. Have you ever been around rust? I hate it so much, because if you get near rust and it rubs off onto your clothes, you cannot get it out again. When you rub against a grumpy person, it is like rust and it can take the whole day to get their grumpiness off of you. Every one of us will have to make a choice at some time in our lives to be full of joy, not grumpy and serious. We must choose to go against the natural flow. Look at the world; the natural flow is grumpy and serious.

The excuse is often, "I have a lot of responsibilities." This is a cop out. When we say we have so many responsibilities that it makes us grumpy, we have allowed "the responsibilities" to be ours. However, when we are getting the work done and we are happy and joyful it is because we've allowed "the responsibilities" to be God's! The Bible says to "roll our cares over on the Lord, because He cares for us" (1 Peter 5:7). God cares for us so much, but often we're *not* doing the rolling over onto Him because "we can handle it." The problem is no one else around us can handle us "handling it." It is important for the sake of what God created Christians to look like: bright, happy, shining-faced Christians everywhere we go; that we learn how to walk in real joy! When we do that, it will literally roll years off of us. Do you want a face-lift? Just learn how to walk in joy! That is the only *true* face-lift you will ever really need!

God can make us carefree like little children all over again. What is supposed to be the difference between little children and grown-ups? Little children walk in childish happiness. As little children grow into men and women of God, with the many challenges and responsibilities that come with life, they are designed to grow in wisdom. Wisdom produces joy! Where we have lacked joy we have lacked wisdom. Wisdom is supposed to be the main difference between a child and an adult. Children are to have happiness, but adults are supposed to have seasoned joy, which is a much more solid and powerful substance.

Stolen Joy

There are four simple ways joy is stolen:

1. Taking yourself too seriously.
2. Caring too much what other people think.
3. Not being able to recognize the difference between mere inconvenience and major catastrophe.
4. Real crisis.

I will talk about number four (crises) a little later, but right now I want to talk about the first three. We have all been culprits of numbers one, two and three at some time or another. However, they are life stealers! So I thought it would be most effective to share a story with you that illustrates the importance of overcoming the first three flaws.

A True Story

I once heard a true story about a certain lady who was a guest speaker at a large conference.

At this conference, dinner was served first. When this guest speaker was on her last course, she looked down and realized that she hadn't painted her fingernails. Now it would not have been so bad if she had had *no* fingernail polish on, except that she did, and it was badly chipped. Unfortunately, people often look at guest speakers' hands. She thought, "Oh my goodness, I forgot to paint my fingernails! Well, while everyone is eating dessert, I will go to the bathroom and paint them." So she excused herself and made her way to the bathroom.

She decided while in there that she needed to go to the bathroom. So as she sat on the toilet she took out her fingernail polish and began to paint her fingernails. She finished painting her fingernails, and then the reality of what she had done hit her.

She realized that she could not pull up her pantyhose because her nails were wet. So, as gracefully as she could, she got off the toilet and hopped over to the hand dryer, where she put her hands underneath. (Now, for any of you who are unaware of this, if you put wet nail polish under heat, it gets twice as bad as it was before. It gets very, very gloopy.)

So as she was standing with her hands underneath the hand dryer, watching her nail polish get gloopier, she began to panic, thinking, "Maybe if I leave it there a bit longer, it'll get better!" By this time, about ten minutes had already lapsed. People were finished with their desserts and her husband knocked on the door and said, "Honey, they are ready for you to speak."

Now, it was one of those bathroom stalls that only one person fits in, where you can lock the door. She unlocked the door and said, "Honey! Here, quick; come help me!" She said, "Honey, I cannot get my pantyhose up!" So he began to try and help her pull up her pantyhose. (For the uninitiated, when you put on pantyhose you have to give a kick, a jump, or a squat to get them up that last bit. I do not even put on pantyhose around my husband anymore because he laughs at me with the final kick!)

So as her husband tried to help her, she was kicking her legs and trying to help him get her pantyhose back up. The couple were making all kinds of noise, bumping into the walls, etc.! More time had passed, and the lady in charge of the whole conference knocked on the bathroom door. The lady hosting the event said, "We're all finished and are ready for you to speak now." The guest speaker said, "I will be out in a minute. Just give me one more minute."

The poor speaker must have been thinking, "How am I going to explain to the lady in charge of the conference why my husband and I are in the bathroom together and innocently banging against the bathroom walls?" As soon as they could hear the conference lady walk away, they fell on the floor and broke out laughing hysterically. The speaker had little bits of nail polish all up and down her pantyhose! Her fingernails were far worse! Fingernail polish was all over her hands, but they just laughed hysterically. It was so bad. It definitely would have ranked as one of those most embarrassing moments in a person's life. Amazingly, miraculously, she was able to see the humor in the entire thing, but most of us would not. Most of us (women anyway) would have cried. We would have gotten frustrated when we realized what happened, embarrassed when our husband came in and mortified at the end result, not to mention what everyone else could have possibly been thinking (and understandably would have been thinking). The speaker of course gave her speech in all the dignity she could muster.

I want to ask, how many of you would have responded the way she did? When life throws you those unexpected curves, or you make silly decisions that you realize afterward were a mistake; if you laugh hysterically at it, it will make life so much easier.

This woman chose the right response. That situation had a lot of humor in it, and she was able to see it. If we have a problem with: 1.) Taking ourselves too seriously, 2.) Caring too much what other people think, and 3.) Not recognizing the difference between mere inconvenience and major catastrophe, then we would naturally think this was a major catastrophe. However, in the scheme of life, this really was not a major ordeal. It just could have felt like it at the moment. It is important that we are able to grow into this place of discerning the difference. When I read this story I thought, *"This is a great way for me to gauge how I am doing on the joy front!"*

Much of life is a series of incorrect responses. We cry when we should laugh, we get mad when we should see the joy in something, the humor in it all. Obviously, for most people, being able to walk in this level of joy is not natural. If you have a lot going on, if you have children of any size, if you own your own business, etc., then it can be very, challenging to walk in this level of joy. I am believing God that as you read this chapter that you will begin to break through into this next level of joy. How can we possibly ever love our lives unless we can do that? This is paramount in our learning to love our lives! But *joy* is even more than just a step in learning to love your life!

Please read this next statement out loud and ponder it.

Truth:

Joy is the *bridge* between faith and our answer to prayer!

Just like thankfulness, joy can open the door to the miraculous in our lives. If you need a miracle in your life, if you've been praying over the same thing over and over, you've pressed, you've prayed, you've done everything you know how to do, then maybe it is time to add the secret ingredient of joy to bridge your answer to prayer. Joy truly is that important bridge. If you will begin to notice, throughout Scripture joy makes waiting for our answer and staying in faith so much easier. According to James 1:2–4, the patience we learn from going through challenges and staying the course while we are waiting for our answers to prayer is reason enough to be joyful. James says that patience, that all important fruit of the Spirit, will have her perfect work in us, making us *perfect, entire, wanting nothing,* if we let her. Patience is not being learned, however, if we are testy, angry with everyone, or being difficult in general. So how do we stay the course while we are waiting or while we are inconvenienced, or while we are embarrassed? Joy! Joy means that you really believe that God is good and you are going to get your breakthrough, so you are choosing to be happy ahead of time (more on that later). Joy also means that no matter what your present scenario, you love your life! You are not waiting for it to start. You are loving it now and choosing to enjoy today!

Real Crisis

Now for number four: How should we deal with a real crisis? We count it all joy! "My brethren, count it all joy when ye fall into divers temptations; Knowing this, that the trying of your faith worketh patience. But let patience have her perfect work, that ye may be perfect and entire, wanting nothing" (Jas. 1:2–4 KJV).

Job

How many of you would say that Job had a serious crisis on his hands? All of his children died. His wife told him to just curse God and die. He lost all of his money. He lost everything. That's a crisis. Yet, what Scripture do we find in this book? "At destruction and famine thou shalt laugh, neither shalt thou be afraid of the beasts of the earth" (Job 5:22). I didn't say that, God said that. If you're going to believe the Bible, you're going to have to believe Job 5:22. Amazingly, also found in the book of Job is this verse: "He will yet fill your mouth with laughter and your lips with joyful shouting" (Job 8:21 KJV). Many crises are not bearable without the wonderful gift of joy being placed right in the middle of them. The joy of the Lord is our strength and it is a salve to a wounded heart. When we allow the joy of the Lord into our crisis, it helps us remember that this world is not our eternal home and that this life and its tears are only temporary. Joy helps us keep perspective. As difficult as Jobs' trial was, as deep as his valley was, this righteous man came through to become *twice* the man he was before, literally. His "patience" paid tremendous dividends … yours will, too. God will reward you.

Why should we want to rejoice in times of famine? Because praise and shouts of joy will send ambushments against our enemy. "And when they began to sing and to praise, the LORD set ambushments against the children of Ammon, Moab, and mount Seir, which were come against Judah; and they were smitten" (2 Chr. 20:22 KJV). Over and over in the Bible we see this as a pattern. When Israel, under King Jehoshaphat, was facing an army that was so huge it couldn't even be numbered, (the Bible says this army was like the sands of the sea; 2 Chron. 20), God told him to go out, confront the enemy, but let the Lord do the fighting. So the king didn't put the army in array, but rather the choir. They went out thanking and praising God. Sure enough, God went in and fought the battle for Israel. He caused confusion in the Enemy's camp and they destroyed one another. It took Israel three days to collect the spoil. What Satan meant to destroy them God used to bless them! Why? Because God inhabits the praises of His people (Ps. 22:3)! Praise in many ways is the ultimate statement of faith in God, and when we are in a real mess we certainly need God to inhabit it. The quickest way to bring God on the scene is through praising Him. Praise always brings joy and relief, and most importantly it brings God.

Now let's look at Habakkuk 3:17–19 (KJV) "Although the fig tree shall not blossom, neither shall fruit be in the vines; the labor of the olive shall fail, and the fields shall yield no meat; the flock shall be cut off from the fold, and there shall be no herd in the stalls ..." This is a crisis if you are in an agricultural society, as a lot of societies were back then. No figs, no fruit, no meat, no olives, nothing in the field ... yet... *"Yet I will rejoice in the LORD, I will joy in the God of my salvation. The LORD God is my strength, and he will make my feet like hinds' feet, and he will make me to walk upon mine high places."* In the Amplified version, it says: "I will exult in the [victorious] God of my salvation!" We see Habakkuk is definitely expecting a turn around. He's not rejoicing in the sorrow or the lack, he is rejoicing in the victorious God of his salvation. At what point do we decide that God is bigger than our problems? At what point do we decide that God is bigger than famine? God *is* bigger than our circumstances. Every time we magnify our circumstances, we are in reality saying that God is not enough. When we do this we are in essence making the problem our god and bowing down before it in sorrow.

But when we look at the problem and praise in the midst of the problem, what are we saying? We are saying God is bigger than our problem. We are worshipping God and praising God. We are saying, "He is the victorious God of my salvation." In fact, we need to become as good at it as Habakkuk was. Let's look again at how incredible Habakkuk's praise and confidence toward God was in the midst of real crisis. Let's look at verse 19 in the Amplified version. "The Lord God is my Strength, my personal bravery, and my invincible army; He makes my feet like hinds' feet and will make me to walk, [not to stand still in terror, but to walk] and make [spiritual] progress upon my high places [of trouble, suffering, or responsibility]!"

It is so important that we do not let fear paralyze us. Fear is a tactic of the Enemy to keep us away from our victory. Let me give you an example. Back in Texas there are a lot of deer. You have to be careful driving at night, because when deer see a car's headlights they freeze. If they would just move over two feet or keep walking, no one would ever hit them. They normally see the lights in plenty of time to get out of the way, but when they see the car lights, fear grips them and they freeze. That's what many people do when they see a problem, they freeze, or they get mad, as though that's going to help. But that is not God's plan or strategy. His plan is to have you "make (spiritual) progress upon the high places (of trouble, suffering or responsibility)". God has a wonderful plan, an effective and cunning plan. That plan is not inactive but very active and to activate it, you need joy and rejoicing.

What we are really saying when we rejoice, is:

1. "Enemy, you lost!"
2. "I believe Jesus is Lord!"
3. "I believe that God's promises for me will come to pass in my life!"

The book of Philippians 1:28 tells us to be "in no way alarmed by your opponents—which is a sign of destruction for them, but of salvation for you, and that too, from God." When we laugh with a full heart of love and rejoice in the Lord, we have no fear (unlike the deer). It will literally leave our enemies confounded. Joy in God changes everything. It makes speaking the Word in faith so fun. It makes all the "have to's" in life fun. It makes the mundane sparkle. It makes life worth living.

One of the other greatest ways to express joy is laughter. There is nothing like a good ole' belly laugh. In the next chapter, hold on to your hat and get ready to laugh.

Prayer

Dear Heavenly Father,

Thank You for Your power working in me right now to count it *all* joy while I am going through the trials and the valleys of life. You have promised to strengthen me with Your joy. I believe that promise, and I receive it today in Jesus' name. I know that though I have sown in tears,

I will reap in joy and I will doubtless come through this with a smile on my face, carrying my reward with me! (James 1:23; Psalm 126)

In Your mighty Name, Jesus,
Amen.

Truth in Action:

1. Where do you take yourself too seriously? (How can you change it?)

   ____

   ____

   ____

   ____

2. Where do you care too much what others think? How can you change that?

   ____

   ____

   ____

   ____

3. Are you a detailer and unable to recognize the difference (in the heat of the moment) between mere inconvenience and major catastrophe?

   ____

   ____

   ____

4. Are you in a real crisis? Begin to let go of fear and begin to rejoice. Write down how you can do that.

____

____

____

____

____

Steps to Loving Your Journey

- **Repent from the sin of dissatisfaction.**
- **Stop envying others and wishing you had someone else's life.**
- **Learn to love your life:** Do not curse your day by starting it out saying, "If my life was only different," or "I hate my life." Instead say, "God, You gave my today, and I choose to love it! Now, what can I do to make it special?"
- **Get rid of the "ifs":** ("If this or that changed, I would be happy.") No! What are you enjoying now? Those who enjoy what they have receive more!
- **Love the process:** Our lives are a constant journey. If we do not learn to love the process, we miss our entire lives!
- **Contentment for the journey:** "But Godliness with contentment is great gain" (1 Tim. 6:6). Remember that whatever you are going through is not the big picture; it is just today's picture! Enjoy life today!
- **Peace for the journey:**

  a) Settle Salvation
  b) Never be at odds with God
  c) Be at peace with yourself
  d) Be at peace with others
- **Grace for the journey**: "My grace is sufficient for you, for My power is perfected in weakness" (2 Cor. 12:9). Daily ask God for His grace to help you love your life, complete your journey, and go the extra mile.
- **Spend time with God:** This daily time with God will send you out with joy and strength for the day, a heart for your responsibilities, and a passion to glorify God in all you do.
- **Rest for the journey:** "And He said, 'My presence shall go with you and I will give you rest'" (Ex. 33:14). "Therefore let us be diligent to enter that rest …"(Heb. 4:11).
- **Learn not to dread:** Pray, "I am going to do the will of God today without thinking about tomorrow."[79] "Casting *all* your cares upon Him, for He cares for you" (1 Peter 5:7).
- **A journey of love:** "Greater love has no one than this, that one lay down his life for his friends" (John 15:13). Love covers, heals, makes faith work, keeps you from having a critical spirit, teaches you to focus on good, and helps you to forgive.

- **Faith for the journey:** Faith is for getting the job done! It is for reaching the next generation for Jesus. Loving your life starts with making sure you are on the right journey (God's journey for your life, not the world's journey for you).
- **Do not control the journey:** Pray: "Father, forgive me for trying to control my journey and other's journeys. I give my life anew into Your hands and I let go! I place my loved ones into Your loving hands."
- **A word for the journey:** "For he that will love life, and see good days, let him refrain his tongue from evil, and his lips that they speak no guile …" (1 Peter 3:10–11). There is nothing more powerful than the Word of God, especially in your mouth and in your heart!
- **Thanks for the journey:** Cultivating a lifestyle of thanksgiving will increase your capacity to receive! "He who offers a sacrifice of thanksgiving honors Me" (Ps. 50:23).
- **Joy for the journey:** "Count it all joy" (Jas. 1:2)! "When they began singing and praising, the LORD set ambushments against their enemy" (2 Chron. 20:22). "At destruction and famine thou shalt laugh" (Job 5:22).

Chapter Twenty

Get Ready to Laugh

"Then our mouth was filled with laughter
And our tongue with joyful shouting."
Psalm 126:2a

Laughter is truly God's medicine. "A merry heart doeth good like a medicine" (Prov. 17:22a KJV). It appears science is catching onto this fact. Laughter research shows that laughter boosts the immune system and cleans out your lymphatic system. "Laughter increases oxygenation of your body at both the cellular and organ level .... It is also interesting to note that cancer cells are destroyed in the presence of oxygen. In fact, many parasites and bacteria do not survive well in the presence of oxygen, and to the extent that you can circulate extra oxygen throughout your body, you can help prevent, or in some cases treat, these diseases." This research also shows that laughter boosts your circulation and in addition to that, "when you laugh, you generate a wealth of healing biochemicals."[80]

The Cancer Treatment Centers of America report, "After evaluating participants before and after a humorous event (e.g., a comedy video), studies have revealed that episodes of laughter helped to reduce pain, decrease stress-related hormones and boost the immune system in participants ... CTCA offers humor therapy sessions, also known as Laughter Clubs or humor groups, to help cancer patients and their families use and enjoy laughter as a tool for healing. These leader-led groups take patients through a number of laugh-related exercises including fake laughter and laughter greetings."[81]

"Laughing Clubs" similar to this meet together each morning around the world. British comedian John Cleese asked a physician in charge of one such therapy group in Mumbai about the effects. The doctor proceeded to explain how laughing strengthens the immune system and more. Doubtful, John responded, "Well, it feels like we're all only faking the laugh." "True," said the doctor, "But the body does not actually know the difference." Ahh! How interesting! We can see the importance in beginning to act on something before we feel it. This is actually an important principle. This is true not only in the area of laughter, but in any area. If we are dictated to by our emotions, we are doomed to a life of failure. A plane has to begin to move fast on the ground before it will ever lift off the ground. There is an initial momentum that must happen before the law of lift and thrust will take over. It is always uncomfortable and feels artificial to break inertia, however, the results are well worth it.

Here's Where it Gets Fun!

The long and the short of it is: when God created laughter, He really created something special! And as we will find out, faith in God expressed through laughter not only heals the body, but also heals circumstances. Remember that life is never so perfect for anyone that it is easy to be satisfied. You have to choose to love your life because there are always reasons not to. There will always be something you cannot have (remember Adam and Eve). Do not let that stop you from enjoying what you do have! If we can learn to sing in those moments that we want to cry, we can learn to love our lives.

Guideposts

Here is a true story that Joyce Meyer read out of *Guideposts* magazine:

> This is a true story about a man that worked down on a Southern farm in the United States. He said, "I remember the summer afternoon in 1925, because that was the day Mama told me how she kept going when she was all tuckered out. On that hot afternoon, Mama and I and my seven brothers and sisters had just come in from the field where we had been picking beans in the scorching Alabama sun. We were tired right to the bone. We all flopped down, everyone except Mama. She went to the sink and started to wash her face because she had to go out again. Mama was raising us by herself and she needed two jobs. She worked in the fields all day long, and then in the evenings she left home to cook for another family. I often wondered how she found her strength. The answer somehow lay in her singing. Mama would sing in church of course, but she would sing with just as much heart in the fields or in the kitchen. Always she was making music, like she was pulling energy from her songs. And that summer afternoon when I was just a little boy of ten and very tired, she put her secret into words. "John, when you're down, that is the time to sing." Mama told me as she headed out the door for the foreman's house. "John, sing until the power comes down!" [82]

That is the power of joy! What an amazing mom! What an amazing choice! We all have that choice and many times under easier circumstances. Remember, God really inhabits the praises of His people. Praise brings God, and God brings joy, and joy brings strength for the task at hand!

Viktor Frankl

Viktor Frankl, a concentration camp survivor, said this: "The last of all human freedoms is the ability to choose one's own attitude regardless of circumstances." He said that while in a concentration camp, where he was being tortured, he felt he could still choose a good attitude, and he did.[83] Yet so many times we find it hard to have a good attitude at work, where no one is really torturing us. We're not in a concentration camp, we're not behind barbed wire, and yet it is still a challenge. However, the choice is always ours. We cannot forget that.

We need to choose joy and laughter. Do not be angry and do not choose to want to get even, even if something is not right or another employee or a customer does not treat you well. Getting even is like taking poison and then expecting your enemy to die. It is important that we do things God's way.

Thomas Edison

It took Thomas Edison hundreds of tries to perfect the light bulb, and yet he kept seeing each failure as a lesson learned on how not to do something a certain way. He refused to give in to discouragement. In December of 1914, the famous inventor's laboratory caught on fire and burned to the ground. "Legend has it that the fire was so extraordinary that, upon seeing and understanding the scope of the disaster, Edison sent word to friends and family to 'Get down here quick .... You may never have another chance to see anything like this again!' Within hours after the fire had been extinguished, Edison began a complete rehabilitation of the plant."[84] That is the kind of attitude we need to have. Some people would have seen that as a catastrophe, but Edison clearly did not. He just started all over again without all the negative emotion or grieving the loss. We have to get to that point of seeing catastrophes for what they truly are and not what we think they are!

Of course, many of us are not faced with the challenges of an early inventor or the tyranny of a concentration camp. We would all like to think that in such extreme circumstances we would choose joy, but would we in reality? The following stories are a few examples from more recent years and hopefully will help you see the principle at work in normal day-to-day scenarios. Certainly, if we are to ever choose joy in the midst of major trial, then it must first start in our everyday lives.

Thelma Wells

Known as a trailblazer for black women and prominent international speaker and author, Thelma Wells, a vast resource of wisdom, says:

> "As a mother, I find solace in praying for my children during the good times and the bad. To help my children and myself get focused on how to deal with problems, I ask my children if they have listened to praise music before they called to tell me about their woes. If they haven't, I ask them to call back after they have—unless, of course, it is an emergency.
>
> I believe one of the best ways to get in a praying mood is to listen to music that ushers you into a spirit of adoration. That, in turn, takes your mind off the problem and helps you focus on the Problem-Solver. While I wait for them to call back, I follow my own instructions. I sing, listen to Gospel music, and pray. Usually, when they phone me again, both of us are in harmony with each other and the Lord … [85]

Imagine if every time someone called you with a woe that was your response, and that was what you did also. It is time each of us takes a giant step forward in the ways of God.

Barbara Johnson

Award-winning Christian author and "Women of Faith" Speaker Emeritus, Barbara Johnson won the hearts of millions with her trademark wit and humor formed in the fire of adversity. She writes:

> Christians sometimes have more trouble handling trouble than the world does, because we think everything should be perfect … We think we should handle it perfectly, we think our lives should be perfect, we think everything should be perfect. Too often our

faith is shallow. We cling to the padded cross instead of the 'old rugged cross' of the hymn. What should set us apart is our trust, our ability to let God loose in our circumstances rather than forever trying to control them ourselves." [86]

"The Bible shows that we are an Easter Sunday people living in a Good Friday World. That means we are destined for joy no matter how difficult our daily life. Something in us responds to the happiness other people experience because we glimpse life as God intends it to be! It is an image imprinted in the spirit of Easter morning: pure, powerful, and potent, like the resurrection."[87]

"So go out there and help create all the happy endings you can. Do not be afraid of tears- or those of neighbors, family, friends, or strangers. You will have your share of Good Fridays, but Easter will come… Remember, moist eyes are good. Trembling lips are acceptable. Quivering voices will not hurt anyone. Those tears may disorient some people, or send others running for cover, they are signals there is something deeper to be understood." [88]

First Peter says, "That the trial of your faith, being much more precious than of gold that perisheth, though it be tried with fire, might be found unto praise and honor and glory at the appearing of Jesus Christ: Whom, having not seen, ye love; in whom, though now ye see him not, yet believing, ye rejoice with joy unspeakable and full of glory: Receiving the end of your faith, even the salvation of your souls" (1 Peter 1:7–9 KJV). God considers the trying of our faith more precious than gold. This fallen world is a trial, yet if we look to the author and finisher of our faith (Heb. 12:2) our faith can become as precious as gold. Always remember: "The thief cometh not, but for to steal, and to kill, and to destroy: I am come that they might have life, and that they might have it more abundantly" (John 10:10).

Also remember, laughter is a fantastic way to get out of the "furnace" (probably one of the best ways to get out of the furnace). If you have patience with faith *and* joy, you win! Why? Because the Enemy has no patience. He has no fruit of the Spirit. He is impatient. The Enemy is a quitter. So if you will not quit, he will quit. If we realize that and begin to develop patience, how great is this life going to look! We will have every victory. If we do not quit, he does! Counting it all joy helps you to be patient as you wait in faith, believing!

I have heard it said, "If I do not rejoice, the Devil will think he won!" Why? Because the Enemy is not omniscient, he is not omnipresent. He does not know if he's winning or losing except by looking at your face. So when we begin to laugh, he thinks, "I am losing!" He doesn't know! We are the ones who give him the clues. The Enemy may say, "You are good-for-nothing. You are horrible." And if you mutter, "I am good-for-nothing. I am horrible." he knows you received his words because you are speaking what he said. But we were created to speak what God said, not what the Enemy says. Instead, when a thought like that comes, begin to say out loud "I am very valuable and I am made in God's image!" Thoughts can be so powerful that we often can only overcome them with the spoken Word. So remember, the Enemy may say, "Your children are never going to change in that area," and if you repeat that thought out loud, "My children are never going to change in that area," he's won. Do not let him do that.

There is terrific power in agreement, especially when that agreement is with what God is speaking to you. His Word will not return void without accomplishing what He sent it to do (Isa. 55:8–10). Do not give the Enemy the same privilege by agreeing with him and repeating what he has said to you. Refuse to live out his prophecy over your life! God has a better plan. Agree with Him and rejoice all the way!

Laughing: The Faith Agent

We see the book of Job says, "At destruction and famine thou shalt laugh" (Job 5:22a KJV). But is there anyone else in the Bible that laughed? "And Sarah said, God hath made me to laugh, so that all that hear will laugh with me" (Gen. 21:6 KJV). Sarah laughed and laughed at the absurdity of a ninety-year old woman having a baby. She knew everyone that saw her would laugh with joy, too! How fun! This is, of course, in contrast to the first time she laughed at hearing this divine plan: she laughed then, too, doubting, but after an encounter with God, she believed. Her laugh of faith had power in it. Joy gives strength, as we've said before. And this is exactly what happened to Sarah: "Through faith also Sarah herself received strength to conceive seed, and was delivered of a child when she was past age, because she judged him faithful who had promised" (Heb. 11:11 KJV). How did Sarah receive her strength to conceive? "For the joy of the LORD is your strength" (Neh. 8:10 KJV). Sarah started out laughing in unbelief, but ended up laughing in faith! [89]

Why laughter? Because God is interested in you receiving strength to conceive and birth His promises! The Scottish writer, George MacDonald (1824–1905), said, "It is the heart that is not yet sure of its God that is afraid to laugh in His presence." [90] We need strength for our miracle, and laughter is key.

The Bible says that God sits in the heavens and laughs at the scheming Enemy (Psa. 2:4). He is not afraid and neither should we be. We can be confident in His loving arms. If we know that we are loved, we laugh. Little children giggle and laugh, especially when they feel secure. It is a great delight to a parent when a child is giggling with joy and laughter. We too need to realize we are secure in God's arms. God loves it when we are so excited about Him and so unimpressed by the problems that we laugh and magnify Him. (Thus minimizing the problems.)

"A happy heart is good medicine and a cheerful mind works healing, but a broken spirit dries up the bones" (Prov. 17:22 Amp). A merry heart actually brings healing into your life and body. Now for us to have a happy heart, God wants us to begin to realize that the former things are past. When we focus on the past it steals our joy! God will turn it all around if we trust in Him. God is going to do His part, but we have got to do our part. God wants to do something new and wonderful in your life. Will you let Him? Will you let go of the past? Can you let go of anger and offenses? Can you throw your head back and laugh?

If things are not going quite right, you may need a new approach (remember Einstein's definition of insanity? Doing the same thing over and over but looking for a different result.[91]) God says He will not "put new wine in an old wineskin." (Matt. 9:17) Do not be afraid to throw out an old mindset. Try a joyful approach (Luke 5:37). It brings God on the scene. "In His presence is fullness of joy" (Ps. 16:11).

Let's look at a few men who did just that under extraordinary circumstances.

Laughing at Impossibilities

Norvel Hayes, a minister of the Gospel, had a restaurant business that was failing. He felt moved by the Lord to step out in joyful faith. He started going daily, parking across the street from his restaurant and laughing and rejoicing by faith for twenty minutes. He did it every day until all of a sudden people started pouring in! [92]

Another joyful example: One particular day, the late Rev. Kenneth E. Hagin (who traveled and ministered for nearly seventy years) found that his face had become partially paralyzed, and by the time he went to bed that evening his face was completely and totally paralyzed. The Enemy, "the father of lies," was giving him thoughts like, "This time you're not going to get your healing," etc. Kenneth Hagin answered those thoughts and said out loud, "I do not have to get my healing, because Jesus already got it 2,000 years ago!" You know what he did? He felt led to laugh and rejoice in the Lord. He began to laugh and made himself laugh and rejoice in God's goodness by faith for forty-five minutes. At the end of the forty-five minutes, the entire paralysis left, every bit of it was completely gone.[93] Sounds amazing, but it really happened.

This reminds me of Isaac. Isaac's name, literally translated, means "Ha! Ha!" Sarah laughed so hard she named him "laughter." How's that for a constant reminder of joy for God's promises! Well, when Isaac was a grown man, he came to live in Gerar where his father, Abraham, had once lived.

> "Now all the wells which his father's servants had dug in the days of Abraham his father, the Philistines stopped up by filling them with earth … Then Isaac *dug again* the wells of water which had been dug in the days of his father Abraham… and he gave them the same names which his father had given them" (Gen. 26:15, 18).

So Isaac dug out the wells of Abraham that had been stopped up by the Philistines. Nothing in Scripture is coincidental. I do not think it is a coincidence that Isaac (laughter) undug the wells that had been stopped up by the enemy. Joy has that much power. Joy has enough power to dig up your stopped up wells too. God will empower you to undo the work of the Enemy in your life and reclaim your rightful inheritance just like He did for Isaac. Has anyone dumped "trash" into your well? If your problems have persisted despite *your* best efforts, maybe it is time to add joy to your arsenal!

The Bible says "Therefore with joy shall ye draw water out of the wells of salvation" (Isa. 12:3 KJV). One thing the Body of Christ has been lacking too long is joy. However, *joy* is the ladle or bucket (depending on your joy level) that draws water out of the wells of salvation (Isa. 12:3 KJV). Salvation not only for us, but for our loved ones and friends. When people see the joy you're dipping out despite circumstances, they too will begin to want to dip into the wells of salvation.

Laughing All the Way to the Bank

A story is told of a certain man who became president of a university. He inherited the position, along with a debt of millions. At one of his board meetings they were discussing the amount of debt and what to do about it. The board felt the situation was so bad that they were going to have to close the university.

As I believe the story goes, someone phoned during their board meeting and the man on the other end said, "I want my money," and told them about an additional huge debt that the university owed. At this point, the young president began to laugh right there on the phone. He laughed so hard that he couldn't stop laughing. The board members thought he was having a nervous breakdown, but he was not. He laughed so hard that he had to leave. He laughed all day and maybe into the next day. He then began to tithe off what the University was bringing in; every student fee, every book, anything anyone bought, even if anyone rented the auditorium. Universities do not normally work this way. That is unheard of! Praise God his board of regents allowed him to do this. They were so far in debt that they could not afford to give 10 percent away. (Imagine how many people, churches and missions boards could be helped if CEOs tithed off their company's gross!) But he understood that God's Kingdom works opposite to the world! And do you know that in record time, God sent provisions to pay off all the University's debts! His laughter was faith in a huge God. He knew he didn't have the answer, but he knew God did. He clearly knew anxiety would only make it worse. Laughter gave him the strength he needed to step into God's Word on a whole new level.

Just like this young president and just like Isaac, we have all inherited wells in our lives that are stopped up. Our inheritance is at stake if we do not unstop them, be it business, relationships or poor health. Joy is definitely paramount in having the strength from God to unstop these wells.

Truth:

One of the greatest keys to your success is joy!

"Rejoice in the Lord always: and again I say, Rejoice" (Php. 4:4 KJV). In the four short chapters of the book of Philippians Paul says to rejoice thirteen times. Do you know where he was when he wrote the book of Philippians? Prison. Profound! Why are we told to rejoice so many times? Because God does not want us to live this life with a yoke of iron. In chapter 28 of Deuteronomy we find the blessing and the curse. In this portion of Scripture, we discover that part of the curse is life without joy. "Because you did not serve the LORD your God with joy and a glad heart, for the abundance of all things; therefore you shall serve your enemies … [with] … an iron yoke …" (Deut. 28:47–48). The choice is up to us. We are either serving God in joy, or we are serving the Enemy in sorrow. The Enemy's yoke is iron. God's yoke is easy and light! (Matt. 11:30) As you begin to press into God's easy, light yoke, you will begin to produce the fruit of joy. We need to remember that this fruit of joy is so different from happiness because it is not motivated by circumstances.

Nugget:

If you do not have the fruit of joy in your life, it may be that you are under the wrong yoke. Even as Christians, we often find ourselves making choices each day that put us under the Enemy's yoke of iron. This does not mean we love God less, it just means that daily and throughout our day we have made wrong decisions, thus opening the door to a harsh and cruel task master. The proof of our choices is whether we have the fruit of joy or we do not. If we do not, it opens up the door to a myriad of negative emotions. But a simple shift from trusting in our own strength, to trusting in God again-praising Him, and reclining in Him- will move you to the Savior's light and easy yoke. The result will be joy.

The Wigglesworth Shuffle

The late Dr. Lester Sumrall, tells the story of a conversation he had with one of the pioneers of the Pentecostal revival that occurred a century ago, a great evangelist of faith, Smith Wigglesworth: "Brother Wigglesworth, how is it that you look the same every time I come? How do you feel?" He bellowed at me like a bull and said, "I do not ever ask Smith Wigglesworth how he feels! I tell him!" I asked, "How do you get up in the morning?" He said, "I jump out of bed! I dance before the Lord for at least ten to twelve minutes—high-speed dancing. I jump up and down and run around my room telling God how great He is, how glad I am to be associated with Him and to be His child." After this, he would take a cold shower, read the Bible for an hour, and then open his mail to see what God would have him do that day. He was an extremely remarkable man, totally sold out to God.[94] He died at age eighty-seven with all of his teeth, his body never touched by a surgeons' scalpel.

What would our lives look like if we got up in the morning and began to dance for ten to twelve minutes outside of our bed? For one thing we would be very fit, but for a second, more important side, we would be full of joy. Remember, the ultimate defeat is when you give up on yourself, because God never gives up on you![95]

Let's recall the four ways joy is stolen:

1. Taking ourselves too seriously
2. Caring too much what other people think
3. Not recognizing the difference between mere inconvenience and major catastrophe
4. Real crisis

And count it all joy.

And above all, enjoy everything!

- Enjoy reading your Bible (Do not just do it because you have to).
- Enjoy praying.
- Enjoy giving (If you haven't gotten to the point that you enjoy giving, you are not giving in faith)
- Enjoy your family.
- Enjoy those around you.
- Enjoy little things.
- Overlook digs.
- Overlook distractions.
- Overlook worry.
- Pray that you do not have to lose things to appreciate them.

Let's end with our final truth:

Truth:

If you have joy for the journey, then you know you have strength for the journey!

One thing I can promise you is that when you begin to have so much joy that it breaks into laughter (Ha, ha, ha!), you will begin to conceive. And when you conceive your miracle, you will give birth to your miracle, if you can keep laughing and rejoicing. The famous, late Smith Wigglesworth said, "Faith laughs at impossibilities."[96] And he certainly saw people overcome impossibilities, perhaps more than any minister in his era. Smith would pray and the blind would see, the deaf were healed, people came out of wheelchairs, and cancers were destroyed. Everywhere he went he would teach and move in the power of God. Hundreds would be healed at one time. Over Smith's ministry it was confirmed that fourteen people were raised from the dead. Thousands were saved and healed, and he impacted whole continents for Christ.[97]

Now it's our turn. God designed us to experience His resurrection power actively in our lives. We know the end of the story. We know that Jesus rose again. We know that He sticks closer to us than a brother. We know that when we cannot handle everything, all we have to do is turn to Him. The world is still without hope. It is our job to let them know the resurrection has happened! We are resurrection people, and we need to make sure that we do not revert back into Good Friday people. We have hope and we have joy! Let's go out there and truly love and live our lives!

Prayer

Dear Lord,

I thank you for turning my captivity and setting me free so that my mouth is filled with laughter and my tongue with singing. You are the great God of restoration! You are restoring my joy and my laugh, making my dreams to come true! Indeed, oh God, there is none like You! Hallelujah!

In Jesus' Name,
Amen.

Truth in Action:

1. Can you recognize what triggers a joyless attitude or what challenges your joy level? How can you respond differently?

   ____
   ____
   ____
   ____
   ____
   ____

2. What trash has stopped up your wells? What lies have you believed and lost your joy over? It's time to dig up the wells and rejoice again!

   ____
   ____
   ____
   ____
   ____
   ____
   ____
   ____

3. What mountains are you facing that are so huge you should laugh at? Speak to the mountain (of debt, lack, etc.), and command it to be moved and laugh at it!

____

____

____

____

____

____

4. Take time to rejoice in God's goodness! Thank Him for His answers, His promises, and dance and rejoice before your God! Humble yourself and dance! Don't let yourself be embarrassed. It's only you and God.

Appendix A: Prayer of Salvation

Why a new birth?

This is such a good question, and such an important one, I wanted to take a moment to explain it to the uninitiated. The answer is very simple but sometimes gets lost or convoluted in religious or lofty words and concepts. Man was never meant to die. That's why death is so hard for humans to experience and cope with. It is, indeed, foreign to man, as we were made in the image of God. So, in order to rescue us from the state of death, God had to actually come down to us. That is what the "incarnation" was all about. Since the only door into the world is birth, God had to come through the same door we do. In fact, Jesus explained that the thief does not come through the door but climbs up another way. The thief, of course, is Satan, who didn't use the door of birth but borrowed the body of the serpent.

So we see that the only entrance into this world is the natural birth. How awesome it is to ponder what God did in order to redeem humanity. He came as a child (Isa. 9:6): *"For unto us a child is born, unto us a son is given: and the government shall be upon his shoulder: and his name shall be called Wonderful, Counselor, The mighty God, The everlasting Father, The Prince of Peace."*

So now that we know how Jesus came to Earth, how does one get to Heaven? In answering, Scripture teaches the simple truth that we must get to Heaven the same way we get to Earth: we must be born to get to

Earth, without exception. We must be "born again" to get to Heaven, without exception. Only instead of a natural birth, we need a spiritual birth. This new birth happens to us when we release faith in Christ to save us. Then our names are written in Heaven's record, the Lamb's Book of Life. We have a new citizenship, even heavenly documents to prove it. This is important, as the Bible teaches that in the last judgment, the books will be opened before the Great White Throne. Everyone whose name is not written in the Book of Life will be cast into the Lake of Fire. This is the second death (Rev. 20:14, 15). Those who are only born once will actually die twice. They will die physically and then, on that fateful Day of Judgment, they will be eternally excused from the presence of God and the eternal plan of bliss and blessing that was prepared for them. But those who are born twice will only die once. They will die physically and then be escorted to Heaven by the chariot of the Lord, where they will share in the eternal bliss of God's plan and presence. Praise God! Make sure that, above all else, you have your name written in that Book. As Jesus said in Luke 10:20, *"rejoice, because your names are written in Heaven."* Amen.

Prayer

Heavenly Father,

I come to You in the name of Jesus. Your Word says, "Whoever shall call on the name of the Lord shall be saved." I am calling on You. I pray and ask Jesus to come into my heart and be Lord over my life. Your Word says, "If I confess with my mouth that Jesus is Lord, and believe in my heart that God raised Him from the dead, I will be saved." I give my entire self to You, Lord Jesus, now and forever. Heal me, change me, strengthen me in my body, soul, and spirit. Cover me with Your precious blood and fill me with your Holy Spirit. I ask You to go before me today and prepare the way. I shall do my utmost to follow you every day of my life. (Acts 2:21, Romans 10:9–10)

In Jesus' Name,
Amen.

If you prayed this prayer for the first time, please contact us. We would love to encourage you with other materials and resources to help on this great journey of faith!

Appendix B: Recommended Resources

Visit your local Christian bookstore to find these items or visit the websites below.

Bible translations:

New American Standard
King James Version
New King James Version
New International Version
New Living Translation: translated into modern speech
The Amplified Bible: elaborates on the original Hebrew/Greek meanings of key words
God's Word Translation: an accurate yet simple translation highly recommended for children

Bible study aids:

One Year Bible:	Online Bible reading plans available for free download:	www.oneyearBibleonline.com
E-Sword	Free software download with various Bible translations and search aids	www.e-sword.net
Bible Gateway	Online Bible with multiple languages and translations:	www.biblegateway.com
Strong's Exhaustive Concordance of the Bible		www.christianbook.com
Hebrew/Greek Lexicon:		www.christianbook.com
Vine's Complete Expository Dictionary		www.christianbook.com www.e-sword.net

Bible study courses:

Drawing Near	by John Bevere	www.messengerinternational.org
Experiencing God	by Henry Blackaby	www.blackaby.org
Financial Peace University	by Dave Ramsey	www.daveramsey.com
God's Master Plan for Your Life	by Gloria Copeland	www.godsmasterplanforyourlife.com

Scripture promises:

God's Promises Series	by Various Authors	www.christianbook.com
God's Creative Power	by Charles Capps	www.charlescapps.com
God's Creative Power for Healing	by Charles Capps	www.charlescapps.com
Healed of Cancer	by Dodie Osteen	www.joelosteen.com
Prayers That Avail Much	by Germaine Copeland	www.prayers.org

Devotionals:

Choosing Life	by Dodie Osteen	www.lakewood.cc
Faith to Faith	by Kenneth and Gloria Copeland	www.kcm.org
My Utmost for His Highest	by Oswald Chambers	www.utmost.org

Devotional charts:

Download a free devotional chart	www.howtoloveyourlife.org

Other recommended reading or sermon resources:

Apologetics:

Evidence That Demands a Verdict	by Josh McDowell	www.josh.org
More Than a Carpenter	by Josh McDowell	www.josh.org

Christian Living:

Psalm 91: God's Umbrella of Protection	by Peggy Joyce Ruth	www.peggyjoyceruth.org
Those Who Trust the Lord Will Not be Disappointed	by Peggy Joyce Ruth	www.peggyjoyceruth.org
Tormented: Eight Years and Back	by Peggy Joyce Ruth	www.peggyjoyceruth.org

Christian Living:

Other authors with many books or resources on this subject:

Kevin & Heather Sanford		www.kevinsanfordministries.com
Joel Osteen		www.joelosteen.com
Joseph Prince		www.josephprince.org
Joyce Meyer		www.joycemeyer.org
Lisa Osteen Comes		www.lisacomes.com
Victoria Osteen`		www.victoriaosteen.com

Family:

Family Fragrance	by J. Otis & Gail Ledbetter	www.heritagebuilders.com
Family Traditions	by J. Otis Ledbetter & Timothy Smith	www.heritagebuilders.com
Your Heritage	by J. Otis Ledbetter & Kurt Bruner	www.heritagebuilders.com

Healing:

God's Creative Power for Healing	by Charles Capps	www.charlescapps.com
God's Medicine	by Kenneth E. Hagin	www.rhema.org
Healed of Cancer	by Dodie Osteen	www.joelosteen.com
Healing Promises	by Gloria Copeland	www.kcm.org
Healing Confessions	by Kenneth Copeland	www.kcm.org
Multiple healing resources	by Benny Hinn	www.bennyhinn.org
Multiple healing resources	by Joseph Prince	www.josephprince.org

Inspirational:

Nick Vujicic		www.lifewithoutlimbs.org

Parenting:

Baby Wise Series	by Gary Ezzo and Dr. Robert Bucknam	www.ezzo.org
Growing Kids God's Way	by Gary and Anne Marie Ezzo	www.growingkids.org
The Power of a Praying Parent	by Stormie O'Martian	www.stormieomartian.com

PRAYER:

God's Creative Power	by Charles Capps	www.charlescapps.com
Prayers That Avail Much	by Germaine Copeland	www.prayers.org
The Power of a Praying series	by Stormie O'Martian	www.stormieomartian.com

VICTORIOUS, FAITH-FILLED LIVING:

Authors with many books or resources on this subject:

Kevin & Heather Sanford	www.kevinsanfordministries.com
Bill Winston	www.billwinston.org
Creflo Dollar	www.creflodollarministries.org
Jan Aldridge	www.janaldridge.org
Kate McVeigh	www.katemcveigh.org
Keith Moore	www.moorelife.org
Kenneth & Gloria Copeland	www.kcm.org
Kenneth Hagin	www.rhema.org
Mark Hankins	www.markhankins.org
Walter Hallam	www.alcc.org, www.walterhallam.com

WOMEN'S MINISTRY:

A Woman After God's Own Heart	by Elizabeth George	www.elizabethgeorge.com
The Power of a Praying Wife	by Stormie O'Martian	www.stormieomartian.com

Music for your quiet time:

PRAISE:

Gateway Worship	www.gatewayworship.com
Hillsongs	www.hillsong.com
Judy Jacobs	www.judyjacobs.com
Shekinah Glory	www.shekinahglory.com

WORSHIP:

Cece Winans	www.cecewinans.com
Sarah Hart Pearsons	www.sarahhartpearsons.com
The Imperials	www.theclassicimperials.com
Traditional Hymn compilations	www.christianbook.com
Wow Worship	www.christianbook.com

Contemporary:

Casting Crowns	www.castingcrowns.com
Chris Tomlin	www.christomlin.com
Mercy Me	www.mercyme.org
Michael W. Smith	www.michaelwsmith.com
Steven Curtis Chapman	www.stevencurtischapman.com
Wow (best of Christian music today)	www.christianbook.com

Pop/Youth:

Hillsong United	www.hillsongyouth.com
Jump 5	www.jump5.com
Pure NRG	www.purenrgonline.com

Children:

Crazy Praize	www.brentwood-benson.com
Hillsong Kids	www.hillsongkids.com
Kellie Copeland	www.kcm.org

Baby Lullabies:

Kellie Copeland	www.kcm.org
Michael Card	www.michaelcard.com

Notes

Chapter 1

1. By permission. From *Merriam-Webster's Collegiate® Dictionary, 11th Edition©2011* by Merriam-Webster, Incorporated (www.merriam-webster.com).
2. 2 Timothy 2:15

Chapter 2

3. Judith Stein, "The White-Haired Girl" A Feminist Reading," *Grandma Moses in the 21st Century* (Alexandria, VA: Art Services International, 2001), pp. 48-63.
4. Eleanor Early, "Just a Mother,"*True Confessions*, May 1947, p. 47.

Chapter 4

5. Kendall, Jackie and Jones, *Debby, Lady in Waiting*: Expanded Edition, Destiny Image Publishers, Shippensburg, PA. 2005, p. 29-30
6. Wells, H.G., *In the Fourth Year: Anticipations of a World Peace* (1918), Project Gutenburg Publishers. 1918
7. Hancock, John Lee, Director, "The Rookie," Walt Disney Pictures. 2002

Chapter 5

8. Titelman, Gregory Y., *Random House Dictionary of Popular Proverbs and Sayings,* Random House, New York. 1996

Chapter 6

9. Hart, Anna, "7 Leading Causes of Stress," (Article), http://ezinearticles.com/?7-Leading-Causes-of-Stress&id=473303
10. Holy Bible, 1 Thessalonians 5:18
11. Eldridge, Emma L., A Child's Reader in Verse, American Book Co. Publishers, 1911, public domain.
12. Monroe, Lewis B., adapted from "How Amy Learned to Work", The third reader, E.H. Butler & Co. Publishers, 1873, public domain. Pg. 137
13. "Agent Sully," 25 Tips to Become More Productive and Happy at Work, http://lifelearningtoday.com/2007/08/23/25-tips-to-become-more-productive-and-happy-at-work/
14. Kumar, David Prakash, "Tips to enjoy your work week," July 10, 2009 http://www.saching.com/Article/A-few-tips-to-enjoy-your-work-/2985
15. List compiled from the following sources:
    Jenkins, Lucia, "Have More Fun at Work: Great Tips to Enjoy Work Each Day," Oct 6, 2009, http://www.suite101.com/content/have-more-fun-at-work-a156301; Tejvan Pettinger, Tejvan, "How to Work 9 to 5 and Enjoy It," http://www.dumblittleman.com/2007/10/how-to-work-9-to-5-and-enjoy-it.html; Parab, Priyanka, "7 Tips to enjoy Work," http://www.medimanage.com/my-health-at-work/articles/7-Tips-to-enjoy-work.aspx
16. Lin, Sing, "Optimum Strategies for Creativity and Longevity" 2002 (Article) http://www.ptarmigannest.net/wp-content/uploads/2008/04/retirement-age-vs-life-span.pdf

Chapter 7

17. McDowell, Josh, *More Than a Carpenter*, Living Books, Carol Stream, IL. 2004
18. McDowell, Josh, *The New Evidence That Demands A Verdict,* Fully Updated To Answer The Questions Challenging Christians Today, Heres Life Publishers Inc, San Bernardino, CA. 1992

19. *Strong's Exhaustive Concordance,* Updated Edition KJV, Hendrickson Publishers, Peabody, MA. 2007
20. Copeland, Gloria, *True Prosperity,* (Article), http://www.kcm.org/real-help/article/true-prosperity
21. Vujicic, Nick, www.lifewithoutlimbs.org
22. Vujicic, Nick, www.lifewithoutlimbs.org

Chapter 8

23. Moore, Keith, "Rest and Recovery" (CD), Moore Life Ministries, Branson MO www.moorelife.org
24. Moore, Keith, "Rest and Recovery" (CD), Moore Life Ministries, Branson MO, www.moorelife.org
25. Moore, Keith, "Rest and Recovery" (CD), Moore Life Ministries, Branson MO, www.moorelife.org
26. Moore, Keith, "Rest and Recovery" (CD), Moore Life Ministries, Branson MO, www.moorelife.org
27. Osborne, T. L. – used by permission of Osborne Ministries International, Box 10 Tulsa, Oklahoma 74102
28. Moore, Keith, "Rest and Recovery" (CD), Moore Life Ministries, Branson MO, www.moorelife.org
29. Moore, Keith, "Rest and Recovery" (CD), Moore Life Ministries, Branson MO, www.moorelife.org
30. Moore, Keith, "Rest and Recovery" (CD), Moore Life Ministries, Branson MO, www.moorelife.org

Chapter 9

31. *Strong's Exhaustive Concordance,* Updated Edition KJV, Hendrickson Publishers, Peabody, MA. 2007

Chapter 10

32. Hankins, Mark, *Revolutionary Revelation,* Mark Hankins Ministries, Alexandria LA. 2005, pp. 89, 96, 99

Chapter 11

33. Prince, Joseph, "Rest: God is Working Behind the Scenes" (CD), www.josephprince.org

34. Procter, Bob, *Your Achievement* Ezine - Issue No. 176, "Your Success Store," 2010 http://www.yoursuccessstore.com

35. Moore, Keith, "Rest and Recovery" (CD), Moore Life Ministries, Branson MO, www.moorelife.org

36. Copeland, Gloria, *God's Master Plan for your Life,* Putnam Praise Publishers, New York, New York. 2008. Chapter 12

37. Copeland, Gloria, *God's Master Plan for your Life,* Putnam Praise Publishers, New York, New York. 2008. Chapter 12

38. Andrew Murray, *The Holiest of All, An Exposition of the Epistle to the Hebrews, Abridged Edition* (Fort Worth: Kenneth Copeland Ministries, abridgement of retypeset edition, 1996).

Chapter 12

39. Andrew Murray, *The Holiest of All, An Exposition of the Epistle to the Hebrews, Abridged Edition* (Fort Worth: Kenneth Copeland Ministries, abridgement of retypeset edition, 1996).
40. Used with permission, Peggy Joyce Ruth Ministries, Brownwood TX www.peggyjoyceruth.org
41. Dale, Edgar, Audio-Visual Methods in Teaching, 3rd Edition, Holt, Rinehart & Winston, New York, 1969, p. 108
42. Andrew Murray, *The Holiest of All, An Exposition of the Epistle to the Hebrews, Abridged Edition* (Fort Worth: Kenneth Copeland Ministries, abridgement of retypeset edition, 1996).
43. William R. Cashion and Joseph D. White. PhD, Study by Hering (1994). Quoted in article: "Seven Secrets of Successful Marriage," 2005 http://www.austindiocese.org/yotf/downloads/7SECRETSOFSUCCESSFULMARRIAGE.pdf
44. Splinter, Dr. John P., *Biblical Sexuality, Part V Cohabitation vs.*

Marriage: A Bible Study for Mature Christ-followers, http://www.purehope.net/stlouisArticlesDetail.asp?id=191

45. Rushnell, SQuire and DuArt, Louise, *Couples Who Pray,* Thomas Nelson, Nashville, TN. 2007 http://www.coupleswhopray.com/challenge/
46. Beer, Michael "Jewish Weddings," www.wildolive.co.uk, http://www.wildolive.co.uk/weddings.htm, 30 April 2011
47. *Strong's Exhaustive Concordance,* Updated Edition KJV, Hendrickson Publishers, Peabody, MA. 2007
48. *Strong's Exhaustive Concordance,* Updated Edition KJV, Hendrickson Publishers, Peabody, MA. 2007
49. Elliot, Elizabeth, *Through Gates of Splendour,* Tyndale House Publishers Inc, Carol Stream, IL. 1981

Chapter 13

50. Mallette, Wanda (Songwriter); Morrison, Bob (Songwriter); Ryan, Patti (Songwriter); Music City Music, Inc. (Publisher), 1980.
51. Andrew Murray, *The Holiest of All, An Exposition of the Epistle to the Hebrews, Abridged Edition* (Fort Worth: Kenneth Copeland Ministries, abridgement of retypeset edition, 1996).
52. Kitchen, Kenneth A. and J.D. Douglas, eds. *The New Bible Dictionary,* Tyndale House Publishers, Wheaton, IL. second edition, 1982.
53. *The International Inductive Study Bible,* NASB, Introductory study notes on Esther, Harvest House Publishers, Eugene Oregon, Study notes compiled by K. Arthur and the staff of Precept Ministries. Page 807
54. Artscroll Tanach Series, Mishlei Vol. 2 Chapters 16–31 Mesorah Publications, Ltd.
55. Author unknown, Jonathan Edwards, 1703–1758, Bib.Scholar, Preacher, Posted on: 03/17/2003, Category: Biographies, Source: CCN, http://www.believersweb.net/view.cfm?ID=118
56. Article: *"Leaving a Family Legacy"* Posted on February 2, 2011 by "Glen". *http:"www.faith4families.org/articles/leaving-a-family-legacy/* Accessed 24 May 2011

57. Article: *"Leaving a Family Legacy"* Posted on February 2, 2011 by "Glen". *http:"www.faith4families.org/articles/leaving-a-family-legacy/* Accessed 24 May 2011
58. Taylor, Dr. and Mrs. Howard, *Hudson Taylor's Spiritual Secret,* Moody Publishers, Chicago, IL. 2009

Chapter 14
59. Andrew Murray, *The Holiest of All, An Exposition of the Epistle to the Hebrews, Abridged Edition* (Fort Worth: Kenneth Copeland Ministries, abridgement of retypeset edition, 1996).
60. Lewis, C.S., *The Lion, the Witch and the Wardrobe,* Harper Collins Publishers, New York, NY. 2009
61. Benge, Janet and Benge, Geoff, *Harriet Tubman: Freedombound,* Emerald Books. 2002

Chapter 15
62. Andrew Murray, *The Holiest of All, An Exposition of the Epistle to the Hebrews, Abridged Edition* (Fort Worth: Kenneth Copeland Ministries, abridgement of retypeset edition, 1996).
63. Segall, Grant, *John D. Rockefeller: Anointed with Oil,* Published by Oxford University Press, Inc., 198 Madison Avenue, NY, 2001, p. 26

Chapter 16
64. Andrew Murray, *The Holiest of All, An Exposition of the Epistle to the Hebrews, Abridged Edition* (Fort Worth: Kenneth Copeland Ministries, abridgement of retypeset edition, 1996).
65. Nave, Orville J., *Nave's Topical Bible,* Hendrickson Publishers, Peabody, MA. 1997
66. By permission. From *Merriam-Webster's Collegiate® Dictionary, 11th Edition©2011* by Merriam-Webster, Incorporated (www.merriam-webster.com)
67. Levy, Rabbi Chai, Article: We all have the power to deliver God's blessings, Thursday December 31, 2009, http://www.jweekly.com/

article/full/40891/we-all-have-the-power-to-deliver-gods-blessings/; Accessed 25th May 2011.

68. Pradervand, Pierre, *The Gentle Art of Blessing,* Atria Paperback, A Division of Simon and Scuster, Inc. New York, NY, 2009.
69. Artscroll Tanach Series, Mishlei Vol. 2 Chapters 16–31 Mesorah Publications, Ltd.

Chapter 17

70. Andrew Murray, *The Holiest of All, An Exposition of the Epistle to the Hebrews, Abridged Edition* (Fort Worth: Kenneth Copeland Ministries, abridgement of retypeset edition, 1996).
71. Ten Boom, Corrie, *The Hiding Place,* Random House, Inc., New York, NY. 1982
72. Wyatt, Ron, Wyatt Archeological Research http://www.wyattarchaeology.com/red_sea.htm
73. *Strong's Exhaustive Concordance,* Updated Edition KJV, Hendrickson Publishers, Peabody, MA. 2007; literal "loud" = Gk: mega
74. *Strong's Exhaustive Concordance,* Updated Edition KJV, Hendrickson Publishers, Peabody, MA. 2007; literal "voice" = Gk: phone
75. Osteen, Dodie, *Healed of Cancer,* A Lakewood Church Publication, Houston TX. 1986, p. 53
76. Comes, Lisa Osteen http://www.lisacomes.com/Pages/About.aspx
77. Benge, Janet and Benge, Geoff, *Harriet Tubman: Freedombound,* Emerald Books. 2002

Chapter 18

78. Andrew Murray, *The Holiest of All, An Exposition of the Epistle to the Hebrews, Abridged Edition* (Fort Worth: Kenneth Copeland Ministries, abridgement of retypeset edition, 1996).
79. Andrew Murray, *The Holiest of All, An Exposition of the Epistle to the Hebrews, Abridged Edition* (Fort Worth: Kenneth Copeland Ministries, abridgement of retypeset edition, 1996).
80. Adams, Mike, "Laughter is Good Medicine for Reducing Stress,

Enhancing Brain Chemistry" (article), Natural News.com, 2005, http://www.naturalnews.com/007551.html

81. Cancer Treatment Centers of America, Laughter Therapy (article), http://www.cancercenter.com/complementary-alternative-medicine/laughter-therapy.cfm
82. *Guideposts Magazine,* Harlan IA, http://www.guideposts.org/
83. Frankl, Viktor E., *Man's Search For Meaning: The classic tribute to hope from the Holocaust,* Rider Publishing, 2004.
84. Robert Edward Auctions, "1914 Thomas Edison Signed Letter—Laboratory Fire Content" (article) http://robertedwardauctions.com/auction/2007/1453.html
85. Wells, Thelma, Various Authors, *Joy for a Woman's Soul: Promises to Refresh the Spirit,* Inspirio, A branch of Zondervan Publishers, Grand Rapids MI. 2006
86. Johnson, Barbara, Various Authors, *Joy for a Woman's Soul: Promises to Refresh the Spirit,* Inspirio. A branch of Zondervan Publishers, Grand Rapids MI. 2006
87. Johnson, Barbara, Various Authors, *Joy for a Woman's Soul: Promises to Refresh the Spirit,* Inspirio, A branch of Zondervan Publishers, Grand Rapids MI. 2006
88. Johnson, Barbara, Various Authors, *Joy for a Woman's Soul: Promises to Refresh the Spirit,* Inspirio,. A branch of Zondervan Publishers, Grand Rapids MI. 2006
89. Hankins, Mark, *Let the Good Times Roll,* Mark Hankins Ministries, Alexandria, LA. 2006, pp101
90. Walsh, Sheila, Various Authors, *Joy for a Woman's Soul: Promises to Refresh the Spirit,* Inspirio, A branch of Zondervan Publishers, Grand Rapids MI. 2006
91. Tangredi, Danny, Einstein - Definition of Insanity, http://ezinearticles.com/?Einstein---Definition-of-Insanity&id=12047, 20 April 2011.
92. Hankins, Mark, "The Secret Power of Joy" (CD), Mark Hankins Ministries, Alexandria LA, www.markhankins.org
93. Hankins, Mark, "The Secret Power of Joy" (CD), Mark Hankins Ministries, Alexandria LA, www.markhankins.org

94. Sumrall, Dr. Lester, *Pioneers of Faith,* Sumrall Publishing, South Bend, IN. 1995
95. Hankins, Mark, "The Secret Power of Joy" (CD), Mark Hankins Ministries, Alexandria LA, www.markhankins.org
96. Hankins, Mark, *Let the Good Times Roll,* Mark Hankins Ministries, Alexandria, LA. 2006
97. Healing and Revival Press, Copyright © 2004, http://healingandrevival.com/BioSWigglesworth.htm, April 20, 2011

More resources from
HEATHER SANFORD

If you have been blessed and challenged by *How to Love Your Life*, you may be interested in the following resources available from Heather Sanford.

How to Love Your Life Series
Living Safe in Dangerous Days
Seeds to Success
Possessing the Promise
Why the Holy Spirit
Fruit of the Spirit
Walking by Faith
How to Birth the Vision of God in Your Life
How to Fulfil Your Destiny
Possessing the Promise

Available online at:
WWW.ABUNDANTLIFE.IE
WWW.HOWTOLOVEYOURLIFE.ORG

Resources from

KEVIN SANFORD

If you have been blessed and challenged by *How to Love Your Life*, you may be interested in the following resources available from Kevin Sanford.

AUDIO TEACHINGS

BY KEVIN SANFORD

In His Image
How to Worship
In Christ
The Ten Commandments
How to Pray
The Story of the Glory
Relationships
You Have Something to Offer

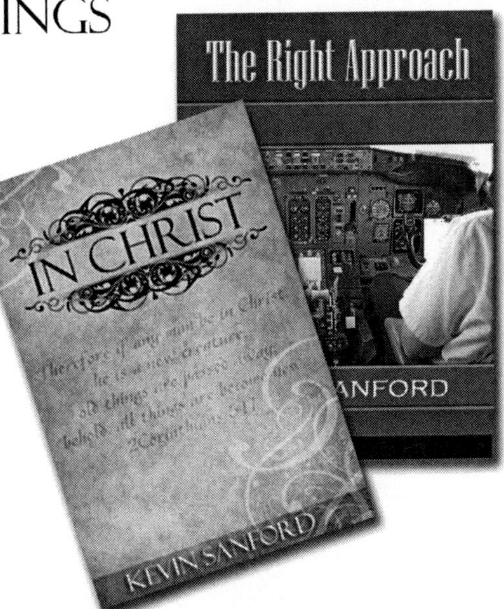

To book Pastor Kevin for a conference or other speaking engagement, contact him at the websites below.

Available online at:

WWW.ABUNDANTLIFE.IE
WWW.KEVINSANFORDMINISTRIES.COM